African Accents

CW00969834

This is a comprehensive workbook for actors, covering the key characteristics and profiles of a wide range of African accents of English. Its unique approach not only addresses the methods and processes by which to go about learning an accent, but also looks in detail at each example. This lets the reader plot their own route through the learning process and tailor not only their working methods but also their own personal idiolect.

Full breakdowns of each accent cover:

- an **introduction** giving a brief history of the accent, its ethnic background, and its language of origin
- preparatory **warm-up** exercises specific to each accent
- a directory of **research materials** including documentaries, plays, films and online resources
- key **characteristics** such as melody, stress, pace and pitch
- descriptions of **physical articulation** in the tongue, lips, jaw, palate and pharynx
- **practice sentences**, **phoneme tables** and **worksheets** for solo study.

African Accents is accompanied by a website at www.routledge.com/cw/mcguire with an extensive online database of audio samples for each accent. The book and audio resources guide actors to develop their own authentic accents, rather than simply to mimic native speakers. This process allows the actor to personalize an accent, and to integrate it into the creation of character rather than to *play* the accent on top of character.

Beth McGuire is a professional dialect and vocal coach for theatre and film. She is Director of Speech and Dialects at Yale School of Drama.

The Adinkra symbol above – Ese Ne Tekrema, which means "the teeth and the tongue" – was created by the Ashanti of Ghana and the Gyaman of Côte d'Ivoire. The interdependent play between the teeth and tongue symbolizes friendship and interdependence.

African Accents

A Workbook for Actors

Beth McGuire

Routledge
Taylor & Francis Group

LONDON AND NEW YORK

First published 2016
by Routledge
2 Park Square, Milton Park, Abingdon, Oxon OX14 4RN

and by Routledge
711 Third Avenue, New York, NY 10017

Routledge is an imprint of the Taylor & Francis Group, an informa business

© 2016 Beth McGuire

The right of Beth McGuire to be identified as author of this work has been asserted by her in
accordance with sections 77 and 78 of the Copyright, Designs and Patents Act 1988.

All rights reserved. No part of this book may be reprinted or reproduced or utilised in any form
or by any electronic, mechanical, or other means, now known or hereafter invented, including
photocopying and recording, or in any information storage or retrieval system, without permission
in writing from the publishers.

Trademark notice: Product or corporate names may be trademarks or registered trademarks, and
are used only for identification and explanation without intent to infringe.

British Library Cataloguing-in-Publication Data
A catalogue record for this book is available from the British Library

Library of Congress Cataloging-in-Publication Data
McGuire, Beth, 1955– author.
  African accents : a workbook for actors / By Beth McGuire.
    pages cm
  Includes bibliographical references and index.
  1. English language–Pronunciation by foreign speakers. 2. English language–Dialects–
Africa–Handbooks, manuals, etc. 3. Acting. I. Title.
  PN2071.F6M36 2015
  792.02′8–dc23

                                                                    2015003173

ISBN: 978-0-415-70591-2 (hbk)
ISBN: 978-0-415-70592-9 (pbk)
ISBN: 978-1-315-85020-7 (ebk)

Typeset in Times New Roman
by Graphicraft Limited, Hong Kong

IPA Chart, http://www.internationalphoneticassociation.org/content/ipa-chart, available under a
Creative Commons Attribution-Sharealike 3.0 Unported License. Copyright © 2005 International
Phonetic Association.

Contents

Acknowledgments

I would first like to thank the many Africans who so graciously volunteered to be interviewed. Without their many voices, this book would not exist.

I am extremely grateful to my extraordinarily talented and dedicated research assistants, Jenna Sofia and Peter Nyong'o. They went above and beyond and I am deeply indebted to them. I would also like to thank Lupita Nyong'o and Madeline Ruskin for their research assistance in the beginning stages of the work. This book would not have been possible without the collective effort of these four marvelous human beings.

I would also like to pay homage to my extended community of support:

Jane Guyer Fujita and Maggie Surovell for their eagle eyes, keen ears and stellar editing skills.

Sylvia Hove, Bimbo Benson, Blake Segal, Zainab Jah, Allison Oman, Ron Kunene, Jeri Silverman, Emery Bright, Melody Louisdhon and Kona Khasu for their unique contributions.

Ben Piggott at Routledge Press for his belief, support and encouragement and Sarah May for her resourcefulness and humor.

I would particularly like to thank Danai Gurira and Liesl Tommy, who were my original inspirations to make resources like this available.

Last but not least, I would like to thank my students at the Yale School of Drama and the many professional actors whom I have coached in African accents. It is they who inspired and continue to inspire me to travel into unknown territories.

Chapter 1

How to Use This Workbook

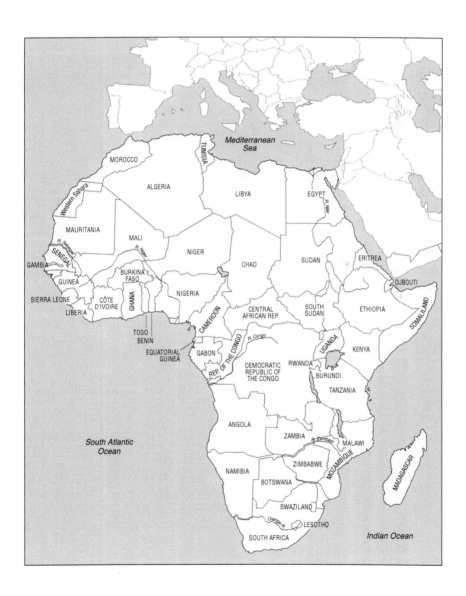

Ways of Approaching an Accent

Improvisation, Research, Finding the Idiolect, Working with Text

Please refer to the Glossary when terms are unclear!

Improvisation and Technique: Getting the Accent into Your Body and Imagination

1. Remember that you are an *actor, not a linguist*. Your purpose is to *illuminate character and text and to tell a story*, not to fool the indigenous speakers of the accent.
2. First and foremost: engage your sense of humor and sense of <u>play</u>.
3. Be willing to commit and enjoy broad strokes at the beginning of your transformation into character with the accent.
4. Studying accents can get overly analytic, therefore be conscious in allowing the accents to inform your ENTIRE psychological and physical being. As you explore the accents keep your IMAGINATION alive and engaged.
5. Employ a CONSCIOUS mimicry[1] as you listen to the accent. It can be quite useful to work with an earbud in <u>one</u> ear only. Leave the other ear free to listen to yourself consciously mimicking what you are hearing through the earbud.
6. REVEL in your mistakes, don't cover them up! They are extremely helpful points of reference, and often very funny.
7. Be conscious of what is happening in your mouth. What is your tongue doing? What are your lips doing? What is your jaw doing? etc. Refining and adding to this awareness will create flexibility for adapting to the many different vocal postures that accent work requires.
8. Take your accents "on the road". Find places that you can try them out in your daily life.

Grounding the Accent in Character: Finding Your Own Idiolect in the Character's Particulars

An author will give you clues about who the character is by how s/he speaks. Virtually all of the elements that make up an accent can inform character.

1. The character's age, gender, sexual preference, socioeconomic status, education, place in history, place of residence, work, self-perception and relationship to her/his body, mind and spirit will all work towards creating the character's particular idiolect.
2. Each of us speaks differently even if we have the same general accent. The individual way we speak is referred to as <u>idiolect</u>. For the actor, idiolect is part of what creates character. It is the "how" of the accent, and influences how we craft our thoughts through language.
3. Research the culture of the people who speak in the accent. What is their music like? Their dance, art, politics and climate?
4. Above all, as an actor, your use of accent will need to be grounded in the character and his/her circumstances.

Bringing the Accent Work to Text: a Conversation Between the Accent and the Text

1. Choose a scene or monologue that uses the accent and transcribe at least six lines using IPA or the sound symbols in the accent breakdowns.
2. It is very easy to fall into a melody or rhythm when working on a role with an accent. For this reason, it is extremely useful to begin to choose the operative words that carry the thoughts, early on in your process. You can focus the elements of the accent on the operative words, bringing your thoughts into action. This will help you speak the accent with need, rather than becoming general, and "playing" the accent. Listen to where and how the accent interviewees stress operative words or where and how they don't.
3. When you receive accent notes in rehearsal from your accent coach or director, or if you notice slippage yourself, identify words and phrases in the script where this is happening and create sentences with these words or phrases that are out of context of the script. Practice these self-constructed sentences <u>in character</u>. This will allow you to take the pressure off of the particular lines in the script, while encouraging the accent to be spoken from the point of view of the character. Jot the challenging words down in the Sound Shifts tables in the *Your Key Words* column for your ready reference.
4. Finally, put together a clear warm-up for yourself and execute it before you rehearse or perform. When you finish the *Mapping Your Accent* worksheet, you will have discovered personal elements for your own warm-up. You can fold these elements into the warm-up in the *Getting Your Instrument Ready* section at the beginning of each chapter. It is disheartening to see an actor warm up into his/her accent during the first scene of a play or at the beginning of a film shoot. Please don't be that actor.

Note

1 In conscious mimicry, one intentionally notes the shifting of one's own articulators and changes in vocal variety, while intuitively mimicking.

How to Work with the Accent in Each Chapter

The accent breakdowns in this book are models. Please find your own variations as you work with the models. Allow the accent to evolve with the character that you are playing. This will be your particular idiolect of the accent.

1. Listen to the accent samples in the Workbook's audio library and choose at least two samples to keep close at ear. It is preferable to choose samples of the same gender as the role you are playing. The reasons being 1) vocal production manifests differently in men and women because of the difference in length of vocal folds, and 2) cultural socialization in relation to gender often affects vocal production and elements of vocal variety including melody, rhythm, pace and volume. That said, it can also be useful to listen to the opposite gender, because it is both close enough and far enough away to provide a helpful perspective. When exploring Vocal Posture, many actors find it helpful to listen to the actual language that is shaping the accent. If you are one of these actors, please listen to one of the language samples that are included in the audio library.

2. Each Chapter contains thirteen sections that are labeled at the top of each page. The sections are listed below:

   Introduction and Resources: This section contains a little history and information about the language, along with lists of documentaries, films, television, music and plays, etc. of the accent and/or language of origin.

   Down & Dirty Warm-up and Quick Look: This section contains 1) a warm-up for your articulators, 2) a quick look at the Vocal Posture for the accent, 3) a Resonator warm-up in the accent, 4) a quick look at the Source & Path of Resonance for the accent, 5) a warm-up to help get the accent's sound changes into your body and imagination,[1] and 6) Articulation exercises in the accent.

   Key Points of Focus: This section does an in depth examination of 1) the accent's Characteristics: Melody/Pitch/Lilt, Rhythm/Stress/Pace, and Source & Path of Resonance, and 2) the accent's Vocal Posture: physical adjustments of the Tongue, Lips, Jaw, Soft Palate, Pharynx, and Focus of Articulation.

Distinct Sounds: This section looks at some of the distinct sounds of the language and/or the accent. This will heighten your physical understanding of the accent's Vocal Posture and Source & Path of Resonance.

Consonant Sound Shifts: This table lists the consonant sound shifts for the accent. From left to right, each table has a list of 1) Key Words, 2) the Detailed American English (D.A.E.) frame of reference for the phoneme in question, 3) the Shift for that phoneme in the particular African accent under investigation, 4) the phonetic Shifts written out in the Key Words, and 5) an empty box for you to list Your Key Words, from your script, containing the particular sound shifts.

All Detailed American English (D.A.E.) phonemes, phoneme shifts and Key Word Shifts appear in formats of both phonetic symbols (above) and sound symbols (below). (Please see the glossary for a definition of D.A.E.)

Example:

$$\frac{3}{\text{ZH}}$$

There will also be a *Sentence for Practice*, containing key consonant shifts, at the beginning of the table.

Front Vowel Sound Shifts: This table lists the vowel shifts that are articulated in the front of the mouth for D.A.E. There is a sentence for practice with the front vowel shifts at the top of the table. This table is in the same format as the consonant table.

Middle Vowel Sound Shifts: This table lists the vowel shifts that are articulated in the middle of the mouth for D.A.E. There is a sentence for practice with the middle vowel shifts at the top of the table. This table is in the same format as the consonant table.

Back Vowel Sound Shifts: This table lists the vowel shifts that are articulated in the back of the mouth for D.A.E. There is a sentence for practice with the back vowel shifts at the top of the table. This table is in the same format as the consonant table.

Diphthong Sound Shifts: This table lists the diphthong sound shifts. There is a sentence for practice with the diphthong shifts at the top of the table. This table is in the same format as the consonant table.

Diphthongs of R Sound Shifts: This table lists the diphthongs of R sound shifts. There is also a sentence for practice with the diphthongs of R shifts at the top of the table. This table is in the same format as the consonant table.

Key Sentences for Practice: This section lists all of the sound shift sentences. In some cases there will be additional sentences added.

Making Your Own Map of the Accent: This is the true workbook section of the chapter and can act as a guide for you to personalize the accent.

You can work through the shifts from the points of view of Vocal Posture, and Accent Characteristics, shifting back and forth between your own home *idiolect of English* and the *accent* you are building. **Observe** the shifts <u>ONE by ONE</u> in your articulators, Focus of Articulation, use of Melody/Pitch/ Lilt, Rhythm/Stress/Pace, and Source & Path of Resonance as you shift back and forth between the two accents. You can note the shifts in the table provided. Putting your understanding of the shifts into your <u>own words</u> will encourage you to develop a more clear and personal idiolect.

Note

1 The sequence in this section is based on Kristin Linklater's pyramid in *Freeing Shakespeare's Voice*.

How to Work with the Sound Shifts Tables

On Detailed American English (D.A.E.)

This is an American English accent model that Dudley Knight synthesized to teach a model of American English that employs the details of phonemes without regional variation. He referred to this model in his article on Standard Speech in *The Vocal Vision*. Although he changed the name of this model to *Formal Speech* in his book *Speaking with Skill*, this workbook will use the older term D.A.E. when referring to the model. This is a model, and is used as one, since no one speaks this way all of the time. Elements of it are used, discarded, or modified, depending on the character the actor is playing. The model is a linguistic work-out for American English and provides a clear frame of reference for accent work. D.A.E. is the base accent used in exploring the sound changes for the African accents in this workbook.

To British Actors

As you know, many African accents of English are influenced by their colonial history, England being one of the colonists. This workbook assumes an American English frame of reference for the accent shifts, specifically D.A.E. Many of the accents' sound changes (except for Liberia) will include sounds that are more familiar to British English speakers than Americans so it should not be difficult for you brilliant Brits to make the leap into the sound changes.

To IPA Users

As you begin to investigate the sound shifts in the tables, you will notice diacritics for the sounds. Don't let them intimidate you. Start by looking at the word sets with keys (↝) and notice how the phonemes change, <u>before</u> looking at the diacritics. If the phoneme does not change, then take a look at the diacritics for information. If you are not versed in diacritics, give yourself time to get comfortable with them. Once you've done this, you may find yourself more curious about the specificity in the sound changes. This is the time when you may want to fully investigate the diacritics. ***Also, keep listening to your accent samples*** *as you work with the tables. This is where you will hear invaluable primary sources illustrate the sound shifts.*

To Symbol Users

As you begin to investigate the sound shifts in the tables, you will notice symbol modifiers for the sounds. Don't let them intimidate you. Start by looking at the word sets with keys (↤) and notice how the sound symbols change, <u>before</u> looking at the symbol modifiers. If the sound symbol does not change, then take a look at the symbol *modifiers* for information. If you are not versed in symbol modifiers, give yourself time to get comfortable with them. Once you've done this, you may find yourself more curious about the specificity in the sound changes. This is the time when you may want to fully investigate the symbol modifiers. *Also, keep listening to your accent samples as you work with the tables. This is where you will hear invaluable primary sources illustrate the sound shifts.*

How to Work with
the Vowels and Diphthongs
in the Sound Shifts Tables

About the Vowel and Diphthong Tables

• In the vowel and diphthong tables, there is a lexical sub-set for *[æ]/[A] that shifts to the lexical set [a]/[Ah] or [ɑ]/[AH] when speaking British Received Pronunciation (R.P.). This sub-set is included in the ask/bath list later on in this chapter.

  This shift usually occurs for African speakers influenced by British English.

  Example: *bath* – D.A.E. → bæθ/BAth changes to R.P. → baθ/BAhth

• In the vowel and diphthong tables, there are lexical sub-sets for *[ɔ]/[AW] and *[ɑ]/[AH] that shift to the phoneme [ɒ]/[O] when speaking R.P.

  This shift usually occurs for African speakers influenced by British English.

  Example: *cloth* – D.A.E. → klɔθ/KLAWth changes to R.P. → klɒθ/KLOth
  Example: *lot* – D.A.E. → lɑt/LAHT changes to R.P. → lɒt/LOT

• In the vowel table, *[ʌ]/[UH] is considered a *back vowel* by the IPA, but we use the diacritic [¨] to indicate a shift in articulation toward the middle of the tongue [ʌ̈] for D.A.E.

• In some accents, the sound shifts are inconsistent because of spelling. For this reason, vowels, diphthongs and diphthongs of R (in the *Key Words* column) sometimes include different representative spellings.

Anatomy of the Vocal Tract

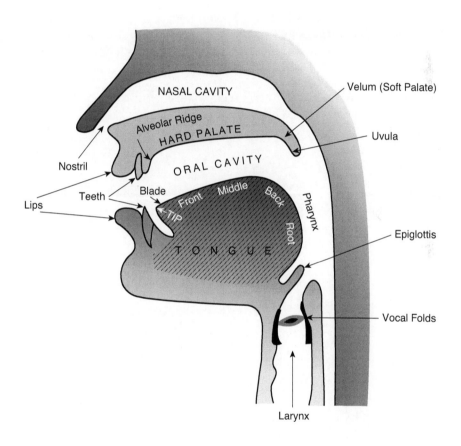

Key Sentences for Pronunciation of Vowels and Diphthongs in *Detailed American English (D.A.E.)*

Below are sample sentences for the vowels and diphthongs of Detailed American English (D.A.E.). This model is the base accent used in exploring the sound changes for the African accents in this workbook.

Front Vowels: Vowels that are pronounced with the front section of the tongue arching or cupping toward the front of the hard palate.

IPA	i	ɪ	ɛ	æ
SYMBOLS	EE	I	EH	A

He hid Henry's hat.

Middle Vowels: Vowels made by arching or cupping the middle section of the tongue toward the middle of the hard palate.

IPA	ɝ	ə	ʌ̈	ɚ
SYMBOLS	ER	uh	UH	er

Spurn a lover.

Back Vowels: Vowels made by arching or cupping the back section of the tongue toward the back of the hard palate.

IPA	u	ʊ	ɔ	ɑ
SYMBOLS	OO	U	AW	AH

Who should call father?

Diphthongs: When two vowels are combined in one syllable.

IPA	eɪ	aɪ	ɔɪ	oʊ	aʊ
SYMBOLS	AY	EYE	OY	OH	OW

Gay fly boys know how.

Diphthongs of R: A diphthong in which the second vowel is rhotic.
Triphthongs of R: A combination of three vowel sounds, in which the third vowel is rhotic.

IPA	ɪɝ	ɛɝ	ʊɝ	ɔɝ	aɝ	aɪɚ	aʊɚ
SYMBOLS	EAR	AIR	UR	AWR	AHR	EYER	OWR

Here's their poor Ford car direly underpowered

Key for International Phonetic Alphabet (IPA) and Symbol Equivalents Referred to in the Workbook

The following is a table of symbols, which requires some clarification. The first column contains the sounds as represented by the *International Phonetic Alphabet (IPA)*, the second column contains *Sound Symbols* for those of you not familiar with the IPA, and the third column contains *Key Words* to more easily identify the sounds. If there is no *Key Word*, there is a brief description of how to make the sound.

There will be some sounds in the chapter Accent Breakdowns that will not need explanation, and therefore are not included here.

IPA Users

Diacritics are marks added to phonetic symbols that indicate the sound has been modified. For instance if you were in Liberia, and you had a friend named "Skip" the final [p] would not have a release of air after it, as it would in Detailed American English. The diacritic would indicate this: [p˺].

Below is a short list of diacritics for your reference. The full IPA list of diacritics is on page 19.

International Phonetic Alphabet (IPA) Diacritics Referred to in the Workbook

a̝	The sound is articulated higher in the mouth
a̞	The sound is articulated lower in the mouth
a̟	Tongue advances forward from tongue root
a̠	Tongue retracts back toward tongue root
a̟	The sound is articulated more forward in the mouth
a̱	The sound is articulated further back in the mouth
ä	The sound is centralized in the mouth
ã	The sound is nasalized
u̹	Lips more rounded
u̜	Lips less rounded
ŭ	The sound is short

ŭ̆ The sound is very short
uː/lː The sound is long
t̪ The sound is articulated on the back of the teeth (dentalized)
t̻ The sound is articulated on the hard palate with the blade rather than the tip of the tongue (laminal)
d̥ Voiced sound is produced without voice (voiceless)
t̬ Unvoiced sound is produced with voice (voiced)
t^h The sound is aspirated
p̚ No audible release
n̩ The sound has become syllabic (taken the place of the vowel)
ɫ The sound is velarized or pharyngealized

Symbol Users

Symbol Modifiers are marks added to a sound symbol indicating the sound has been modified. For instance if you were in Liberia, and you had a friend named "Skip", the final [P] almost sounds like a [P] with a [B] following it because it does not have a release of air after it, as it would in an American accent of English. The Symbol Modifier would indicate this: [P^B].

Below is a list of the modifiers that will be used in the workbook.

Symbol Modifiers Referred to in the Workbook

<o> When a symbol is <bracketed>, this means to use less lip rounding. An example of this would be in a Cockney accent when <o> is used rather than a final [L]: Bill → BI-<o>

>UHR< When a word is >reverse bracketed<, this means lips are more rounded. An example of this is in many American dialects when [UHR] is made with rounded lips: bird → B>UHR<D

O͞O When [‾] appears above a symbol, the sound is lengthened.

O͝O When [˘] appears above a symbol, the sound is shortened.

A̟W When [₊] appears below a symbol, the sound is articulated toward a place further forward in the mouth.

A̠W When [_] appears below a symbol, the sound is articulated toward a place further back in the mouth.

P^B When there is no release of air after plosive sounds [P], [T], [K]. This makes the unvoiced plosive have a slight voiced quality after it.

Sounds that are *italicized* are nasalized: man → M*A*N

International Phonetic Alphabet (IPA)	Symbol	Key Words
IPA will most often be in lower case and Symbol equivalents will most often be in upper case.		
Front Vowels		
i	EE	fl<u>ee</u>ce, sn<u>ee</u>ze, pl<u>ea</u>d
ɪ	I	k<u>i</u>t, p<u>i</u>tch, d<u>i</u>m, l<u>i</u>p
e	e	dr<u>e</u>ss, b<u>e</u>d, f<u>ea</u>ther, s<u>e</u>nd Same lexical set as D.A.E. [ɛ]/[EH]
ø	>e<	[e] with rounded lips
ɛ	EH	dr<u>e</u>ss, b<u>e</u>d, f<u>ea</u>ther, s<u>e</u>nd
æ	A	tr<u>a</u>p, m<u>a</u>d, r<u>a</u>t, c<u>a</u>ndle
a	Ah	b<u>a</u>th, <u>a</u>sk, <u>a</u>fter, d<u>a</u>nce Origin in British English.[1]
Middle Vowels		
ɘ	<u>e</u>	[e] articulated further back in the mouth
ɵ	<u>o</u>	[o] articulated more forward in the mouth
ɝ	UHR	n<u>ur</u>se, b<u>ir</u>d, w<u>or</u>k, s<u>er</u>vice, l<u>ear</u>n
ɜ	UH[R]	n<u>ur</u>se, b<u>ir</u>d, w<u>or</u>k, s<u>er</u>vice, l<u>ear</u>n Origin in British English. This is a non-rhotic (no r-coloration) version of [ɝ]/[UHR]
ɞ	>UH[R]<	UH[R] made with rounded lips
ə	uh (unstressed sound)	<u>a</u>bout, banan<u>a</u>
ɚ	er (unstressed sound)	sist<u>er</u>, trait<u>or</u>, hang<u>ar</u>
Λ̈	UH	str<u>u</u>t, c<u>u</u>rry, c<u>o</u>me, fl<u>oo</u>d This is represented as a centralized vowel in D.A.E. because the sound is made more in the middle of the mouth for American English. In R.P. it is a back vowel, made in the back of the mouth. The IPA refers to the R.P. pronunciation as the home base for this vowel: [ʌ]/[UH]

International Phonetic Alphabet (IPA)	Symbol	Key Words

International Phonetic Alphabet (IPA)	Symbol	Key Words
Back Vowels		
u	OO	f<u>oo</u>d, gr<u>ew</u>, tr<u>ue</u>, tw<u>o</u>
ʊ	U	f<u>oo</u>t, p<u>u</u>t
o	o	<u>o</u>bey Origin in British English
ɤ	<o>	[o] with lip corners pulled back rather than rounded. This sound is used in a Cockney accent, in place of a final [l]/[L]. Example: Bi<u>ll</u> → bɪɤ/BI<o>
ɔ	AW	th<u>ou</u>ght, t<u>a</u>ll, c<u>au</u>lk, <u>aw</u>ful
ɒ	O	cl<u>o</u>th, d<u>o</u>g, c<u>ou</u>gh, w<u>a</u>sh, h<u>o</u>rrid [ɒ]/[O], origin in British English.[2]
ɒ	O	l<u>o</u>t, sq<u>ua</u>d, w<u>a</u>nder [ɒ]/[O], origin in British English[2]
ɑ	AH	f<u>a</u>ther
Diphthongs		
eĭ	AY	f<u>a</u>ce, p<u>ai</u>n, d<u>ay</u>, w<u>eigh</u>t, st<u>ea</u>k
aĭ	EYE	pr<u>i</u>ce, <u>eye</u>s, d<u>i</u>aper, fl<u>y</u>, g<u>uy</u>, h<u>eigh</u>t
ɔĭ	OY	ch<u>oi</u>ce, b<u>oy</u>s
oŭ	OH	g<u>oa</u>t, s<u>ew</u>, g<u>o</u>
aŭ	OW	m<u>ou</u>th, t<u>ow</u>n
Diphthongs of R		
ɪɚ	EAR	n<u>ear</u>, b<u>eer</u>
ɛɚ	AIR	h<u>air</u>, st<u>are</u>, p<u>ear</u>, squ<u>are</u>, th<u>ere</u>
ʊɚ	UR	s<u>ure</u>, p<u>oor</u>, y<u>our</u>
ɔɚ	AWR	n<u>or</u>th, Ge<u>or</u>ge, p<u>our</u>, w<u>ar</u>p, <u>oar</u>
aɚ	AHR	st<u>ar</u>t, h<u>ear</u>t
aĭɚ	EYER	f<u>ire</u>
aŭɚ	OWR	h<u>our</u>

International Phonetic Alphabet (IPA)	Symbol	Key Words
		Consonants
ð	TH (voiced)	<u>th</u>ese, brea<u>the</u>
θ	th (no voice)	<u>th</u>in, mou<u>th</u>
ɹ	R	<u>r</u>ed, me<u>rr</u>y
r	RR (trilled)	<u>R</u>oberto, <u>r</u>ojo, pe<u>rr</u>o (Spanish)
ɾ	R^R (tapped)	pe<u>r</u>o, ama<u>r</u>illo (Spanish)
ŋ	NG	si<u>ng</u>, ha<u>ng</u>er
ʃ	SH	<u>sh</u>oe, fi<u>sh</u>
ʒ	ZH	bei<u>g</u>e
tʃ	CH	<u>ch</u>ur<u>ch</u>
dʒ	J	<u>j</u>u<u>dg</u>e
j	Y	<u>y</u>ou
ʔ	ʔ	This sound is often inserted before a vowel at the beginning of a word in many accents. In American English it is referred to as a glottal stop. Example: apple → 'ʔæ.pəl/**ʔA**.PuhL

Notes

1 In the D.A.E. vowel and diphthong tables in this workbook, there is a lexical sub-set for [æ]/[A] that shifts to the [a] and is commonly referred to as the *ask/bath* list or set. This shift usually occurs for African speakers influenced by British English.

   Example: *bath* – D.A.E. → bæθ/BAth changes to R.P. → baθ/BAhth.

2 In the D.A.E. vowel and diphthong tables in this workbook, there are lexical sub-sets for *[ɔ]/[AW] and *[ɑ]/[AH] that shift to the phoneme [ɒ]/[O] when speaking R.P. This shift usually occurs for African speakers influenced by British English.

   Example: *cloth* – D.A.E. → klɔθ/KLAWth; R.P. – klɒθ/KLOth.
   Example: *lot* – D.A.E. → lɑt/LAHT; R.P. – lɒt/LOT.

International Phonetic Alphabet (IPA) Charts for Consonants (Pulmonic) and Vowels

Below are three excellent websites for audio pronunciation of phonemes in the following IPA tables:

University of Victoria:
http://web.uvic.ca/ling/resources/ipa/charts/IPAlab/ipachart.htm

UCLA:
http://www.phonetics.ucla.edu/course/chapter1/chapter1.html

Paul Meier Dialect Services:
http://www.paulmeier.com/ipacharts/

THE INTERNATIONAL PHONETIC ALPHABET (revised to 2005)

CONSONANTS (PULMONIC)   © 2005 IPA

	Bilabial	Labiodental	Dental	Alveolar	Postalveolar	Retroflex	Palatal	Velar	Uvular	Pharyngeal	Glottal
Plosive	p b			t d		ʈ ɖ	c ɟ	k ɡ	q ɢ		ʔ
Nasal	m	ɱ		n		ɳ	ɲ	ŋ	N		
Trill	ʙ			r					R		
Tap or Flap		ⱱ		ɾ		ɽ					
Fricative	ɸ β	f v	θ ð	s z	ʃ ʒ	ʂ ʐ	ç ʝ	x ɣ	χ ʁ	ħ ʕ	h ɦ
Lateral fricative				ɬ ɮ							
Approximant		ʋ		ɹ		ɻ	j	ɰ			
Lateral approximant				l		ɭ	ʎ	L			

Where symbols appear in pairs, the one to the right represents a voiced consonant. Shaded areas denote articulations judged impossible.

On p. 19 is the IPA chart of vowel sounds. Speakers of English dialects use about half of these sounds. *Front, Central (Middle), and Back* indicate where the sounds are made. If you can envision a very large left profile of someone's head, the positions of the phonemes would be in the approximate places in the mouth where the tongue would be making them.

VOWELS

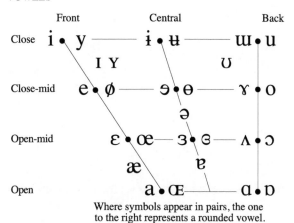

Where symbols appear in pairs, the one
to the right represents a rounded vowel.

DIACRITICS   Diacritics may be placed above a symbol with a descender, e.g. ŋ̊

̥	Voiceless	n̥ d̥	̤	Breathy voiced	b̤ a̤	̪ Dental	t̪ d̪
̬	Voiced	s̬ t̬	̰	Creaky voiced	b̰ a̰	̺ Apical	t̺ d̺
ʰ	Aspirated	tʰ dʰ	̼	Linguolabial	t̼ d̼	̻ Laminal	t̻ d̻
̹	More rounded	ɔ̹	ʷ	Labialized	tʷ dʷ	̃ Nasalized	ẽ
̜	Less rounded	ɔ̜	ʲ	Palatalized	tʲ dʲ	ⁿ Nasal release	dⁿ
̟	Advanced	u̟	ˠ	Velarized	tˠ dˠ	ˡ Lateral release	dˡ
̠	Retracted	e̠	ˤ	Pharyngealized	tˤ dˤ	̚ No audible release	d̚
̈	Centralized	ë	̴	Velarized or pharyngealized	ɫ		
̽	Mid-centralized	e̽	̝	Raised	e̝	(ɹ̝ = voiced alveolar fricative)	
̩	Syllabic	n̩	̞	Lowered	e̞	(β̞ = voiced bilabial approximant)	
̯	Non-syllabic	e̯	̘	Advanced Tongue Root	e̘		
˞	Rhoticity	ɚ a˞	̙	Retracted Tongue Root	e̙		

IPA Chart, http://www.internationalphoneticassociation.org/content/ipa-chart, available under a Creative Commons Attribution-Sharealike 3.0 Unported License. Copyright © 2005 International Phonetic Association.

Ask/Bath List of Words

Below are some of the most common ask/bath words, as defined in Edith Skinner's *Speak With Distinction* and J.C. Wells' *Accents of English 1.*

The list is skeletal and does not include the many variations of these root words, including their placement in compound words.

advance	Chancellor	giraffe	prance
advantage	chandler	glance	raft
after	chant	glass	rascal
alabaster	clasp	graft	rasp
answer	class	graph	raspberry
ask	command	grasp	rather
aunt	craft	grass	reprimand
bask	daft	half	sample
bath	dance	lance	shaft
blanch	demand	last	slander
blast	disaster	laugh	slant
branch	draft	mask	staff
brass	draught	mast	taft
calf	enchant	master	task
can't	enhance	nasty	trance
cask	entrance (verb)	pass	vantage
cast	example	past	vast
caste	fast	pastor	waft
castle	flask	pasture	wrath
castor-oil	France	path	
chaff	gasp	plant	
chance	ghastly	plaster	

Accent Diagnostic Passage and Sentences

The following diagnostic passage and sentences are read by many of the inter-viewees in the Workbook's accent library.

A poor fool, sitting high on a mountain, heard a mournful tune coming from the forest below. His pulse quickened. He had the gift of second sight and knew at once that it was not a bird's song he heard. It was the voice of the orphan princess Mary. Mary's strict and evil uncle had seized power of her kingdom, and placed an ugly curse on her, banishing her from the town. Her once merry and golden eyes had turned sad and orange. Thick fur had grown all over her body. The poor woman was doomed to wander in fear, unless she could solve the riddle of her uncle's curse. The fool knew in his heart that he must save her. He hurried down the mountain, drawn by the princess' singing. He found her standing at the edge of a cliff. As soon as he saw her, he burned with desire, fell to his knees, and asked her to marry him. Wouldn't you know, that when he dared to look up, she calmly graced him with golden eyes. Her fur gently fell to her feet, revealing a glistening human form. The irreversible riddle had been solved by a fool's true love.[1]

I'll meet you at the ferry in an hour with the ten children.
The thief will tell me after we trap him.
In the summer, workers burned the underbrush.
I thought my father would not stop being a bully but the truth is, I was wrong.
I'd like to fly away someday and go south to the mountains with the boys.
Our friends started the fire, near your north orchard, an hour before we got there.

Note

1 This diagnostic passage targets key phoneme changes that commonly occur in accent work. This was composed with my colleague Pamela Prather in 2005.

Chapter 2

Ugandan (Luganda) Accent of English

Introduction and Resources

The Luganda Language in Uganda

In the late 19th century when the English colonized Uganda, they began to impose English as the official language. The Baganda ethnic group was less cooperative than others in culturally adapting to the English, and held onto their Luganda language. They became the country's government leaders in 1962 when Uganda became independent. This ensured that although English is the official language, Luganda is one of the most widely spoken in the country.

Luganda (or Ganda), a member of the Bantu branch of the Niger-Congo languages, is spoken by the Baganda people and is taught in many schools in the Buganda, a south central region of Uganda. Bagandans make up the largest ethnic group in Uganda and major publications in Kampala are published in Luganda. Swahili is also considered a national language. Luo is the official language of the Acholi in Northern Uganda. There are at least forty-one African languages spoken in the country.

Documentaries

Lord's Children (Betty Bigome speaks in English on this PBS video), *Invisible Children* (this documentary contains Sudanese, Congolese, Achiola Luo and Ugandan (Luganda) accents), *The Drunkest Place on Earth*, *God Loves Uganda*

Films

divisionz, Innocent Tears, Candle in the Wind, The Step Mom, The Blame, Betrayal Balyake, School Times, Abasama Vacation, Feelings Struggle

Television

Bukedde TV, NTV, T Nation

Plays with Ugandan (Luganda) Characters

Book of Mormon by Matt Stone, Robert Lopez and Trey Parker, *That Uganda play* by Theroun D'Arcy Patterson, *Witness Uganda* by Matt Gould and Griffin Matthews

Music

Akazinga by Stella Kayaga, *Nze Wuwo By* by Stecia Mayanja, *Badilisha* by Dr. Jose Chameleone, Sheila Nvanungi

Radio

Radio Simba, Akaboozi FM, Dembe FM, Bukedde FM

Personalities

Emmanuel Arnold Okwi (soccer player), Ronald Muwenda Mutebi II (King of Buganda), Yoweri Musevni (President 2015), Idi Amin (former President of Uganda), Gravity Omutujju (rapper), John Aki-Bua (Olympic gold medalist), Kassim Ouma (boxer), Juliana Kanyomozi (actress and musician), Janet Museveni (First Lady of Uganda 2015), Patrick Amama Mbabazi (former Prime Minister of Uganda), Rebecca Kadaga (Speaker of the House of Parliament 2015)

Down & Dirty Warm-up and Quick Look

Note!

On Symbols

- International Phonetic Alphabet Symbols will be listed first and Sound Symbols will be listed second. Example: [i]/[EE]
- Sound Symbol Users: bold-faced letters indicate the syllable is stressed.

1) **The Muscles:** Wake your mouth up so you can more easily discover the physical transformation of the accent.

   a. Scratch the front, middle and back of your tongue with your front top teeth.

   b. Rub the front, middle and back of your hard palate with the tip of your tongue.

   c. Imagine your mouth is numb from being at the dentist and you want to wake it up. Make tongue circles pressing against the back of your lips first clockwise, then counter clockwise (you are waking up your orbicularis muscle).

   d. To get the breath flowing, blow through your lips, getting them to flap together. Travel up and down in pitch on a BBBB and PPP, feeling the vibration as you wiggle up and down your spine.

2) **Vocal Posture for a Ugandan (Luganda) Accent:** The tongue is relaxed and wide and the blade cups up from a dip in the middle back of the tongue. The lips are suppler in Ugandan articulation than in American English. The corners of the lips are active in rounding; the lower lip is more active in the rounding than the upper lip. The jaw is half closed, and articulation is somewhat jaw driven. Articulation is focused in the middle back of the mouth with the lips bringing the sound forward and out. The soft palate remains fairly wide as the pharynx narrows, creating a twang.

3) **Resonators:** "occupy" the following spaces. This will prepare you to find the Source & Path of Resonance for a Ugandan (Luganda) accent. (By

"occupy", I mean just that; be in the space of it and find the pathway and flow of resonance, rather than "putting" the resonance there.)

a.   CHEST – Generously laugh at something – hạ hạ hạ / HAh HAh HAh
b.   HARD PALATE – As if you were discovering something – hoː hoː hoː / Hō Hō Hō
c.   THE BONES AT THE BASE OF YOUR SKULL (THE OCCIPITAL BONE) – Use your hands to scoop the sound from the base of your skull with a Mississippi African-American dialect as if you're flirting with someone nearby – hɚ· hɚ· hɚ· / Hē̠ Hē̠ Hē̠
d.   FLICK THE SOUND OUT OF YOUR CHEEKBONES with an Italian-American flourish, as if calling to someone across the street – hɚ· hɚ· hɚ· / Hē̠ Hē̠ Hē̠
e.   WITH YOUR HANDS NEXT TO YOUR TEMPLES, SHAKE THE SOUND OUT WITH LOOSE FISTS – As if you were somewhat crazed – jị jị jị / YEE̠ YEE̠ YEE̠
f.   IMAGINE A METAL DISK EXTENDING FROM YOUR HANDS THROUGH YOUR SKULL. Bring your hands to the sides of your head just above the temples, with your palms facing the floor, thumbs hooked behind your skull. *Lid* the vibration to create a muted brassy sound. Like a robot saying "Hi" – haɨ haɨ haɨ / Hah-EE̠ Hah-EE̠ Hah-EE̠
g.   GIGGLE OUT OF THE TOP OF YOUR HEAD – As if you were tickled pink by something – hɨ hɨ hɨ / HEE̠ HEE̠ HEE̠

4)   **Source & Path of Resonance for a Ugandan (Luganda) Accent:** The resonance starts robustly, filling the chest, traveling through a slightly contracted pharynx, creating a pharyngeal twang. Think of it then going through a widened soft palate to the bones at the base of the skull (see #3c above). It then spreads fully into the sinuses, without becoming nasalized, and gets lidded in the "metal disc" area of the skull (see #3f above).

5)   **Get the sound changes into your body and imagination.**
     Say these phrases occupying the following places in your body, suggesting to yourself the following energetic associations:

- pubic bone to tail bone – survival instinct

     zʉː / ZŌO
     I need it – a nị̠d ï̠t / Ah NEED EE̠T

- pubic bone to navel & sacrum in back – sexuality, big feelings

     woː / Wō
     I desire it – a d̥ɪˈza.jɚɪ ï̠t / Ah DEE̠.**ZEYE**-YUHR̠ ̠EE̠T

- rib cage to below heart – will

     ʒɒ̠ː / Zhō
     I want it – a wɒn̠t ï̠t / Ah WONT EE̠T

- heart – love

  mḁː / MĀh
  I love it – a lʌv ï̠ṭ / Ah LUHV Ḛ̄T

- throat – communication (think of talking at a party)

  bə / Bȩ
  I have to say it – a hɛɣ ̥tʉ sə· ï̠ṭ / Ah HEHVᶠ TỠO Sȩ̄ Ḛ̄T

- forehead – intelligence/wisdom

  kəː / Kȩ̄
  I know it – a noː ï̠ṭ / Ah Nō Ḛ̄T

- crown of head – spirituality

  ɹ̠iː / Ṟ̠EE
  I believe it – a biˈlịv ï̠ṭ / Ah BEE.**LEE̱V** Ḛ̄T

6) **Articulation** – using playful physical actions: punching, flicking, dabbing, slashing

   d̪ʊ· d̪ɪ kʊ· d̪ʊ· d̪ɪ kʊ· d̪ʊ· d̪ɪ kʊ· – d̪ị̈
   d̪ʊ· d̪ɪ kʊ· d̪ʊ· d̪ɪ kʊ· d̪ʊ· d̪ɪ kʊ· – d̪ə·
   d̪ʊ· d̪ɪ kʊ· d̪ʊ· d̪ɪ kʊ· d̪ʊ· d̪ɪ kʊ· – d̪aɨ
   d̪ʊ· d̪ɪ kʊ· d̪ʊ· d̪ɪ kʊ· d̪ʊ· d̪ɪ kʊ· – d̪o
   d̪ʊ· d̪ɪ kʊ· d̪ʊ· d̪ɪ kʊ· d̪ʊ· d̪ɪ kʊ· – d̪ʉ

Repeat as needed, replacing [d̪] with [t], [p], [b], [k], [g], [f], [v]

   DŪ DI KŪ DŪ DI KŪ DŪ DI KŪ – DEE̱
   DŪ DI KŪ DŪ DI KŪ DŪ DI KŪ – Dȩ̄
   DŪ DI KŪ DŪ DI KŪ DŪ DI KŪ – DAh-EE̱
   DŪ DI KŪ DŪ DI KŪ DŪ DI KŪ – Dō
   DŪ DI KŪ DŪ DI KŪ DŪ DI KŪ – DO̧O

Repeat as needed, replacing [D] with [T], [P], [B], [K], [G], [F], [V]. [D] & [T] are made with the blade (rather than the tip) of the tongue on the alveolar ridge.

Key Points of Focus
Characteristics and Vocal Posture

Ugandan (Luganda) Accent Characteristics

Note!
On Melody/Lilt/Pitch and Rhythm/Stress/Pace
Every accent contains shifts for some, but not necessarily all, of these elements of vocal variety.

Note!
On Use of Musical Notes
Follow the "musical notes" up and down to get a feel for the melody of the accent. The filled-in notes are shorter than the open notes. For those who are musically inclined, think of them as approximating quarter notes and half notes. This distinction will give you a feel for the rhythm of the accent.

Melody/Lilt/Pitch

Luganda is a lively, tonal language. Vowels have a high tone, a low tone, or a falling high-to-low tone. The pitch change is mostly major. This can be heard clearly in *Richard Story Part 2*, in which he speaks Luganda.

This lively pitch change of vowels is a salient characteristic of a Ugandan (Luganda) accent.

1. Note that the pitch change is mostly from syllable to syllable rather than within the syllable, although sometimes when the vowel has shifted from a diphthong to a monophthong, speakers will elongate the vowel on a glide up or down.

2.   Note that, unlike English, there can be a lift in pitch at the end of a declarative thought.

Example: Martha Story (Part 1) – 1:02

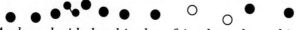

And we decided as his close friends to throw him

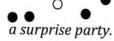

a surprise party.

Martha's pitch play is sometimes surprising, as in her final high pitch in the final syllable of *party* (#2 above). She illustrates syllable-to-syllable pitch change, as well as the use of a glide in tone from high to low in the middle syllable of the word *deci̲ded*.

Example: Thembo Story – 2:40

Everybody in the party we we laughed a lot because we saw

that this thing what the la̲dy has done to the man.

In this sentence, Thembo, too, embodies lively pitch play. The pitch changes from syllable to syllable (rather than within a syllable), except in the word *la̲dy*, in which the diphthong [eī]/[AY] is replaced by the monophthong [ɘˑ]/[ē] (#1 above). He also ends his thought going up in pitch on the word *ma̲n* (#2 above).

Rhythm/Stress/Pace

There is a somewhat syncopated feel to the accent because of the following characteristics.

1.   The vowels in operative words are often elongated on an even pitch.
2.   Diphthongs most often become monothongs and are elongated in operative words.
3.   The "e" in prefixes like *re, be, pre* is often elongated, which brings stress to an otherwise unstressed syllable.
4.   The second to last syllable in words with three or more syllables is often stressed.
5.   The predominant use of strong forms of vowels rather than weak forms.

Example: Richard Story (Part 1) – 0:07

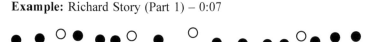

I was bitten by a fox that morning and as a result I was

admitted to the hospital.

Richard elongates the vowels in his operative words: *bitten, morning, admitted, hospital* (#1 above). In the word *morning*, he pronounces the diphthong of R as a monophthong: [ɔɹ]/[AWR] becomes [o]/[o] (#2 above). In the word *hospital*, the second to last syllable is elongated, and shifts toward a stronger form of the vowel: [ɪ]/[I] becomes [ɨ]/[EE] (#4 and #5 above).

Example: Olivia Story – 1:02

As if they were eating cheese without realizing the butter

was supposed to be spread on the buns...

Because Olivia's pitch play is somewhat more subdued than Richard's, stress and rhythm shifts are singularly apparent. The vowels in her operative words are all lengthened: *eating, cheese, butter, supposed, spread, bun* (#1 above). In the word *supposed*, she also pronounces the diphthong [oʊ]/[OH] as a monophthong [oː]/[o] (#2 above). In the word *realizing*, the diphthong in the second to last syllable is elongated (#4 above).

Source & Path of Resonance

The resonance starts robustly, filling the chest. Then, it travels through a slightly narrowed pharynx, which creates pharyngeal twang. Think of it then going through a widened soft palate to the bones at the base of the skull (see #3c on page 28). It then spreads fully into the sinuses, without becoming nasalized, and gets lidded in the "metal disc" area of the skull (see #3f on page 28).

You can hear the Source & Path of Resonance as described, quite clearly in all of the Ugandan (Luganda) interviews on the accent library. Tona, Olivia and Thembo have more pharyngeal twang than the others, but besides that, they are consistent in the other characteristics.

Ugandan (Luganda) Accent Vocal Posture

Note!

On Vocal Posture

These adjustments enable you to integrate the accent through physical transformation rather than solely relying on sound shifts.

- **Focus of Articulation:** Articulation is focused in the middle back of the mouth with the lips bringing the sound forward and out.
- **Tongue:** The tongue is relaxed and wide. The blade cups up from a dip in the middle back of the tongue.
- **Lips:** The lips are suppler in Ugandan articulation than in American English. The corners of the lips are active in rounding. The lower lip is more active in the rounding than the upper lip.
- **Jaw:** The jaw is half closed, and articulation is somewhat jaw driven.
- **Soft Palate and Pharynx:** The soft palate remains fairly wide as the pharynx narrows, creating a twang.

Distinct Sounds of the Language and/or Accent

Note!

On Distinct Sounds

These are some of the sounds that Ugandans use and American speakers do not. In speaking the sounds and/or the words that contain them, you can heighten your physical understanding of the Ugandan (Luganda) accent's *Vocal Posture* as compared to your own. This frame of reference will both inform and strengthen your accent.

Consonants

1. *IPA:* [c] → Voiceless palatal plosive.
   Symbol: [$\underset{+}{K}^Y$] → [K] made more forward in the mouth with a little [^{Y}] following.
   This sound is used in speaking the Ugandan (Luganda) language.
2. *IPA:* [ɟ] → Voiced palatal plosive.
   Symbol: [$\underset{+}{G}^Y$] → [G] made more forward in the mouth with a little [^{Y}] following.
   This sound is used in speaking the Ugandan (Luganda) language.
3. *IPA:* [ɱ] → Labiodental nasal.
   Symbol: [M] made with the upper teeth on the lower lip.
   This sound is used in speaking the Ugandan (Luganda) language.
4. *IPA:* [ɲ] → Palatal nasal.
   Symbol: [$\underset{+}{NG}^Y$] → [NG] made more forward in the mouth with a little [^{Y}] following.
   Used in place of [ŋ]/[NG]: *sing*
   This sound is used in speaking both the language and accent of Ugandan (Luganda).
5. *IPA:* [r] → Alveolar trill.
   Symbol: [RR] → Trilled [R].
   Used in place of [ɹ]/[R]: *ran, ferry*
   This sound is used in speaking both the language and accent of Ugandan (Luganda).

6. *IPA:* [ɾ] → Alveolar tap.
   Symbol: [R^R] → This is a tapped [R]. It is made by lightly tapping the blade of the tongue on the post alveolar ridge.
   Used in place of [ɹ]/[R]: <u>r</u>an, fe<u>rr</u>y
   This sound is used in speaking both the language and accent of Ugandan (Luganda).

Pre-nasalized Consonants

These are consonants that, in addition to standing on their own, also have a nasalized counterpart in Luganda.

   IPA: [ɱf], [ɱv], [mp], [mb], [nt], [nd], [nc], [ɲɟ], [ng], [ns], [nz]
   Symbol: [MF], [MV], [MP], [MB], [NT], [ND], [NK̟], [NG̟], [NG], [NS], [NZ]

Although these sounds are only used in the Ugandan (Luganda) language, they indicate the prevalence of nasality, which manifests as sinus resonance in a Ugandan (Luganda) accent.

Vowels

The vowels of Ugandan (Luganda) include:

   IPA: [i], [e], [a], [u], [o]
   Symbol: [EE], [e], [Ah], [OO], [o]

Knowing the vowels for the Ugandan (Luganda) language will provide clues for the vowel shifts in the accent.

7. *IPA:* [e]
   Symbol: [e] This is the first sound in the D.A.E. diphthong [AY] as in f<u>a</u>ce.
   [e]/[e] used in place of [ɛ]/[EH]: dr<u>e</u>ss, b<u>e</u>d
   This sound is used in speaking both the language and accent of Ugandan (Luganda).
8. *IPA:* [a]
   Symbol: [Ah] This is the first sound in the diphthong [EYE] as in sk<u>y</u>.
   Used in place of [æ]/[A]: tr<u>a</u>p, b<u>a</u>th
   This sound is used in speaking both the language and accent of Ugandan (Luganda).
9. *IPA:* [ɨ] → centralized [i].
   Symbol: [E̱E̱] → [EE] made in the middle of the mouth rather than in the front of the mouth.
   Used in place of [i]/[EE]: fl<u>ee</u>ce, sn<u>ee</u>ze, pl<u>ea</u>d
   This sound is used in speaking a Ugandan (Luganda) accent of English.
10. *IPA:* [ʉ] → centralized [u].
    Symbol: [O̱O̱] → [OO] articulated in the middle of the mouth rather than the back of the mouth.

Used in place of [u]/[OO]: *f<u>oo</u>d, gr<u>ew</u>*

This sound is used in speaking a Ugandan (Luganda) accent of English.

11. *IPA:* [ə] → centralized [e].

   Symbol: [e̞] → [e] made in the middle of the mouth.

   Used in place of [ʌ]/[UH]: *str<u>u</u>t, c<u>u</u>rry, c<u>o</u>me*

   Used in place of [eɪ]/[AY]: *f<u>a</u>ce, p<u>ai</u>n, d<u>ay</u>*

   This sound is used in speaking a Ugandan (Luganda) accent of English.

12. *IPA:* [ɵ] → centralized [o].

   Symbol: [o̞] → [o] made in the middle of the mouth.

   Sometimes used in place of [ʌ]/[UH]: *str<u>u</u>t, c<u>u</u>rry, c<u>o</u>me*

   This sound is used in speaking a Ugandan (Luganda) accent of English.

13. *IPA:* [ɜ]

   Symbol: [UH^R]

   Used in place of [ɝ]/[ER]: *b<u>ir</u>d, n<u>ur</u>se, w<u>or</u>k*

   This sound is used in speaking a Ugandan (Luganda) accent of English.

14. *IPA:* [ɤ] → [o] with no lip rounding and lip corners slightly pulled back.

   Symbol: [<o>] → [o] with no lip rounding and lip corners slightly pulled
      back. The sound is much like a [W].

   Used in place of [l]/[L] at the end of a word: *exce<u>l</u>, fa<u>ll</u>, tab<u>le</u>*

   This sound is used in speaking a Ugandan (Luganda) accent of English.

15. *IPA:* [o]

   Symbol: [o] → This is the first sound in the D.A.E. diphthong OH as in *g<u>o</u>*.

   Used in place of [ɔ]/[AW]: *th<u>ou</u>ght, t<u>a</u>ll, c<u>au</u>lk*

   Used in place of [oʊ]/[OH]: *g<u>oa</u>t, s<u>o</u>, g<u>o</u>*

   This sound is used in speaking both the language and accent of Ugandan
      (Luganda).

16. *IPA:* [ɒ]

   Symbol: [O] → This is the British *h<u>o</u>t, c<u>o</u>pper, c<u>o</u>ffee, p<u>o</u>t* sound.

   Used in place of [ɑ]/[AH] in many words spelled with "o": *l<u>o</u>t, squ<u>a</u>d,
      w<u>a</u>nder*

   This sound is used in speaking both the language and accent of Ugandan
      (Luganda).

Consonant Sound Shifts

- ☛ indicates that this sound is a key sound shift
- You can begin to fold melody and rhythm with the sound changes by speaking the sample sentences that are before each section of sound changes.

Consonant Shifts

Example: Dennis Story (Part 1) – 0:21

We foun_d_ our fa_ther_ sea_ted_ a_t the front_ of the_ wha_t?...the hou_se.

IPA: wɪ̈ föˀnḍ 'a.wə̣ 'fạ.ð̟ə sɨ.tɪ̈d aṭ ð̟ï fronṭ əv ð̟ï ʍạt ð̟ï haüs

SYMBOLS: WEE FUᵘʰND **Ah**.WUH **FAh**.THUH SEE.TEED AhT THEE FRᴿǫNT
ǫv THEE HWAhT THEE HAh-ŲS

I'_ll_ mee_t_ _you_ a_t the ferry_ in an hour wi_th the ten children._

IPA: aɪʏ mɪ̣t ʃ‿ʉ aṭ ð̟ə 'fɛ.ɹ̣i ïn an 'a.wə wɪ̈θ̟ ð̟ə ṭen 'tʃ ïʏ.ḍɾen

SYMBOLS: Ah-EE-<o> MEETCH‿OO AhT THuh **Fe**.REE EEN AhN **Ah**.WUH
WEEth THuh TeN **CHEE**-<o>.DRᴿeN

Key Words	Detailed American English Accent	Shift to Ugandan (Luganda) Accent of English	Key Words Shifts	Your Key Words
	IPA	IPA	IPA	
	Symbol	Symbol	Symbol	
team de_bt_, _did_	[t]/[d]	[ṭ]/[ḍ]	ṭim, ḍeṭ, ḍiḍ	
	[T]/[D]	[T]/[D] are both made with the blade of the tongue on the alveolar ridge	TEEM, DeT, DEED	
☛ _the_se _th_ere, brea_the_	ð	ð̟	ð̟iz, ð̟ɛ', bɹ̣ið̟	
	[TH]	[TH] made with the blade of the tongue on the back of the top front teeth (dentalized)	THEEZˢ, THEH, BREETH	

Key Words	Detailed American English Accent IPA / Symbol	Shift to Ugandan (Luganda) Accent of English IPA / Symbol	Key Words Shifts IPA / Symbol	Your Key Words
☞ thin thick, mouth	θ --- th	θ̬ --- [th] (dentalized)	θ̬ïn, θ̬ïk, maöθ̬ --- thEEN, thEEk, MAh-Uth	
☞ red dress, merry, sorry	ɹ --- R	[ɹ̬] or [ɾ] --- [R̬] or [Rᴿ]	ɹ̬ed, dɹ̬es, 'me.ɹ̬i, 'sɒ.ɹ̬i or red, dres, 'me.ri, 'sɒ.ri --- R̬eD, DR̬eS, Me.REE, SO.REE or RᴿeD, DRᴿeS, Me.RᴿEE, SO.RᴿEE	
☞ excel fall, table (final *l* in spelling)	l --- L	sometimes ɣ --- sometimes [<o>] ([o] made with lip corners pulled back rather than rounded)	ek.seɣ, fɔɣ, tɘˑ.bɣ --- eK.Se-<o>, FAW-<o>, Tê.B<o>	
judge	dʒ --- J	d̬ʒ̊ --- Jˢᴴ	d̬ʒ̊ɘd̬ʒ̊ --- JˢᴴeJˢᴴ	
church	tʃ --- CH	ᵗʃ --- ᵀSH	ᵗʃɜᵗʃ --- ᵀSH UHᴿ ᵀSH	
☞ boys (final *s* in spelling when pronounced [z])	z --- Z	z̬ --- Zˢ	boiz̬ --- Bo-EEZˢ	
sing (final *ng* in spelling)	ŋ --- NG	sometimes ɲ --- sometimes [NG̟ʸ]	sïɲ --- SEENG̟ʸ	
reading (final *ing* in spelling)	ɪŋ --- ING	sometimes iɲ̊ --- sometimes EENG	'ɹi.d̬iɲ̊ --- REE.DEENG	
☞ what which, why (*wh* in spelling for words consistent with this change in RP)	w --- W	ʌ --- HW	ʌɒt̬, ʌïtʃ, ʌaɪ --- HWOT, HWEECH, HWAh-EE	

Front Vowel Sound Shifts

Note!

On Vowels

The vowels of the Ugandan (Luganda) language include:

IPA: [i], [e], [a], [o]
SYMBOLS: [EE], [e], [Ah], [o]

Knowing the vowels of the Luganda language will provide clues for the vowel shifts in the accent.

		Front Vowel Shifts		
The thi̯e̱f wi̱ll te̱ll me̱ a̱fter we̱ tra̱p hi̱m.				
IPA: ð̯ə θi̯f wïl te̯ɤ mɨ 'a̯f.tə̯ wɨ tre̯p hïm				
SYMBOLS: THuh thE̱E̱F WE̱E̱L Te̱-<o> MEE **AhF**.Tuh WEE TRᴿEHP HE̱E̱M				
Key Words	*Detailed American English Accent* IPA --- Symbol	*Shift to Ugandan (Luganda) Accent of English* IPA --- Symbol	*Key Words Shifts* IPA --- Symbol	*Your Key Words*
☞ fle̱e̱ce sne̱e̱ze, ple̱a̱d	i --- EE	i̱ --- [E̱E̱] [EE] made in the middle of the mouth	flis, sni̱z, pli̱d --- FLE̱E̱S, SNE̱E̱Zˢ, PLE̱E̱D	
☞ ki̱t pi̱tch, di̱m, lip	ɪ --- I	ï --- [E̱E̱] [I] made more like an [EE]	kït, pïtʃ, dïm --- KE̱E̱T, PE̱E̱CH, DE̱E̱M	

Key Words	Detailed American English Accent	Shift to Ugandan (Luganda) Accent of English	Key Words Shifts	Your Key Words
	IPA ----------- Symbol	IPA ----------- Symbol	IPA ----------- Symbol	
country (*y* in final position of spelling)	ɪ ----------- EE	ɪ̆ ----------- EE	ˈkʌn.tɾɪ̆ ----------- KUHN-TRᴿEE	
berated	[ɪ] in prefix ----------- [EE] in prefix	i̤ ----------- EE	bi.ɾe̬.tɪ̤d ----------- BEE.Rᴿē.TEED	
☛ dress bed, feather, send	ɛ ----------- EH	e ----------- e̬	dɹes, bed̬, ˈfe̬.ðə ----------- DReS, BeD, Fe̬.THUH	
☛ trap mad, rat, candle	æ ----------- A	[ɛ̤] or [a] ----------- [EH] or [Ah]	tɾɛ̤p, mɛd̬, ɹɛt or tɾap, mad̬, ɹat ----------- TRᴿEHP, MEHD, REHT or TRᴿAhP, MAhD, RAhT	
☛ bath *[a]/[Ah] ask, after, dance, example, half, mask, rascal, transfer In Chapter 1, there is a list of these words called the BATH or ASK list of words.	æ ----------- A	a̤ ----------- [Ah] ([Ah] made in the middle of the mouth)	ba̤θ, a̤sk, ˈa̤f.tə ----------- BAhth, AhSK, AhF.TUH	

Middle Vowel Sound Shifts

Middle Vowel Shifts				
In the summer, workers burned the underbrush. *IPA:* ɪ̈n ðə 'sə.mə̰ 'wə.kə̰z bɜnd̪ ð̪ɪ̈ 'ən.d̪ʌ.bɹʌʃ *SYMBOLS:* E̠E̠N THuh Se̠.MUH **W>UH^R<**.KUHZ^S BUH^RND THE̠E̠ e̠N.DUH.BRUHSH				
Key Words	*Detailed American English Accent* *IPA* ------------------ *Symbol*	*Shift to Ugandan (Luganda) Accent of English* *IPA* ------------------ *Symbol*	*Key Words Shifts* *IPA* ------------------ *Symbol*	*Your Key Words*
ɝ nurse bird, work, service, learn ER	ɝ ------------------ ER	[ə] or [ɜ] ------------------ [>UH^R<] or [UH^R]	nəs, bəd̪, wək, 'sə.vïs, lən or nɜs, bɜd̪, wɜk, 'sɜ.vïs, lɜn ------------------ N>UH^R<S, B>UH^R<D, W>UH^R<K, **S>UH^R<.VE̠E̠S,** L>UH^R<N or NUH^RS, BUH^RD, WUH^RK, **SUH^R.VE̠E̠S,** LUH^RN	
sister traitor, hangar er	ɚ ------------------ er	ə̰ ------------------ UH	'sïs.tə, 'tɹɪə'.tə, 'hɛɲ.ə̰ ------------------ **SE̠E̠S.TUH,** **TRɪ̈e̠.TUH,** **HEHNG.UH**	

Key Words	Detailed American English Accent IPA / Symbol	Shift to Ugandan (Luganda) Accent of English IPA / Symbol	Key Words Shifts IPA / Symbol	Your Key Words
☛ strʉt curry, cọme	ʌ̈	ə or ɵ or ʌ̩̈	st̮rɘt̮, ˈkə.ɹ̩i, kəm or st̮rɵt̮, ˈkɵ.ɹ̩i, kəm or st̮rʌ̩̈t̮, ˈkʌ̩̈.ɹ̩i, kʌ̩̈m	
	ỤH	[e̩] ([e] made in the middle of the mouth) or [o̩] ([o] made in the middle of the mouth) or [UH]	STR^R e̩T, Ke̩.REE̤, Ke̩m or STR^R o̩T, Ko̩.REE̤, Ko̩m or STR^R UHT, KUH.REE̤, KUHm	
about banana	ə / uh	ə / uh	əˈbaʊ̈t̮, bəˈna.nə / uh.BAh-ỤT, Buh.NAh.Nuh	

Back Vowel Sound Shifts

	Back Vowel Shifts			
I thought my father would not stop being a bully but the truth is, I was wrong.				
IPA: ai θɒt ma ˈfa.ðə̞ wʊ˙d nɒt stɒp bɪŋ ə ˈbʊ˙.lĭ bʌt ðə̞ t̪ɾʉθ ïz a waz̞ ɹɒŋ				
SYMBOLS: Ah-EE thoT MAh FAh.THUH WŪD NOT STOP BEĔNG uh BŪ.LEĔ BUHT THuh TRᴿOOth EĔZˢ Ah WAhZˢ RONG				
Key Words	*Detailed American English Accent* *IPA* ------------------ *Symbol*	*Shift to Ugandan (Luganda) Accent of English* *IPA* ------------------ *Symbol*	*Key Words Shifts* *IPA* ------------------ *Symbol*	*Your Key Words*
☛ food grew, true, two	u ------------------ OO	ʉ ------------------ [OO] ([OO] made in the middle of the mouth)	fʉd̞, g̞ɾʉ, t̪ɾʉ, t̪ʉ ------------------ FOOD, GROO, TRᴿOO, TOO	
☛ duty tune, news	[ɪʊ̞] when preceded by *t, d, n* in spelling ------------------ [I-OÕ] when preceded by *t, d, n* in spelling	jʉ ------------------ YOO	d̞ᶾjʉ.t̆ĭ, t̪ʲjʉn, njʉz̞ ------------------ DᴶYOO.TEĔ, TᶜᴴYOON, NYOŎZˢ	
foot put	ʊ ------------------ U	ʊ˙ ------------------ Ū	fʊ˙t̪, pʊ˙t̪ ------------------ FŪT, PŪT	
☛ thought tall, caulk, awful	ɔ ------------------ AW	ǫ ------------------ O	θǫt, tǫɾ, kǫk, ˈǫ.fɹ̩ ------------------ thOT, TO-<o>, KOK, O.F<o>	

Key Words	Detailed American English Accent	Shift to Ugandan (Luganda) Accent of English	Key Words Shifts	Your Key Words
	IPA ------------------ Symbol	IPA ------------------ Symbol	IPA ------------------ Symbol	
cl<u>o</u>th *[ɒ]/[O] d<u>o</u>g, c<u>ou</u>gh, w<u>a</u>sh, h<u>o</u>rrid	ɔ ------------------ AW	ɔ̰ ------------------ AW	klɔ̰θ, dɔ̰g, kɔ̰f, wɔ̰ʃ ------------------ KLAWth, DAWG, KAWF, WAWSH	
f<u>a</u>ther	ɑ ------------------ AH	a̰ ------------------ [A<u>h</u>] ([Ah] made further back in the mouth)	ˈfa̰.ðə̰ ------------------ **FAH**.THUH	
⊷ l<u>o</u>t *[ɒ]/[O] sq<u>ua</u>d, w<u>a</u>nder	ɑ ------------------ AH	o or ɒ ------------------ o or O	lot̰, skwod̰, ˈwon.d̰ə̰ or lɒt̰, skwɒd̰, ˈwɒn.d̰ə̰ ------------------ LoT, SKWoD, **WoN**.DUH or LOT, SKWOD, **WON**.DUH	

Diphthong Sound Shifts

Diphthong Shifts				
I'd like to fly away someday and go south to the mountains with the boys.				
IPA: aɪd laɪk tu flaɪ aˈwəˑ səm.dəˑ anḏ goː saöθ tu ðə ˈmaön.tïnz wïθ ðə boɪz				
SYMBOLS: Ah-EED LAh-EEK TOO FLAh-EE Ah-Wē SeM.De AhND Gō SAh-Uth TOO THuh **MAh-UN**.TEENZ^S WEEth THuh Bo-EEZ^S				
Key Words	Detailed American English Accent *IPA* --- *Symbol*	Shift to Ugandan (Luganda) Accent of English *IPA* --- *Symbol*	Key Words Shifts *IPA* --- *Symbol*	Your Key Words
☞ face pain, day, weight, steak	eɪ --- AY	əˑ --- [ē] ([e] made in the middle of the mouth)	fəˑs, pəˑn, ḏəˑ, wəˑṯ --- FeS, PeN, De, WeT	
price eyes, diaper, fly, guy, height	aɪ --- EYE	[a] or [aɪ] --- [Ah] or [Ah-EE]	pɾas, aẕ, ˈda.pə or pɾais, aiẕ, ˈdai.pə --- PR^RAhS, AhZ^S, **DAh**.PUH or PR^RAh-EES, Ah-EEZ^S, **DAh-EE**.PUH	
choice boys	ɔɪ --- OY	oɪ --- o-EE	tʃois, boiẕ --- CHo-EEZ^S, Bo-EEZ^S	
☞ goat sew, go	oŭ --- OH	oː --- ō	goːṯ, soː, goː --- GōT, Sō, Gō	
mouth town	aŭ --- OW	aö --- Ah-U	maöθ, ṯaön --- MAh-Uth, TAh-UN	

Diphthongs and Triphthongs of R Sound Shifts

> **Note!**
> **On r-coloration**
> A Ugandan (Luganda) Accent has no r-coloration in diphthongs and triphthongs of R.

	Diphthongs and Triphthongs of R Shifts			

Our friends started the fire near your north orchard an hour before we got there.

IPA: 'a.wǝ fɹenz 'stɑ.tɪd ðǝ 'fa.jǝ nɪǝ jʊǝ noθ 'o.tʃǝd an 'a.wǝ bɪ.fo wɪ gɒt ðɛˑ

SYMBOLS: Ah.WUH FReNZ^S STAH.TEED THuh Fah.YUH NI-UH YU-UH Noth o.^TSH>UH^R<D AhN Ah.WUH BEE.Fo WEE GOT THEH

Key Words	Detailed American English Accent — IPA / Symbol	Shift to Ugandan (Luganda) Accent of English — IPA / Symbol	Key Words Shifts — IPA / Symbol	Your Key Words
near beer	ɪɚ / EAR	ɪǝ / I-UH	nɪǝ, bɪǝ / NI-UH, BI-UH	
hair stare, pear, square, there	ɛɚ / AIR	[ɛǝ] or [ɛˑ] / [EH-UH] or [EH]	hɛǝ, stɛǝ, pɛǝ, skwɛǝ or hɛˑ, stɛˑ, pɛˑ, skwɛˑ / HEH-UH, STEH-UH, PEH-UH, SKWEH-UH or HEH, STEH, PEH, SKWEH	
sure poor, your	ʊɚ / UR	ʊǝ / U-UH	ʃʊǝ, pʊǝ, jʊǝ / SHU-UH, PU-UH, YU-UH	

Key Words	Detailed American English Accent	Shift to Ugandan (Luganda) Accent of English	Key Words Shifts	Your Key Words
	IPA	*IPA*	*IPA*	
	Symbol	*Symbol*	*Symbol*	
↢ north George, pour, warp, oar	ɔɝ --- AWR	o --- o	noθ, d̠ʒod̠ʒ, po, wop --- Noth, J^{SH}oJ^{SH}, Po, WoP	
↢ start heart	ɑɝ --- AHR	ɑ --- AH	s̪t̪ɑt̪, hɑt̪ --- STAHT, HAHT	
fire	aɪɝ --- EYER	a.jə̞ --- EYE.YUH	ˈfa.jə̞ --- **FEYE**.YUH	
hour	aʊɝ --- OWR	a.wə̞ --- Ah.WUH	ˈa.wə̞ --- **Ah**.WUH	

Key Sentences for Practice

Note!
- By practicing the sentences below, you can work through the sound shifts for a Ugandan (Luganda) accent in the context of a simple thought. I suggest you think, imagine and speak actively from a point of view. As you begin to work with the operative words in the thoughts, the rhythm and melody of the accent will begin to emerge appropriately.

Consonants:

- **Example:** Dennis Story (Part 1) – 0:21

We found our father seated at the front of the what?

...the house.

IPA:	wɨ fö°nd ˈa.wə̦ ˈfa̦.ðə sɨ.tɨ̠d aṯ ðɨ frent ev ðɨ ʍa̠ṯ ðɨ haʊs
SYMBOLS:	WEE FUᵘʰND **Ah.**WUH **FAh.**THUH SEE.TEED AhT THEE FRᴿoNT ov THEE HWAhT THEE HAh-ŲS

- *I'll meet͜ you at the ferry in an hour with the ten children.*

IPA:	aɪʳ miṯ ʃ͜ʉ aṯ ðə ˈfe̠.ɹɨ ïn an ˈa.wə̦ wɨ̠θ ðə ṯen ˈtʃïʳ.dɹen
SYMBOLS:	Ah-EE-<o> MEETCH͜OO AhT THuh **Fe̠.**REE EEN AhN **Ah.**WUH WEEth THuh Te̠N **CHEE**-<o>.DRᴿe̠N

Front Vowels: Vowels made by arching or cupping the front of the tongue toward the front of the hard palate.

- *The thief will tell me after we trap him.*

IPA:	ðə θïf wɨl te̠ʳ mɨ ˈaf.tə̦ wɨ ṯɹep hïm
SYMBOLS:	THuh thEEF WEEL Te̠-<o> MEE **AhF.**Tuh WEE TRᴿEHP HEEM

Middle Vowels: Vowels made by arching or cupping the middle of the tongue toward the middle of the hard palate.

- ***In the summer, workers burned the underbrush.***

    IPA: ïn ðə 'sə.mə̰ 'wɐ.kə̰z bənd̚ ði̥ 'ən.dʌ.bɹʌʃ

    SYMBOLS: EĒN THuh S**e**.MUH **W>UH**^R**<.KUHZ**^S BUH^RND TH**EE** e**N**.DUH.B**R**UHSH

Back Vowels: Vowels made by arching or cupping the back of the tongue toward the back of the hard palate.

- ***I thought my father would not stop being a bully but the truth is, I was wrong.***

    IPA: aɪ θɒt ma 'fɑ.ðə̰ wʊ·d̚ nɒt stɒp bɪɲ ə 'bʊ·.lĭ bʌt ðə tɾu̥θ ïz a waẓ ˌɹɒɲ

    SYMBOLS: Ah-**EE** thoT MAh **FAh**.THUH WŪD NOT STOP B**EE**NG uh **BŪ**.L**EE** BUHT THuh TR^ROOth **EEZ**^S Ah WAhZ^S **R**O**N**G

Diphthongs: When two vowels are combined in one syllable.

- ***I'd like to fly away someday and go south to the mountains with the boys.***

    IPA: aɪd̚ laik t̪u flai a'wə· səm.də· and̚ goː saʊ̈θ t̪u ðə 'maʊ̈n.t̪ĩnz wïθ ðə boɪẓ

    SYMBOLS: Ah-**EE**D LAh-**EE**K T**O**O FLAh-**EE** Ah-W**ē** S**e**M.D**e** AhND G**ō** SAh-**U**th T**O**O THuh **MAh**-**U**N.T**EE**NZ^S W**EE**th THuh Bo-**EE**Z^S

Diphthongs of R: A diphthong in which the second vowel is rhotic (e.g., has r-coloration in the final sound).

Example: near → nɪɚ/NEAR

Triphthongs of R: A combination of three vowel sounds, in which the third vowel is rhotic.

Example: fire → faɪɚ/FEYER

- ***Our friends started the fire near your north orchard an hour before we got there.***

    IPA: 'a.wə fɹenz 'stɑ.t̪ɪd̚ ðə 'fa.jə nɪə̥ jʊə̥ noθ 'o.t̪ʃəd̚ an 'a.wə bi̥.fo wɨ gɒt̚ ðɛ·

    SYMBOLS: **Ah**.WUH F**Re**NZ^S **STAH**.T**EE**D THuh **FAh**.YUH NI-UH YU-UH Noth o.^TSH>UH^R<D AhN **Ah**.WUH B**EE**.Fo W**EE** GOT TH**EH**

Extra Sentences:

- ***I wish I could open up her brain.***

    IPA: a wïʃ a kʊ·d̚ 'o.pen ʌp hɜ bɹɪə·n

    SYMBOLS: Ah W**EE**SH Ah KŪD **O**.P**e**N UHP HUH^R B**R**^R**e**N

Making Your Own Map of the Accent

Listen to the Ugandan (Luganda) accent samples provided and investigate the resources suggested in the *Introduction and Resources* section. Compose (or steal) *Key Phrases* from your listening/viewing that challenge and/or ground you in the accent. Then get more specific and check your sounds against the sounds in the Workbook.

Your take on the sound shifts may be slightly different. That is okay. The breakdown is a tool, not a rule. Recheck what you hear and, if you still stand behind your discoveries, go with them. This will help you to develop **your own** idiolect of the accent.

> *Note!*
> **What is an Idiolect?**
> Each of us speaks differently even if we have the same general accent.
> The individualized way that each of us speaks is referred to as an idiolect.
> For the actor, idiolect is part of what creates character. It is the "how" of
> the accent, and influences the way we craft our thoughts through language.

KEY PHRASES WITH KEY SOUND SHIFTS

Speak your *Key Phrases*, shifting back and forth between your own home *idiolect of English* and the ·*Ugandan (Luganda) accent* you are building. **Observe** the shifts <u>ONE by ONE</u> in your Articulators, Focus of Articulation, use of Melody/Pitch/Lilt, Rhythm/Stress/Pace, and Source & Path of Resonance as you shift back and forth between the two accents. Make note of the shifts in the table provided. Putting your understanding of the shifts into your <u>own words</u> will encourage you to develop a more clear and personal idiolect.

UGANDAN (LUGANDA) ACCENT *KEY POINTS OF FOCUS: VOCAL POSTURE AND CHARACTERISTICS*

JAW
LIPS
TONGUE
SOFT PALATE
PHARYNX

FOCUS OF ARTICULATION (TOWARDS TEETH, FRONT/MIDDLE/ BACK OF HARD PALATE, SOFT PALATE, ETC.)

MELODY/PITCH/LILT

RHYTHM/STRESS/PACE

SOURCE & PATH OF RESONANCE – Where does the resonance begin and what is the apparent path it travels through your body (chest, hard palate, sinuses, temples, crown, base of skull, etc.)? Refer to the Source & Path of Resonance and Resonators in the *Ugandan (Luganda) Accent of English: Down & Dirty Warm-Up and Quick Look* on page 28.

OTHER CHARACTERISTICS (What are your observations?)

PERSONAL IMAGES (For many actors personal images can be the most powerful and effective triggers for their transformation into an accent)

Chapter 3

Kenyan (Dholuo) Accent of English

Introduction and Resources

The Dholuo Language in Kenya

Dholuo is the language of the Luo people. It is a Nilotic sub-branch of the Char-Nile family of languages. The first Luo migration to Kenya was probably from Sudan in the 16th century. There have been at least five more Luo waves of migration since.

The Luo are the third largest ethnic group in Kenya, behind the Kikuyu and the Luhya. Although the Kikuyu are currently in governmental control, the Luo along with the Kikuyu were the ethnic groups that inherited most of the power from the British when Kenya established independence in 1963.

The Luo were one of the first ethnic groups to adopt the English language. It seems that at the end of the 19th century when the Luo chief Odera Akang'o helped the British fight against the Nandi by providing Luo porters, he became interested in British health practices, fashion, and education. As he encouraged his people to adopt British customs, he also encouraged them to learn English.

The two national languages of Kenya are English and Kiswahili.

Documentaries

Darwin's Nightmare (both Tanzanian and Kenyan Luos), *In My Genes*: Wycliffe, *The World of Ronah* (documentary in process at time of publication of this book; has an active Vimeo page)

Films

Fernando Mereilles' film adaptation of *The Constant Gardener*, *Kibrit* (a video recorded play by Albert Wandago), Albert Wandago's *Naliaka Is Going*

Television

Shuga: the actor Wilfred Maina Olwenya plays "Uncle Joe" (a very creepy guy)

Music

Awino Lawi (Benga), Poxy Pressure (Rap), Giddi Giddi & Maji Maji (Hip-Hop/Pop), Ayub Ogada (Folk), Suzanne Owiyo (Folk), Tony Nyadundo (Ohangla), Chris Adwar (Ohangla)

Plays with Kenyan (Dholuo) Characters

Duogo by Albert Wandago, *Lwanda Magere* by Okoiti-Omtatah, *Simbi Nyaima* by A.B. Odaga, the group Heartstrings Ensemble adapts all sorts of plays into Luo

Radio

Ramogi FM

Personalities

Jalang'o, Otoyo (Kazungu Matano), Eric Omondi, Fred Omondi, Wilbroda & Owago, Jaramogi Oginga Odinga, Robert Ouko, Raila Odinga, Winnie Odinga, Patrick Lumumba

Down & Dirty Warm-up and Quick Look

Note!

On Symbols

● International Phonetic Alphabet Symbols will be listed first and Sound Symbols will be listed second. Example: [i]/[EE]

● Sound Symbol Users: bold-faced letters indicate the syllable is stressed.

1) **The Muscles:** Wake your mouth up so you can more easily discover the physical transformation in speaking the accent.

   a. Scratch the front, middle and back of your tongue with your front top teeth.

   b. Rub the front, middle and back of your hard palate with the tip of your tongue.

   c. Imagine your mouth is numb from being at the dentist and you want to wake it up. Make tongue circles pressing against the back of your lips first clockwise, then counter clockwise (you are waking up your orbicularis muscle).

   d. To get the breath flowing, blow through your lips, getting them to flap together. Travel up and down in pitch on a BBBB and PPP, feeling the vibration as you wiggle up and down your spine.

2) **Vocal Posture for a Kenyan (Dholuo) Accent:** The back of the tongue is high, shooting articulation forward in the mouth, focusing the articulation on the front-middle of the hard palate. The soft palate is slightly raised because of the raised back of tongue and there is a somewhat rounded feeling in the back of the mouth. The lips are slightly pursed and ready for rounding on rounded vowels and consonants. The pharynx actively narrows to create oral twang.

3) **Resonators:** "occupy" the following spaces. This will prepare you to find the Source & Path of Resonance for a Kenyan (Dholuo) accent. (By "occupy", I mean just that; be in the space of it and find the pathway and flow of resonance, rather than "putting" the resonance there.)

a.   CHEST – Generously laugh at something – ha ha ha / HAh HAh HAh

b.   HARD PALATE – As if you were discovering something – ho ho ho / Ho Ho Ho

c.   THE BONES AT THE BASE OF YOUR SKULL (THE OCCIPITAL BONE) – Use your hands to scoop the sound from the base of your skull with a Mississippi African-American dialect as if you're flirting with someone nearby – he̤ː he̤ː he̤ː / hē̤ hē̤ hē̤

d.   FLICK THE SOUND OUT OF YOUR CHEEKBONES with an Italian-American flourish, as if calling to someone across the street – he̤ː he̤ː he̤ː / hē̤ hē̤ hē̤

e.   WITH YOUR HANDS NEXT TO YOUR TEMPLES, SHAKE THE SOUND OUT WITH LOOSE FISTS – As if you were somewhat crazed – ji̤ ji̤ ji̤ / YEE YEE YEE

f.   IMAGINE A METAL DISK EXTENDING FROM YOUR HANDS THROUGH YOUR SKULL. Bring your hands to the sides of your head just above the temples, with your palms facing the floor, thumbs hooked behind your skull. *Lid* the vibration to create a muted brassy sound. Like a robot saying "Hi" – haˑ˘ɪ haˑ˘ɪ haˑ˘ɪ / HĀH-Ĭ HĀH-Ĭ HĀH-Ĭ

g.   GIGGLE OUT OF THE TOP OF YOUR HEAD – As if you were tickled pink by something – hi̤ hi̤ hi̤ / HEE HEE HEE

4)   Source & Path of Resonance for a Kenyan (Dholuo) Accent: There is a full chest resonance that travels to the middle of the hard palate, up into the *lidded metal disk* resonator in the skull (see #3f above). The sound is forward in the mouth.

5)   Get the sound changes into your body and imagination.
Say these phrases occupying the following places in your body, suggesting to yourself the following energetic associations:

- pubic bone to tail bone – survival instinct

  zṳ / Z>OO<
  I need it – aːˑ˘ɪ ni̤d̪ ɪt̪ / ĀH-Ĭ NEED EĔT

- pubic bone to navel & sacrum in back – sexuality, big feelings

  woː / Wō
  I desire it – aˑ˘ɪ ˌd̪iˈzaˑˑ.jə̠ɹ‿ɪt̪ / ĀH-Ĭ DEE.ZĀH-YUHRᴿ‿EĔT

- rib cage to below heart – will

  ʒɔ̞ / ZHo
  I want it – aˑ˘ɪ wɒ̞nt̪ ɪt̪ / ĀH-Ĭ WǪNT EĔT

- heart – love

  mɑ / MAH
  I love it – aˑ˘ɪ lʌv ɪt̪ / ĀH-Ĭ LUHV EĔT

- throat – communication (think of talking at a party)

  bʌ / BUH
  I have to say it – aˑɪ̆ hav tʊ seː ɪt̪ / Ah̄-Ĭ HAhV TU Sē̱ ĔET

- forehead – intelligence/wisdom

  ke̱ː / Kē̱
  I know it – aˑɪ̆ noː ɪt̪ / Ah̄-Ĭ Noː ĔET

- crown of head – spirituality

  ri̱ / RᴿEE
  I believe it – aˑɪ̆ biˈli̱v ɪt̪ / Ah̄-Ĭ BEE-**LEEV** ĔET

6) **Articulation –** using playful physical actions: punching, flicking, dabbing, slashing

   d̪ʊ d̪ɪ kʊ d̪ʊ d̪ɪ kʊ d̪ʊ d̪ɪ kʊ – d̪ɪ
   d̪ʊ d̪ɪ kʊ d̪ʊ d̪ɪ kʊ d̪ʊ d̪ɪ kʊ – d̪eː
   d̪ʊ d̪ɪ kʊ d̪ʊ d̪ɪ kʊ d̪ʊ d̪ɪ kʊ – d̪aˑɪ̆
   d̪ʊ d̪ɪ kʊ d̪ʊ d̪ɪ kʊ d̪ʊ d̪ɪ kʊ – d̪oː
   d̪ʊ d̪ɪ kʊ d̪ʊ d̪ɪ kʊ d̪ʊ d̪ɪ kʊ – d̪u

Repeat as needed, replacing [d̪] with [t̪], [p], [b], [k], [g], [f], [v]

   D>U< DĒĔ K>U<   D>U< DĒĔ K>U<   D>U< DĒĔ K>U< – DEE
   D>U< DĒĔ K>U<   D>U< DĒĔ K>U<   D>U< DĒĔ K>U< – Dē̱
   D>U< DĒĔ K>U<   D>U< DĒĔ K>U<   D>U< DĒĔ K>U< – DAh̄-Ĭ
   D>U< DĒĔ K>U<   D>U< DĒĔ K>U<   D>U< DĒĔ K>U< – Dō
   D>U< DĒĔ K>U<   D>U< DĒĔ K>U<   D>U< DĒĔ K>U< – D>OO<

Repeat as needed, replacing the [D] with [T] (dentalized), [P], [B], [K], [G], [F], [V]. [D] & [T] are both articulated with the blade of the tongue against the back of the top front teeth (dentalized).

Key Points of Focus

Characteristics and Vocal Posture

Kenyan (Dholuo) Accent Characteristics

Note!

On Melody/Lilt/Pitch and Rhythm/Stress/Pace

Every accent contains shifts for some, but not necessarily all, of these elements of vocal variety.

Note!

On use of Musical Notes

Follow the "musical notes" up and down to get a feel for the melody of the accent. The filled-in notes are shorter than the open notes. For those who are musically inclined, think of them as approximating quarter notes and half notes. This distinction will give you a feel for the rhythm of the accent.

Melody/Lilt/Pitch

There is an easy rise and fall in the melody, sometimes accompanied by internal lilts within words. You may also notice minor interval steps down or up in pitch between words at the end of thoughts.

Example: Mary Story – 1:15

If they are late to go to their own homes, they were spending

the night with them.

Mary illustrates both lilt and an easy rolling up and down melody in her speech. Notice the lilts in *were* and *them*. Also notice the minor interval step down from *own* to *homes*.

Example: Ben Story – 0:38

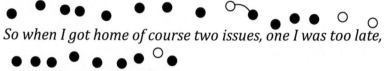

So when I got home of course two issues, one I was too late,

and I had no milk to deliver.

The way Ben speaks is a good example of an easy rolling up and down in melody but without much lilt in his speech. Notice how this helps to create a slightly different idiolect than Mary. Notice the minor lilt down in the second syllable of *issues*, much like the minor interval step down between *own* and *homes* in Mary's sentence.

Rhythm/Stress/Pace

Because vowels in Kenyan (Dholuo) are rarely pronounced in their *weak* form, weak syllables are often stressed through lengthening of the vowel and changing the pitch. There is also a tendency to elongate consonants, especially nasal consonants [n]/[N] and [m]/[M], in stressed syllables. Both of these characteristics help to create a somewhat syncopated rhythm.

Example: Peter (50s) Story (Part 1 & 2)
In both of Peter's stories you can hear how elongation of vowels and non-weak usage of "ing" and "y" endings both contribute in creating a unique rhythm in his Dholuo accent of English. Some of these words include:

- Words where Peter elongates his vowels: starting, certain, father, patterns
- Words where Peter uses a non-weak usage for his *ing* and *y* endings: starting, using, reading, discovery

Example: Peter (50s) Story (Part 1) – 1:50

Even if the discovery have no initial utility value, it's quite

a fulfilling venture.

In the sample sentence above you can hear Peter's vowel elongation in addition to the elongation of *n* in the word *venture*. Notice how the melodic play intersects with the rhythm.

Source & Path of Resonance

There is a full chest resonance that travels up into the middle of the hard palate, and on into the *lidded metal disk* resonator in the skull (see #3f on page 58). The sound is forward in the mouth.

You can hear these characteristics very clearly in Juliana speaking Dholuo and in all of the speakers as they speak English.

Kenyan (Dholuo) Accent Vocal Posture

Note!
On Vocal Posture
These adjustments enable you to integrate the accent through physical transformation rather than solely relying on sound shifts.

- **Focus of Articulation:** The effort is easy and sensual and centered in the front-middle of the hard palate.
- **Tongue:** The back of the tongue is high, shooting articulation forward in the mouth.
- **Lips:** The lips are slightly pursed and ready and active to round for the back rounded vowels: [u̜]/[>OO<], [ʊ]/[>U<], [o]/[o], [o̜]/[Ǫ]
- **Jaw:** The jaw is somewhat active in articulation and is generally half open.
- **Soft Palate:** The soft palate is slightly raised because of the raised back of tongue.
- **Pharynx:** The pharynx actively narrows to create oral twang.

Distinct Sounds of the Language and/or Accent

On Distinct Sounds
These are some of the sounds that Kenyan (Dholuo) speakers use and American speakers do not. In speaking the sounds and/or the words that contain them, you can heighten your physical understanding of the Kenyan (Dholuo) accent's *Vocal Posture* as compared to your own. This frame of reference will both inform and strengthen your accent.

Consonants

1. *IPA:* [c] → voiceless palatal plosive.
   Symbol: [K̟ᶻ] → [K] made on the hard palate with a little [ᶻ] following.
   This sound is used in speaking the Kenyan (Dholuo) language.
2. *IPA:* [ɟ] → voiced palatal plosive.
   Symbol: [G̟ᶻ] → [G] made on the hard palate with a little [ᶻ] following.
   This sound is used in speaking the Kenyan (Dholuo) language.
3. *IPA:* [ɾ] → alveolar tap.
   Symbol: [Rᴿ] → tapped [R].
   Used in place of [ɹ]/[R]: r̲ed, fer̲r̲y
   This sound is used in speaking both the language and accent of Kenyan (Dholuo).
4. *IPA:* [h] → voiceless glottal fricative.
   Symbol: [H̲] → [H] made with some frication at the glottis.
   This sound is used in speaking the Kenyan (Dholuo) language.

Pre-nasalized Consonants

[n]/[N] or [m]/[M] is inserted before articulation of the following consonants when speaking the Kenyan (Dholuo) language. Although these consonants are not used in the accent, the nasality in the resonance does carry over.

5. *IPA:* [ᵐb] → pre-nasalized labial plosive.
   Symbol: [ᵐB] → Make a quick [M] and explode it into a [B].
   This sound is used in speaking the Kenyan (Dholuo) language.
6. *IPA:* [ⁿd̪] → pre-nasalized dentalized plosive.
   Symbol: [ⁿD] → Make a quick [N] and explode it into a [D] that is articulated
      on the back of the top front teeth.
   This sound is used in speaking the Kenyan (Dholuo) language.
7. *IPA:* [ⁿd] → pre-nasalized alveolar plosive.
   Symbol: [ⁿD] → Make a quick [N] and explode it into a [D].
   This sound is used in speaking the Kenyan (Dholuo) language.
8. *IPA:* [ⁿɟ] → pre-nasalized palatal plosive.
   Symbol: [ⁿG] → Make a quick [N] and explode it into a [G] that is made
      on the hard palate rather than the soft palate.
   This sound is used in speaking the Kenyan (Dholuo) language.

Vowels

The vowels of the Kenyan (Dholuo) language include:

IPA: [i], [e], [a], [u], [o]
Symbol: [EE], [e], [Ah], [OO], [o]

There are variations of these vowels depending on whether the tongue root is
advanced or remains neutral.
   Knowing the vowels of the Kenyan (Dholuo) language will provide clues for
the vowel shifts in the accent.

9. *IPA:* [e]
   Symbol: [e] → This is the first sound in the D.A.E. diphthong [AY] as in *face*.
   Used in place of [ɛ]/[Eh]: *dr_e_ss, b_e_d*
   This sound is used in speaking both the language and accent of Kenyan
      (Dholuo).
10. *IPA:* [a]
    Symbol: [Ah] → This is the first sound in the D.A.E. diphthong [EYE].
    Used in place of [æ]/[A]: *tr_a_p, b_a_th*
    This sound is used in speaking both the language and accent of Kenyan
       (Dholuo).
11. *IPA:* [ə] → centralized [e].
    Symbol: [e̠] → [e] made in the middle of the mouth.
    Sometimes used in place of [ɝ]/[ER]: *n_u_rse, w_or_k*
    This sound is used in speaking a Kenyan (Dholuo) accent.
12. *IPA:* [ɞ] → [ɜ] made with rounded lips.
    Symbol: >UHᴿ< → [UHᴿ] made with rounded lips.
    Sometimes used in place of [ɝ]/[ER]: *b_i_rd, l_ear_n, s_e_rvice*
    This sound is used in speaking a Kenyan (Dholuo) accent.

13. *IPA:* [ɵ] → centralized [o].
    Symbol: [o̝] → [o] made in the middle of the mouth.
    Sometimes used in place of [ɝ]/[ER]: b<u>ir</u>d, l<u>ear</u>n, s<u>er</u>vice
    This sound is used in speaking a Kenyan (Dholuo) accent.

14. *IPA:* [o]
    Symbol: [o]. This is the first sound in the D.A.E. diphthong [OH].
    Used in place of [oʊ]/[OH]: g<u>oa</u>t, s<u>ew</u>
    This sound is used in speaking both the language and accent of Kenyan (Dholuo).

Consonant Sound Shifts

- ⊷ indicates that this sound is a key sound shift
- You can begin to fold melody and rhythm with the sound changes by speaking the sample sentences that are before each section of sound changes.

Note!

On Consonants

Consonants, but especially nasal consonants tend to elongate: mou̲n̲tain

IPA: ˈma̤ŭn·t̤ən

SYMBOLS: **MA̅h-O̅O̅N̄.TUHN**

Consonant Shifts

Example: Juliana Story 0:45

And she looked around, under the bed our cat was busy

eating the fish.

Example: Juliana Story – 1:25

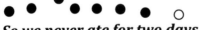

So we never ate for two days.

Notice the shifts in → t, d, th, final s, l, r and the lengthening in sh and n.

IPA: an ʃi̤ lʊ̤kt̤ aˈraund ˈʌnː.də ð̤ə bed̤ ˈaˑ.wə̤ kaˑt̤ wəz̤ ˈbi̤.zi̤ ˈi̤.t̤ɪn̤ ð̤ə fi̤ʃ so wi̤
         ˈneˑ.və et̤ fo̤ t̤u dez̤

SYMBOLS: Ahn SHEE L>U<KT Ah.R^RA̤h-O̅O̅ND UHN̄.DUH THuh BeD
         A̅h.WUH KA̅hT WuhZ^s **BE̅E̅.ZE̅E̅ E̅E̅.TE̅E̅NG THuh FE̅E̅SH̄.** So WEE
         Ne.Vṳh eT F>o< T>OO< De Z^s

I'll meet̲ ̲you at̲ t̲he ̲ferry in an hour wit̲h t̲he t̲en chil̲dr̲en.

IPA: aĭl mi̤t̚ ̲ju at̤ ð̤ĭ ˈfe.ɾɪ ɪn an aˑ.wə̤ wi̤θ ð̤ĭ ten ˈt̤ʃi̤l.dɾen

SYMBOLS: Ah-Ĭ̲L MEET^SH ̲Y>U< AhT THE̅E̅ **Fe.**R^RE̅E̅ E̅E̅N AhN Ah-WṲH
         WE̅E̅th THE̅E̅ TeN **CHE̅E̅L-**DR^ReN

Key Words	Detailed American English Accent IPA	Shift to Kenyan (Dholuo) Accent of English IPA	Key Words Shifts IPA	Your Key Words
	Symbol	Symbol	Symbol	
☞ team debt, did	[t]/[d] [T], [D]	[t̪] or [d̪] [T] or [D] dentalized	t̪im, d̪et̪, d̪id̪ TEEM, DeT, DEED	
☞ these there, breathe	[ð] [TH]	ð̪ [TH] dentalized	ð̪iz, ð̪eː, bri̪ð̪ THEEZˢ, Thē, BREETH	
☞ thin thick, mouth	θ [th]	θ̪ [TH] dentalized	θ̪in, θ̪ik, məŭθ̪ thEEN, thEEK, MŲO͡Oth	
☞ red dress, merry, sorry	ɹ R	ɾ [Rᴿ] tapped R	red̪, d̪ɾes, 'me.ɾi, 'sŲ.ɾi Rᴿed, DRᴿeS, **Me.RᴿEĒ, So.RᴿEĒ**	
☞ excel fall, table (final *l* in spelling)	l L	l̪ [L] pressed up toward the front of the hard palate	ek'sel̪, fɔl̪, 'te̪ːbəl̪ eK.**Sel**, FoL, **Te̪.BUHL**	
judge	dʒ J	d̪ʒ̊ Jᶜᴴ	d̪ʒ̊ʌd̪ʒ̊ JᶜᴴUHJᶜᴴ	
☞ reading (final *ing* in spelling)	ŋ ING	ɪn IN	'ɾi̪.d̪ɪn **RᴿEE.DIN**	
hanger (*ng* followed by a vowel)	ŋ NG	ŋ̊ Nᴷ	'han̪.ə **HAhNG.ᴷuh**	
boys (final *s* when pronounced [z])	z Z	z̥ Zˢ	bŲĭz̥ BŲ-EĒZˢ	

Front Vowel Sound Shifts

Front Vowel Shifts				
The thi͙e͙f wi͙ll te͙ll me͙ a͙fter we͙ tra͙p hi͙m.				
IPA: ðə̰ θi̤f wɪ̰l tel mi̤ 'af.tə̰ wi̤ t̰rap˥ hi̤m				
SYMBOLS: THUH thEEF WE͞EL TeL MEE **AhF**.TUH WEE TR^R AhP HE͞EM				
Key Words	*Detailed American English Accent* IPA -------------------- *Symbol*	*Shift to Kenyan (Dholuo) Accent of English* IPA -------------------- *Symbol*	*Key Words Shifts* IPA ------------------ *Symbol*	*Your Key Words*
fle͙e͙ce sne͙e͙ze, ple͙a͙d	i -------------------- EE	i̤ -------------------- EE	fli̤s, sni̤z̰, pli̤d ------------------ FLEES, SNEEZ^S, PLEED	
☛ ki͙t pi͙tch, di͙m, li͙p	ɪ -------------------- I	ɪ̤ -------------------- E͞E	kɪt, pɪt̰ʃ, d̰ɪm ------------------ KE͞ET, PE͞ECH, DE͞EM	
country͙ (*y* in final position of spelling)	ɪ̤ -------------------- E͞E	ɪ̤ -------------------- E͞E	'kʌn.t̰rɪ̰ ------------------ **KUHN**.TR^R E͞E	
be͙rated	[ɪ̰] in prefix -------------------- [E͞E] in prefix	i -------------------- EE	ˌbi'reː.t̰ɪd̰ ------------------ BEE.R^R e͙.TE͞ED	

Key Words	Detailed American English Accent *IPA* ----- *Symbol*	Shift to Kenyan (Dholuo) Accent of English *IPA* ----- *Symbol*	Key Words Shifts *IPA* ----- *Symbol*	Your Key Words
dr<u>e</u>ss b<u>e</u>d, f<u>ea</u>ther, s<u>e</u>nd	ɛ ----- EH	e ----- e	d̪res ----- DR^ReS	
☛ tr<u>a</u>p m<u>a</u>d, r<u>a</u>t, c<u>a</u>ndle	æ ----- A	a ----- Ah	t̪rap⌐, mad̪, ɾat̪ ----- TR^RAhP, MAhD, R^RAhT	
☛ b<u>a</u>th *[a]/[Ah] <u>a</u>sk, <u>a</u>fter, d<u>a</u>nce, ex<u>a</u>mple, h<u>a</u>lf, m<u>a</u>sk, r<u>a</u>scal, tr<u>a</u>nsfer In Chapter 1, there is a list of these words called the BATH or ASK list of words.	æ ----- A	a ----- Ah	baθ, ask ----- BAhth, AhSK	

70

Middle Vowel Sound Shifts

	Middle Vowel Shifts			
In the summer, workers burned the underbrush.				
IPA: ɪn ði ˈsʌː.mˑə ˈwɜ.kəz bənd ði ˈʌːnˑ.də͵brʌʃ				
SYMBOLS: ĒEN THǏ **SŪH**.M̃uh **WUH^R**.KUHZ^S B<u>e</u>ND THǏ **ŪHÑ**.Duh.BR^RUHSH				
Key Words	Detailed American English Accent IPA -------- Symbol	Shift to Kenyan (Dholuo) Accent of English IPA -------- Symbol	Key Words Shifts IPA -------- Symbol	Your Key Words
☛ b<u>ir</u>d l<u>ear</u>n, s<u>er</u>vice (*ir, er, ear* in spelling)	ɝ -------- ER	[ə] or [ɵ] -------- [>UH^R<] or [ɵ̧]	bəd, lən, ˈsə.vɪs or bəd, lən, ˈsə.vɪs -------- B>UH^R<D, L>UH^R<N, S>**UH**^R<.VĒES or BɵD, LɵN, Sɵ.VĒES	
☛ n<u>ur</u>se w<u>or</u>k (*ur, or* in spelling)	ɝ -------- ER	[ɜ] or [ə] -------- [UH^R] or [e̞]	nɜs, wɜk or nəs, wək -------- NUH^RS, WUH^RK or N<u>e</u>S, W<u>e</u>K	
sist<u>er</u> trait<u>or</u>, hang<u>ar</u>	ɚ -------- er	ə -------- uh	ˈsɪs.tə, ˈtreː.tə, ˈhaŋə -------- SĒES.Tuh, TR^Rḛ.tuh, HAhNG.^Kuh	
str<u>u</u>t	Ä -------- U̧H	ʌː -------- ŪH	stɾʌːt -------- STR^RŪHT	

Key Words	Detailed American English Accent IPA ------------------ Symbol	Shift to Kenyan (Dholuo) Accent of English IPA -------------------- Symbol	Key Words Shifts IPA -------------------------- Symbol	Your Key Words
c<u>u</u>rry h<u>u</u>rry (*urr* in spelling)	Ä ------------------ U̟H	ɘ -------------------- e̠	ˈkɘ.r̡ɪ̠ -------------------------- **Ke̠.RʰĒĒ**	
c<u>o</u>me fl<u>oo</u>d (in words spelled with *o* and sometimes *oo*)	Ä ------------------ U̟H	ʌ -------------------- UH	kʌm, flʌd̠ -------------------------- KUHM, FLUHD	
<u>a</u>bout b<u>a</u>nan<u>a</u>	ə ------------------ uh	ə̟ -------------------- UH	ə̟ˈbəṳt̠, bə̟ˈna.na -------------------------- **UH.BU̟-OŌT**, **BUH.NAh**.NAh	

Back Vowel Sound Shifts

	Back Vowel Shifts			
I thought my father would not stop being a bully but the truth is, I was wrong.				
IPA: aˑɪ̆ θɔt maˑɪ̆ ˈfɑ.ðə wʊd nɒt stɒp⌐ bɪŋ ə ˈbʊ.lɪ bət ðə tɾuθ ɪz aˑɪ̆ waz ɾoŋ				
SYMBOLS: Āh-Ĭ thoT MĀh-Ĭ **FAH**.THuh W>U<D NOT STOP BEENG UH **B>U<.LEE BUHT THUH TRᴿ>OO<th EEZˢ Ah-Ĭ WAHZˢ RᴿoNG**				
Key Words	Detailed American English Accent *IPA* ---------------- *Symbol*	Shift to Kenyan (Dholuo) Accent of English *IPA* ---------------- *Symbol*	Key Words Shifts *IPA* ---------------- *Symbol*	Your Key Words
f<u>oo</u>d gr<u>ew</u>, tr<u>ue</u>, tw<u>o</u>	u ---------------- OO	u̞ ---------------- >OO<	fu̞d, gɾu̞, tɾu̞ ---------------- F>OO<D, GRᴿ>OO<, TRᴿ>OO<	
↩ d<u>u</u>ty t<u>u</u>ne, n<u>ew</u>s	[ɪʊ] when preceded by *t, d, n* in spelling ---------------- [I-OO͡] when preceded by *t, d, n* in spelling	ju̞ ---------------- Y>OO<	ˈdju̞.tu̞, tju̞n, nju̞z ---------------- **DY>OO<.TEE͡,** TY>OO<N, NY>OO<Zˢ	
↩ f<u>oo</u>t p<u>u</u>t	ʊ ---------------- U	u̞ ---------------- >U<	fu̞t, pu̞t ---------------- F>U<T, P>U<T	
th<u>ou</u>ght t<u>a</u>ll, c<u>au</u>lk, <u>aw</u>ful	ɔ ---------------- AW	ɔ̞ ---------------- o	θɔ̞t, tɔ̞l, kɔ̞k ---------------- ThoT, ToL, KoK	
↩ cl<u>o</u>th *[ɒ]/[O]* d<u>o</u>g, c<u>ou</u>gh, w<u>a</u>sh, h<u>o</u>rrid	ɔ ---------------- AW	o ---------------- o	kloθ, dog, kof ---------------- KLoTh, DoG, KoF	

Key Words	Detailed American English Accent	Shift to Kenyan (Dholuo) Accent of English	Key Words Shifts	Your Key Words
	IPA	*IPA*	*IPA*	
	Symbol	*Symbol*	*Symbol*	
f<u>a</u>ther	ɑ	ɑ	ˈfɑ.ðə	
	AH	Ah	**FAH**.THuh	
☛ l<u>o</u>t *[ɒ]/[O]* sq<u>ua</u>d, w<u>a</u>nder	ɑ	[ɒ̞] or [ɑ]	lɒ̞t, skwɒ̞d, ˈwɒ̞n.də or lɑt, skwɑd, ˈwɑn.də	
	AH	[Ọ] or [AH]	LỌT, SKWỌD, **WỌN**.DUH LAHT, SKWAHD, **WAHN**.DUH	

Diphthong Sound Shifts

		Diphthong Shifts		

I'd like to fly away someday and go south to the mountains with the boys.

IPA: aˑɪ̌d laˑɪ̌k tʊ flaˑɪ̌ ə'weː 'sʌmˑ.de an goː søʊ̌θ tʊ ð̪ə 'mạʊ̌nˑ.tə̥nẓ wɪ̣θ ð̪ə
bʊ̣ɪ̌ẓ

SYMBOLS: A͞h-Ĭ̠D LA͞h-Ĭ̠K TU FLĀ-Ĭ̠ UH-**Wẹ̄ SUHM̄**.Dē AhN Goː Sọ-O͞Oth TU
THUH **MẠh-O͞ON**.TUHNZˢ WĒEth THUH BỤ-ĒEZˢ

Key Words	Detailed American English Accent IPA — Symbol	Shift to Kenyan (Dholuo) Accent of English IPA — Symbol	Key Words Shifts IPA — Symbol	Your Key Words
↪ fa̲ce pa̲in, da̲y, we̲ight, stea̲k	eɪ̌ — AY	ẹː — ē̠	fẹːs, pẹːn, d̪ẹː — Fẹ̄S, Pẹ̄N, D̪ē̠	
pri̲ce e̲yes, di̲aper, fly̲, guy̲, hei̲ght	aɪ̌ — EYE	aˑɪ̌ — A͞h-Ĭ̠	pɾaˑɪ̌s, aˑɪ̌ẓ, 'daˑɪ̌.pə̥ — PRᴿA͞h-Ĭ̠S, A͞h-Ĭ̠Zˢ, **DA͞h-Ĭ̠.PUH**	
choi̲ce boy̲s	ɔɪ̌ — OY	ụ̌ɪ̌ — Ụ-ĒE	t̠ʃụ̌ɪ̌s, bụ̌ɪ̌ẓ — CHỤ-ĒES, BỤ-ĒEZˢ	
↪ goa̲t se̲w, go̲, toe̲	oʊ̌ — OH	oː — ō	goːt̠, soː, goː — Gō̠T, Sō̠, Gō	
↪ mou̲th tow̲n	aʊ̌ — OW	[ɔə̌] or [øʊ̌] or [ạʊ̌] — [e-u͞h] or [ọ-O͞O] or [Ah-O͞O]	mɔə̌θ, t̠ə̌n or møʊ̌θ, tøʊn, or mạʊ̌θ, tạʊn — Me-u͞hth, Te-u͞hn or Mọ-O͞Oth, Tọ-O͞ON or MAh-O͞Oth, TAh-O͞ON	

Diphthongs of R Sound Shifts

> *Note!*
> **On r-coloration**
> A Kenyan (Dholuo) accent has no r-coloration in diphthongs and triphthongs of R.

	Diphthongs and Triphthongs of R Shifts			

Our friends started the fire near your north orchard an hour before we got there.

IPA: 'aˑ.wə̰ frenz̥ 'staː.tĭd ð̥ĭ 'faˑ.jə nɪˑ jʊə̃ nə̰θ 'ɔ̰.tʃəd an 'aˑ.wə̰ 'bɪ.fə̰ wɪ gʊ̰t ð̥eː

SYMBOLS: A̅h-WUH FRᴿeNZˢ STA̱̅h.TĬD THĬ FA̱̅h.YŬH NE̅E̯ YU-uh Noth o.CHe̱D AhN A̅h.WŬH BE̅E̯.Fo WEE GƆT THe̅

Key Words	Detailed American English Accent IPA ------ Symbol	Shift to Kenyan (Dholuo) Accent of English IPA ------ Symbol	Key Words Shifts IPA ------ Symbol	Your Key Words
⌐ near beer	ɪɚ̯ ------ EAR	ɪˑ ------ EE	nɪˑ, bɪˑ ------ NEE, BEE	
⌐ hair stare, pear, square, there	ɛɚ̯ ------ AIR	eː ------ e̅	heː, stḛː, peː ------ He̅, Stḛ, Pe̅	
sure poor, your	ʊɚ̯ ------ UR	ʊə̃ ------ U-uh	ʃʊə̃, pʊə̃, jʊə̃ ------ SHU-uh, PU-uh, YU-uh	
⌐ north George, pour, warp, oar	ɔɚ̯ ------ AWR	ɔ̰ ------ o	nɔ̰θ, d̥ʒ̰ɔd̥ʒ̰, pɔ̰ ------ NoTh, JᶜᴴoJᶜᴴ, Po	

Key Words	Detailed American English Accent	Shift to Kenyan (Dholuo) Accent of English	Key Words Shifts	Your Key Words
	IPA ------------------ Symbol	IPA -------------------- Symbol	IPA ----------------------- Symbol	
⊷ st<u>art</u> h<u>ear</u>t	ɑɹ˞ ------------------ AHR	aː -------------------- A̱ẖ	sta̱ːt̪, ha̱ːt̪ ----------------------- STA̱ẖT, HA̱ẖT	
f<u>ire</u>	aɪɚ˞ ------------------ EYER	aˑ.jə̧ -------------------- A̱ẖ-YŬH	ˈfaˑ.jə̧ ----------------------- FA̱ẖ.YŬH	
h<u>our</u>	aʊɚ˞ ------------------ OWR	aˑ.wə̧ -------------------- A̱ẖ.WŬH	ˈaˑ.wə̧ ----------------------- A̱ẖ.WŬH	

Key Sentences for Practice

Note!

- By practicing the sentences below, you can work through the sound shifts for a Kenyan (Dholuo) accent in the context of a simple thought. I suggest you think, imagine and speak actively from a point of view. As you begin to work with the operative words in the thoughts, the rhythm and melody of the accent will begin to emerge appropriately.
- Note that less significant words are often unstressed, and articulation of vowels and diphthongs in these words may move toward the neutral *schwa* [ə]/[uh].

Consonants:

- **Example:** Juliana Story (Part 1) – 0:45

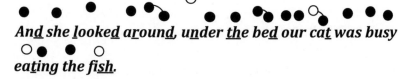

And she looked around, under the bed our cat was busy

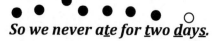

eating the fish.

Example: Juliana Story (Part 1) – 1:25

So we never ate for two days.

Notice the shifts in → t, d, th, final z, l, r and the lengthening in sh and n.

IPA: an ʃi̞ lʊ̞kt̪ aˈraʊ̆nd̪ ˈʌnːdə ð̞ə bed̪ ˈaˑwə̞ kaˑt̪ wəz̞ ˈbɪˌzɪ ˈiˌtin̪ ð̞ə fi̞ʃː so wi̞ ˈneˑvə et̪ fo̞ tu̞ dez̞

SYMBOLS: Ahn SHEE L>Ū<KT Ah.**R**ᴿ**Ah-ŌOND UHÑ**.DUH THuh BeD **Āh**.WUH KĀʰT WuhZˢ **BĔE.ZĔE EE**.TĔENG THuh FĔESH. So WEE **Ne**.Vu̱h eT F>o< T>OO< De̱ Zˢ

- *I'll meet̲ ̮you a̲t the ferry in an hour wi̲th the ̲ten chil̲dren.*

  IPA: aɪ̰l miṭ⌣ju aṭ ð̰ɪ̰ 'fe.rɪ̰ ɪn an aˑwə̰ wɪ̰θ ð̰ɪ̰ ten 'tʃɪ̰l.dren

  SYMBOLS: Ah-Ḭ̆L MEET^SH⌣Y>U< AhT THḚ̆E **Fe.R^RḚ̆E** Ḛ̆EN AhN
            Ah-WṴ̆H WḚ̆Eth THḚ̆E TeN **CHḚ̆EL**-DR^ReN

Front Vowels: Vowels made by arching or cupping the front of the tongue toward the front of the hard palate.

- *The thi̲e̲f wi̲ll te̲ll me̲ a̲fter we̲ tra̲p hi̲m.*

  IPA: ð̰ə̰ θif wɪ̰l tel mḭ 'af.tə̰ wḭ ṭrap⌐ hɪ̰m

  SYMBOLS: THUH thEEF WḚ̆EL TeL MEE **AhF**.TUH WEE TR^RAhP
            HḚ̆EM

Middle Vowels: Vowels made by arching or cupping the middle of the tongue toward the middle of the hard palate.

- *In the̲ su̲mme̲r, wo̲rke̲rs bu̲rned the u̲nderbru̲sh.*

  IPA: ɪn ð̰ɪ̰ 'sʌː.mˑə 'wɜ.kə̰z bənḏ ð̰ɪ̰ 'ʌːnˑ.də̣ˌbrʌʃ

  SYMBOLS: Ḛ̆EN THḬ̆ **SŪ̄H**.M̄uh **WUH^R**.KUHZ^S Be̲ND THḬ̆
            Ū̄H̄N̄.Duh.BR^RUHSH

Back Vowels: Vowels made by arching or cupping the back of the tongue toward the back of the hard palate.

- *I thou̲ght my fa̲ther wou̲ld no̲t sto̲p being a bu̲lly but the tru̲th is, I wa̲s wro̲ng.*

  IPA: aˑĭ θɔ̲t maˑĭ 'fɑ.ð̰ə wʊ̲ḏ nɒ̲t stɒp⌐ biŋ ə̰ 'bʊ̰.lɪ bə̲t ð̰ə̰ ṭru̲θ ɪ̰z aˑĭ
            waz̰ rɒŋ

  SYMBOLS: Ā̄h-Ḭ̆ thoT MĀ̄h-Ḭ̆ **FAH**.THuh W>U<D NO̲T STO̲P BEENG
            UH **B>U<**.LḚ̆E BŬ̄HT THUH TR^R>OO<th Ḛ̆EZ^S Ah-Ḭ̆ WAHZ^S
            R^RoNG

Diphthongs: When two vowels are combined in one syllable.

- *I'd li̲ke to fly awa̲y someda̲y and go̲ sou̲th to the mou̲ntains with the bo̲ys.*

  IPA: aˑĭd laˑĭk ṭʊ flaˑĭ ə̰'weː 'sʌmˑ.de an goː səŭθ̰ ṭʊ ð̰ə 'mɑŭnˑ.ṭ ə̰nz̰
            wɪ̰θ ð̰ə bʊ̰ĭz̰

  SYMBOLS: Ā̄h-Ḭ̆D LĀ̄h-ĬK TU FLĀ̄-Ḭ̆ UH-**We̲** **SUHM̄**.Dē AhN Go: Se̲-ŎŌth
            TU THUH **MA̲h-ŎŌN**.TUHNZ^S WḚ̆Eth THUH BU̲-Ḛ̆EZ^S

Diphthongs of R: A diphthong in which the second vowel is rhotic (e.g., has [R] coloration)

Example: near → nɪɚ/NEAR

Triphthongs of R: A combination of three vowel sounds, in which the third vowel is rhotic.

Example: fire → faɪɚ/FEYER

- ___Our___ *friends st__ar__ted the f__ire__ n__ear__ __your__ n__or__th __or__chard an h__our__ bef__ore__ we got th__ere__.

  IPA: ˈaˑ.wǫ frenẓ ˈstaː.t̬ɪ̆d̬ ð̬ĭ ˈfaˑ.jǝ nɪ̣ˑ jʊɚ nǫ̈θ ˈɔ̣.t̬ʃǝd̬ an ˈaˑ.wǫ̈ ˈbɪ̣.fǫ̈ wị gṇt ð̬eː

  SYMBOLS: A̅h-WUH FRᴿeNZˢ **STA̅h**.TĬD THĬ **FA̅h**.YŬH NĔE YU-uh Noth **o**.CHҽD AhN A̅h.WŬH **BĔE**.Fo WEE GǪT Thē

Making Your Own Map of the Accent

Listen to the Kenyan (Dholuo) accent samples provided and investigate the resources suggested in the *Introduction and Resources* section. Compose (or steal) *Key Phrases* from your listening/viewing that challenge and/or ground you in the accent. Then get more specific and check your sounds against the sounds in the Workbook.

Your take on the sound shifts may be slightly different. That is okay. The breakdown is a tool, not a rule. Recheck what you hear and, if you still stand behind your discoveries, go with them. This will help you to develop **your own** idiolect of the accent.

> *Note!*
> **What is an Idiolect?**
> Each of us speaks differently even if we have the same general accent. The individualized way that each of us speaks is referred to as an idiolect. For the actor, idiolect is part of what creates character. It is the "how" of the accent, and influences the way we craft our thoughts through language.

KEY PHRASES WITH KEY SOUND SHIFTS

Speak your *Key Phrases*, shifting back and forth between your own home *idiolect of English* and the *Kenyan (Dholuo) accent* you are building. **Observe** the shifts <u>ONE by ONE</u> in your Articulators, Focus of Articulation, use of Melody/Pitch/Lilt, Rhythm/Stress/Pace, and Source & Path of Resonance as you shift back and forth between the two accents. Make note of the shifts in the table provided. Putting your understanding of the shifts into your <u>own words</u> will encourage you to develop a more clear and personal idiolect.

KENYAN (DHOLUO) ACCENT *KEY POINTS OF FOCUS: VOCAL POSTURE AND CHARACTERISTICS*

JAW
LIPS
TONGUE
SOFT PALATE
PHARYNX

FOCUS OF ARTICULATION (TOWARDS TEETH, FRONT/MIDDLE/
BACK OF HARD PALATE, SOFT PALATE, ETC.)

MELODY/PITCH/LILT

RHYTHM/STRESS/PACE

SOURCE & PATH OF RESONANCE – Where does the resonance begin and
what is the apparent path it travels through your body (chest, hard palate,
sinuses, temples, crown, base of skull, etc.)? Refer to the Source & Path of
Resonance and Resonators in the *Kenyan (Dholuo) Accent of English: Down
& Dirty Warm-Up and Quick Look* on page 57–8.

OTHER CHARACTERISTICS (What are your observations?)

PERSONAL IMAGES (For many actors personal images can be the most
powerful and effective triggers for their transformation into an accent)

Chapter 4

Zimbabwean (Shona) Accent of English

Introduction and Resources

The Shona Language in Zimbabwe

Shona is a Bantu language of the Benue-Congo subgroup of the Niger-Congo
family of languages. There are three dialects of Shona: Karanga, Zezuru and
Korekore. The Shona spoken in Zimbabwe today is based on a mix of the Karanga
dialect from Masvingo Province and the Zezuru dialect from north and central
Zimbabwe.

English is the official language of Zimbabwe although only 2.5% of the
population, mainly people of white and mixed race, use it as a primary language.
Most of the population speaks Shona. About 20% of the population speaks
Ndebele, mainly in the southwest of the country.

Documentaries

*The Wind of Change, Mugabe and the White African, How the British Stole
Zimbabwe, Rhodesia at War: The Selous Scouts*

Films

Everyone's Child, Yellow Card, Flame (in Shona), *More Time, Mbira – Spirit
of the People* (Thomas Mapfumo, Oliver Mtukudzi), *Zimbabwe Yesterday
Zimbabwe Today: Africa's Hope for a Heritage*

Television

Unscripted, Zimbabwe Broadcasting Corporation (ZBC), Zimbo Live TV,
Nehanda TV, Makosi today, The Dr. Stem Show

Plays by Shona authors and/or with Shona characters

The Convert and *Familiar* by Danai Gurira, *Zuva Crumbling* by Lucian Msamati,
The Epic Adventure of Nhamo the Manyika Warrior and his Sexy Wife Chipo
by Denton Chikura, *The Rise and Shine of Comrade Fiasco* by Andrew Whaley

Music

Derek Mpofu (*Chisikana Changu, Zimbabwe*), Alick Macheso (*Charakupa*), Andy Brown (*Mawere Kongonya*), Bhundu Boys (*Baba Munini Francis*), Cephas Mashakada (*Zvamaronga*), Dumisani Maraire & Ephat Mujuru (*Chemutengure*), Chiwoniso (*Mai*), Devera Ngwena Namatso (*Hombarume*), Hallelujah Chicken Run Band (*Mudzimu Ndiringe*), Leonard Zhakata (*Kumatenga*), John Chibadura (*Zuva Rekufa Kwangu*), Marshall Munhumumwe (*Rudo Imoto*), James Chimombe (*Bindura*), Matemai & Simboti (Nehanda Mudzimu Woye), Nharira (*Mbira Dze-Nharira*), Oliver Mtukudzi (*Neria*), Stella Rambisai Chiweshe Shiri (*Nhengure*), Simon Chimbetu (*Samatenga*), Stella Chiweshe (*The Speech*), Idya Banana, Tsviriyo, Nicholas Zakaraia

Radio

AfromZimRadio, Zimnet Radio Gospel, Visions FM-Harare, Zim FM Sterio 104.3, Zimnet Radio, Radio Zimbabwe Harare

Personalities

Dambudzo Marechera, Godwin Mawuru (director and producer), Musaemura Zimunya (writer), Solomon Mutswairo (author), Yvonne Vera (author), Petina Gappah (attorney and writer), Byron Black (tennis player), Locardia Ndandarika (sculptor), Nehanda Nyakasikana (activist), Tendai Biti (former Minister of Finance), Kirsty Coventry (Olympic medal winning swimmer)

Down & Dirty Warm-up and Quick Look

Note!

On Symbols

- International Phonetic Alphabet Symbols will be listed first and Sound Symbols will be listed second. Example: [i]/[EE]
- Sound Symbol Users: bolded letters indicate the syllable is stressed.

1) **The Muscles:** Wake your mouth up so you can more easily discover the physical transformation in speaking the accent.

   a. Scratch the front, middle and back of your tongue with your front top teeth.

   b. Rub the front, middle and back of your hard palate with the tip of your tongue.

   c. Imagine your mouth is numb from being at the dentist and you want to wake it up. Make tongue circles pressing against the back of your lips first clockwise, then counter clockwise (you are waking up your orbicularis muscle).

   d. To get the breath flowing, blow through your lips, getting them to flap together. Travel up and down in pitch on a BBBB and PPP, feeling the vibration as you wiggle up and down your spine.

2) **Vocal Posture for a Zimbabwean (Shona) Accent:** The jaw is half closed and the tongue is slightly pitched forward with the front of the tongue lightly resting against the back of the lower front teeth. The blade of the tongue is wide. The middle of the tongue is very active in vowel articulation. The back of the tongue is raised high towards the soft palate but is very ready to cup down for the low back vowels: [ɔ]/[AW], [ɒ]/[Q], [ɑ]/[AH]. There is an easy fullness in the lips which actively round for the rounded vowels and consonants. The soft palate is lifted and slightly domed while the pharynx narrows, creating a slight pharyngeal twang (think singing posture for the pharynx). The Focus of Articulation is toward the front-middle of the hard palate.

3) **Resonators:** "occupy" the following spaces. This will prepare you to find the Source & Path of Resonance for the Zimbabwean (Shona) accent. (By "occupy", I mean just that; be in the space of it and find the pathway and flow of resonance, rather than "putting" the resonance there.)

   a. CHEST – Generously laugh at something – hǫ hǫ hǫ / HAH HAH HAH

   b. HARD PALATE – As if you were discovering something – hǫ hǫ hǫ / >Ho< >Ho< >Ho<

   c. THE BONES AT THE BASE OF YOUR SKULL (THE OCCIPITAL BONE) – Use your hands to scoop the sound from the base of your skull with a Mississippi African-American dialect as if you're flirting with someone nearby – heː heː heː / Hē Hē Hē

   d. FLICK THE SOUND OUT OF YOUR CHEEKBONES with an Italian-American flourish, as if calling to someone across the street – heː heː heː / Hē Hē Hē

   e. WITH YOUR HANDS NEXT TO YOUR TEMPLES, SHAKE THE SOUND OUT WITH LOOSE FISTS – As if you were somewhat crazed – jɨ jɨ jɨ / YEE YEE YEE

   f. IMAGINE A METAL DISK EXTENDING FROM YOUR HANDS THROUGH YOUR SKULL. Bring your hands to the sides of your head just above the temples, with your palms facing the floor, thumbs hooked behind your skull. *Lid* the vibration to create a muted brassy sound. Like a robot saying, "Hi" – haɨ haɨ haɨ / HAh-EE HAh-EE HAh-EE

   g. GIGGLE OUT OF THE TOP OF YOUR HEAD – As if you were tickled pink by something – hɨ hɨ hɨ / HEE HEE HEE

4) **Source & Path of Resonance for the Zimbabwean (Shona) Accent:**
There is a rich chest resonance that rolls up into the base of the skull, stroking the back of the hard palate and then resonating boldy in the sinuses. The soft palate often rests high, resulting in a slight hypo-nasality (no nasality). And there is often a bit of "giggle" resonance in the head, especially for women.

5) **Get the sound changes into your body and imagination.**
Say these phrases occupying the following places in your body, suggesting to yourself the following energetic associations:

- pubic bone to tail bone – survival instinct

    zu / ZOO
    I need it – aɨ niḏ ɨt̪ / Ah-EE NEED EET

- pubic bone to navel & sacrum in back – sexuality, big feelings

    wǫ / W>o<
    I desire it – aɨ ˌd̪ɨˈza.jar‿ɨt̪ / Ah-EE DEE.**ZAh**.YAhR[R]‿EET

- rib cage to below heart – will

    ʒǫ / ZH>AW<
    I want it – aɨ wǫnt ɨt̪ / Ah-EE WONT EET

● heart – love

mᶐ / MAH
I love it – aɨ lɔv ɨt / Ah-EE LAWV EET

● throat – communication (think of talking at a party)

ba: / BAh
I have to say it – aɨ hεy ṱu se: ɨt / Ah-EE HEHVᶠ TOO Sē EET

● forehead – intelligence/wisdom

ke: / Kē
I know it – aɨ nọ ɨt / Ah-EE N>o< EET

● crown of head – spirituality

ɾɨ / RᴿEE
I believe it – aɨ 'bɨ'lɨv ɨt / Ah-EE **BEE.LEEV** EET

6) **Articulation** – using playful physical actions: punching, flicking, dabbing, slashing

d̪ʉ d̪ɨ kʉ d̪ʉ d̪ɨ kʉ d̪ʉ d̪ɨ kʉ – d̪ɨ
d̪ʉ d̪ɨ kʉ d̪ʉ d̪ɨ kʉ d̪ʉ d̪ɨ kʉ – d̪e:
d̪ʉ d̪ɨ kʉ d̪ʉ d̪ɨ kʉ d̪ʉ d̪ɨ kʉ – d̪ai
d̪ʉ d̪ɨ kʉ d̪ʉ d̪ɨ kʉ d̪ʉ d̪ɨ kʉ – d̪o
d̪ʉ d̪ɨ kʉ d̪ʉ d̪ɨ kʉ d̪ʉ d̪ɨ kʉ – d̪u

Repeat as needed, replacing [d̪] with [t̪], [pˀ], [b], [k], [g], [f], [v].

> **Note!**
> **For Symbol Users**
> [T] & [D] are made with the blade (rather than the tip) of the tongue on the alveolar ridge.
> [P] is made without the usual puff of air released afterward.

DOO DEE KOO DOO DEE KOO DOO DEE KOO – DEE
DOO DEE KOO DOO DEE KOO DOO DEE KOO – Dē
DOO DEE KOO DOO DEE KOO DOO DEE KOO – DAh-EE
DOO DEE KOO DOO DEE KOO DOO DEE KOO – D>o<
DOO DEE KOO DOO DEE KOO DOO DEE KOO – DOO

Repeat as needed, replacing [D] with [T], [P], [B], [K], [G], [F], [V].

Key Points of Focus

Characteristics and Vocal Posture

Zimbabwean (Shona) Accent Characteristics

Note!
On Melody/Lilt/Pitch and Rhythm/Stress/Pace
Every accent contains shifts for some, but not necessarily all, of these elements of vocal variety.

Note!
On use of Musical Notes
Follow the "musical notes" up and down to get a feel for the melody of the accent. The filled-in notes are shorter than the open notes. For those who are musically inclined, think of them as approximating quarter notes and half notes. This distinction will give you a feel for the rhythm of the accent.

Melody/Lilt/Pitch

The following characteristics contribute to the playful musicality of the accent.

1. Because Shona has both a high and low tone used for sense differentiation and grammar, there is often an unexpected jumping up and down in pitch from syllable to syllable or word to word. It usually manifests in operative words, but can also be surprisingly random.
2. There is often a lift in pitch on an operative word which can then go into a downward lilt.
3. The final word of a thought will normally lift rather than fall in pitch. This lift is often accompanied by a downward lilt.

Example: Yemu Story (Part 1, in English and Shona) – 0:01

My mother always used to tell me

– followed by a segment of Yemu speaking in Shona

In this recording Yemu skillfully switches back and forth between speaking English and Shona. Notice how, when she speaks Shona, her high to low pitch jumps are quite apparent, and when she speaks English this character-istic is also present, but to a lesser degree – (#1 above). She also uses the upward-downward inflectional lilt in her operative words *always* and *me* – (#2 on p. 90).

Example: Edwin Story (Part 1) – 0:35

But I was young enough to let it go

Edwin lifts in pitch on his operative words: *young, go* and also adds stress to the stressed syllable in the operative word *enough*, by not lengthening the vowel and jumping up in pitch. He illustrates the lift in pitch followed by the downward lilt on the final word in this thought: *go* – (#1 and #3 on p. 90)

Rhythm/Stress/Pace

There is a syncopated and somewhat staccato feel to the accent, largely due to the following:

1. Most vowels are pronounced in their strong form rather than their weak form.
2. Diphthongs that turn into monophthongs tend to lengthen and lilt which contributes to a kind of syncopated feel to the accent.
3. There is a tendency to lengthen vowels of operative words.

Example: Batsi Story (Part 1) – 2:58

He just stopped and shooed the dogs away.

You can hear a syncopated and staccato quality in Batsi's sentence. He makes the diphthong in the second syllable of *away* into a monophthong while at the same time lengthening and lilting it – (#2 on p. 90). He also uses a strong form of the vowel in the unstressed first syllable *a* in *away*. This gives the two syllables more equal stress – (#1 above). Finally, he lengthens the vowels in his operative words *st<u>o</u>pped* and *sh<u>oo</u>ed* – (#3 on p. 91).

Example: Nodumo Story (Part 1) – 0:01

So there was a day when I did not want to go to school.

This sentence of Nodumo's is an excellent example of how retaining strong forms of vowels in non-operative words can create a staccato feel. Words such as *was, a, did, to*, which would be considered non-operative words in American English and would therefore be pronounced with weak forms of the vowels they contain, Nodumo pronounces with full value – (#1 on p. 91). She also has the characteristic lilt when she replaces the diphthong in *d<u>ay</u>* with a monophtong – (#2 on p. 91). Interestingly, when she drops the final [l]/[L] in *school* she replaces it with the same characteristic lilt.

> *Note!*
> **A word of caution in relation to Rhythm and Stress:**
> Because the syllables are more evenly stressed than in American English in this accent, it is important not to be seduced by the seemingly staccato quality of the accent. Do text work and personalization in relation to operative words and keep focused on following through to the end of the thought. This will help keep you from playing the stress too randomly.

Source & Path of Resonance

There is a rich chest resonance that rolls up into the base of the skull, stroking the back of the hard palate and then resonating boldly in the sinuses. The soft palate often rests high resulting in a slight hypo-nasality (no nasality). And there is often a bit of "giggle" resonance in the head, especially for women.

Nontsikelelo and Edwin both speak with stronger pharyngeal twang than the other speakers. This may be because they have spent a significant amount of time in America. Besides this variation, all of the Zimbabwean speakers in the accent library clearly represent the Path of Resonance traits described on p. 91.

Zimbabwean (Shona) Accent Vocal Posture

> *Note!*
> **On Vocal Posture**
> These adjustments enable you to integrate the accent through physical transformation rather than solely relying on sound shifts.

- **Focus of Articulation:** Full toward the front-middle of the hard palate.
- **Tongue:** The tongue is slightly pitched forward with the front of the tongue lightly resting against the back of the lower front teeth. The blade of the tongue is wide. The middle of the tongue is very active in vowel articulation. The back of the tongue is raised high towards the soft palate but is very ready to cup down for the low back vowels: [ɔ̞]/[AW], [ɒ̞]/[O], [ɑ̞]/[AH].
- **Lips:** There is an easy fullness in the lips which actively round for the rounded vowels: [u]/[OO], [ʊ]/[U], [o]/[o], [ɔ̞]/[AW], [ɒ̞]/[O].
- **Jaw:** The jaw is half closed.
- **Soft Palate:** The soft palate is lifted and slightly domed.
- **Pharynx:** The pharynx is narrowed, creating a slight pharyngeal twang (think singing posture for the pharynx).

Distinct Sounds of the Language and/or Accent

Note!

On Distinct Sounds

These are some of the sounds that Zimbabweans (Shona speakers) use and American speakers do not. In speaking the sounds and/or the words that contain them, you can heighten your physical understanding of the Zimbabwean (Shona) accent's *Vocal Posture* as compared to yours. This frame of reference will both inform and strengthen your own accent.

Consonants

1. *IPA:* [ɾ] → alveolar tap.
   Symbol: [R^R] → This is a tapped [R]. It is made by lightly tapping the top of the tip of the tongue on the post alveolar ridge.
   Used in place of [ɹ]/[R]: *ran, ferry*
   This sound is used in speaking both the language and accent of Zimbabwean (Shona).
2. *IPA:* [Φ] → voiceless bilabial fricative. [f] made with the lips rather than with the upper teeth on the lower lip.
   Symbol: [F] made with the lips rather than with the upper teeth on the lower lip.
   This sound is used in speaking the Shona language.
3. *IPA:* [β] → voiced bilabial fricative. This is made by flapping the lips lightly on a [b].
   Symbol: [B^H] → This is made by flapping the lips lightly on a [B].
   This sound is used in speaking the Shona language.

Vowels

The vowels of Zimbabwean (Shona) include:

IPA: [i], [e], [a], [u], [o]
Symbol: [EE], [e], [Ah], [OO], [o]

Knowing the vowels for the Shona language will provide clues for the vowel shifts in the accent.

4. *IPA:* [e]
   Symbol: [e] → This is the first sound in the D.A.E. diphthong [AY] as in *face*.
   Used in place of [ɛ]/[EH]: *dress, bed*
   This sound is used in speaking both the language and accent of Zimbabwean (Shona).
5. *IPA:* [a]
   Symbol: [Ah] → This is the first sound in the D.A.E. diphthong [EYE] as in *sky*.
   Used in place of [æ]/[A]: *trap, bath*
   This sound is used in speaking both the language and accent of Zimbabwean (Shona).
6. *IPA:* [i] → centralized [i].
   Symbol: [EE] → [EE] made in the middle of the mouth rather than in the front of the mouth.
   Used in place of [i]/[EE]: *fleece, creep*
   This sound is also used in its lowered form [ɨ]/[EE] to replace [ɪ]/[I]: *kit, ship*
   This sound is used in speaking a Zimbabwean (Shona) accent.
7. *IPA:* [ə] → centralized [e].
   Symbol: [e] → [e] made in the middle of the mouth.
   Used in place of [ʌ]/[UH]: *strut, curry*
   This sound is used in speaking a Zimbabwean (Shona) accent.
8. *IPA:* [ɜ]
   Symbol: [UH^R]
   Used in place of [ɝ]/[ER]: *bird, nurse, were*
   This sound is used in speaking a Zimbabwean (Shona) accent.
9. *IPA:* [ɞ] → [ɜ] made with rounded lips.
   Symbol: [>UH^R<] → [UHR] with no [R] and made with rounded lips.
   Used in place of [ɝ]/[UHR]: *nurse, work, service*
   This sound is used in speaking Zimbabwean (Shona).
10. *IPA:* [ɤ] → [o] with no lip rounding and lip corners slightly pulled back.
    Symbol: [<o>] → [o] with no lip rounding and lip corners slightly pulled back. The sound is much like a [W].
    Used in place of [l]/[L] in a consonant cluster like PL, BL, LD: *build, trouble* or final [l]/[L]: *fall*
    This sound is used in speaking a Zimbabwean (Shona) accent.

11. *IPA:* [o]

    Symbol: [o] → This is the first sound in the diphthong OH as in *go*.

    Used in place of [ɔ]/[AW]: *cloth, dog, cough*

    This sound is used in speaking both the language and accent Zimbabwean (Shona).

12. *IPA:* [ɒ]

    Symbol: [O] → This is the British *hot, copper, coffee, pot* sound

    Used in place of [ɑ]/[AH] in many words spelled with "o": *bomb, involved*

    This sound is used in speaking both the language and accent of Zimbabwean (Shona).

Consonant Sound Shifts

- ↵ indicates that this sound is a key sound shift
- You can begin to fold melody and rhythm with the sound changes by speaking the sample sentences that are before each section of sound changes.

Consonant Shifts
Example: Pishai Story (Part 2) – 0:43

The school which was pretty new you could only go up to

five years of education.

IPA: θi skuḻ ʍɪ̣ʃ wəs 'prɪ̣'tɪ̣ njuː ju kʊ̱d̯ ʔo̱ˑn.li go̱ a̱pˀ t̯u faiɤ jɪ̯ʌz o̱ɤ
'ə.dʒju'keː.ʃə̱n

SYMBOLS: THEE SKUḺ HWEĒSH WuhS **PRᴿEĒ.TEE** NYOO YOO KŎOD
>ō<N.LEE G>o< A̱hP TOO FAh-EĒVᶠ YEĒ-UHZˢ uhVᶠ
e̱.DᴶYOO.Kə̄.SHuhN

I'll meet you at the ferry in an hour with the ten children.

IPA: aiɤ mi̱t̯ ju a̱t̯ ðo̱ə 'fə.ɾi i̱n an 'a'we wi̱θ ðo̱ə t̯ən ''ʃi̱ɹ.dɾən

SYMBOLS: Ah-EĒ<o> MEĒT YOO AhT THuh **Fe̱**.RᴿEE EĒN AhN **Ah-We**
WEĒ.th THuh Te̱N ᵀ**SHEĒR**.DRᴿe̱N

Key Words	Detailed American English Accent IPA ——— Symbol	Shift to Zimbabwean (Shona) Accent of English IPA ——— Symbol	Key Words Shifts IPA ——— Symbol	Your Key Words
☞ <u>t</u>eam deb<u>t</u>, di<u>d</u>	t/d ——— T/D	<u>t̯</u>/<u>d̯</u> ——— [T] and [D] are both made with the blade rather than the tip of the tongue on the post alveolar ridge	<u>t̯</u>im, <u>d̯</u>o̯t̯, <u>d̯</u>i<u>d̯</u> ——— TEEM, DeT, DEED	
☞ <u>p</u>ee<u>p</u>	p ——— P	p˺ ——— very little air is let out after [P] (non-audible release)	p˺i̯p˺ ——— PEEP	
☞ <u>th</u>ese <u>th</u>ere, brea<u>the</u>	ð ——— TH	[ḏ̯] or [d̯] ——— [TH] or [D] dentalized	ḏ̯iz, ḏ̯ɔ̯ː, brið̯̯ or d̯iz, d̯ɔ̯ː, brid̯ ——— THEEZ, THe, BRᴿEETH or DEEZ, De, BRᴿEED	
☞ <u>th</u>in <u>th</u>ick, mou<u>th</u>	θ ——— th	θ̯ ——— [th] dentalized	θ̯i̯n, θ̯i̯k, me̯o̯θ̯ ——— thEEN, thEEK, MA-OOth	
☞ <u>r</u>ed d<u>r</u>ess	ɹ ——— R	[r] or [ɹ̯] ——— [Rᴿ] or [R̯]	rə̯d̯, d̯rəs or ɹ̯ə̯d̯, d̯ɹ̯əs ——— RᴿeD, DRᴿeS or R̯eD, DR̯eS	
☞ exce<u>l</u> fa<u>ll</u>, tab<u>le</u> (final *l* in spelling)	l ——— L	[ɤ] or [ɫ] or [ɹ̯] ——— [<o>] or [L̯] [L] made by lifting the back of the tongue toward the soft palate or [R̯]	ˈɔk.sɔɤ, fɔɤ, ˈteː.bɤ or ˈɔk.sɔɫ, fɔɫ, ˈteː.bəɫ or ˈɔk.sɔɹ̯, fɔɹ̯, ˈteː.bəɹ̯ ——— eK.Se-<o>, F>AW<-<o>, Te.B<o> or eK.SeL, F>AW<L, Te.BuhL or eK.SeR, F>AW<R, Te.BuhR	

Key Words	Detailed American English Accent IPA Symbol	Shift to Zimbabwean (Shona) Accent of English IPA Symbol	Key Words Shifts IPA Symbol	Your Key Words
ju<u>dg</u>e	dʒ ---- J	d̥ʒ ---- J^SH	dʒaːd̥ʒ ---- J^SH A̱J^SH	
<u>ch</u>ur<u>ch</u>	tʃ ---- CH	ˈʃ ---- ^CHSH	ˈʃeˈʃ ---- ^CHSHe^CHSH	
<u>h</u>ome (initial *h* in spelling)	h ---- H	sometimes dropped sometimes dropped	ʌːŏm ---- ŪH-ŬM	
⊢ boy<u>s</u> (final *s* when pronounced [z])	z ---- Z	z̧ ---- Z^S	bʊiz̧ ---- BUE̱Z^S	
readi<u>ng</u> (final *ing* in spelling)	ŋ ---- ING	i̧n ---- E̱EN	ˈɾi.ḑin ---- R^REE̱.DE̱EN	

Front Vowel Sound Shifts

The vowels of Zimbabwean (Shona) include:

IPA: [i], [e], [a], [u], [o]
Symbol: [EE], [e], [Ah], [o]

Knowing the vowels for the Shona language will provide clues for the vowel shifts in the accent.

Front Vowel Shifts				
The thief will tell me after we trap him.				
IPA: ðə θif wɨɫ ţəɫ mɨ ˈaf.ţə wɨ ţɾɛpˀ hɨm				
SYMBOLS: THuh thEEF WEE<o> TeL MEE **Ahf.**Tuh WEE TRᴿEHP HEEM				
Key Words	*Detailed American English Accent* *IPA* -------------------- *Symbol*	*Shift to Zimbabwean (Shona) Accent of English* *IPA* -------------------- *Symbol*	*Key Words Shifts* *IPA* -------------------- *Symbol*	*Your Key Words*
☛ fleece sneeze, plead	i -------------------- EE	ɨ -------------------- EE [EE] made in the middle of the mouth	flis, kɾipˀ, pɹiḍ -------------------- FLEES, KRᴿEEP, PREED	
☛ kit ship, pitch, dim, lip	ɪ -------------------- I	ɨ -------------------- EE	kɨţ, ʃɨpˀ, pˀɨtʃ -------------------- KEET, SHEEP, PEECH	
country (*y* in final position of spelling)	ɪ -------------------- EE	ɨ -------------------- [EE]	ˈkaːn.ţɹɨ -------------------- **KAHN.**TREE	

Key Words	Detailed American English Accent	Shift to Zimbabwean (Shona) Accent of English	Key Words Shifts	Your Key Words
	IPA -------------------- Symbol	IPA -------------------- Symbol	IPA -------------------- Symbol	
☛ berated	[ɪ] in prefix -------------------- [EE] in prefix	i̵ -------------------- E̱E̱	ˈbi̵.ɹeː͵t̪i̵d̪ -------------------- B**E̱E̱**.R^Rē̱.TE̱E̱D	
☛ dress bed, feather, send	ε -------------------- EH	ə -------------------- [e] ([e] made in the middle of the mouth)	d̪ɾəs, bəd̪, ˈfə.d̪ə -------------------- DR^Re̱S, BeD, Fe.Duh	
member empty (*em* in spelling)	ε -------------------- EH	sometimes [ɪ] -------------------- sometimes [I]	ˈmɪm.bə, ˈɪm.t̪i̵ -------------------- MIM-Buh, IM.TE̱E̱	
☛ trap mad, rat, candle	æ -------------------- A	[ε] or [a] -------------------- [EH] or [Ah]	t̪ɾɛp̚, mɛd̪, ɾɛt̪ or t̪ɾap̚, mad̪, ɾat̪ -------------------- TREHP, MEHD, R^REHT or TRAhP, MAhD, R^RAhT	
☛ bath *[a]/[Ah] ask, after, dance, example, half, mask, rascal, transfer In Chapter 1, there is a list of these words called the BATH or ASK list of words.	æ -------------------- A	a -------------------- Ah	bað̪, ask -------------------- BAhth, AhSK	

Middle Vowel Sound Shifts

Middle Vowel Shifts				
In the summer, workers burned the underbrush.				
IPA: ɪ̈n ðə̈ ʂ̣ 'saː.mə 'wə.kəʐ bənḓ ð̣ị 'aːn.ḓə'braːʃ				
SYMBOLS: Ĕ̱EN THuh **SAI̱h**.Muh **W>UHᴿ<**.KuhZˢ Be̱ND THĔ̱E **A̱I̱hN**.Duh.**BRᴿA̱I̱hSH**				
Key Words	*Detailed American English Accent* *IPA* ------ *Symbol*	*Shift to Zimbabwean (Shona) Accent of English* *IPA* ------ *Symbol*	*Key Words Shifts* *IPA* ------ *Symbol*	*Your Key Words*
↤ nu̲rse (*ur* in spelling)	ɝ ------ ER	ɐ or ɔ ------ >UHᴿ< or e̱	nɐs or nɔs ------ N>UHᴿ<S or Ne̱S	
↤ bi̲rd (*ir* in spelling)	ɝ ------ ER	ɜ ------ UHᴿ	bɜḓ ------ BUHᴿD	
↤ wo̲rk (*or* in spelling)	ɝ ------ ER	ɐ ------ >UHᴿ<	wɐk ------ W>UHᴿ<K	
se̲rvice lea̲rn (*er, ear* in spelling)	ɝ ------ ER	e ------ e	'se.vị̈s, len ------ **Se**.VĔ̱ĔS, LeN	
siste̲r traito̲r, hanga̲r	ɚ ------ er	ə ------ uh	'sị̈s.ṭə, 'ṭɹəːṭə, hɛŋ.ə ------ **SĔ̱ĔS**.Tuh, **TRᴿe̱**.Tuh, **HENG**.uh	

Key Words	Detailed American English Accent	Shift to Zimbabwean (Shona) Accent of English	Key Words Shifts	Your Key Words
	IPA	*IPA*	*IPA*	
	Symbol	*Symbol*	*Symbol*	
str<u>u</u>t c<u>u</u>rry	ʌ̈ U̟H	aː A̲h	st̬raːt̬, kaː.ɹi STR^RA̲ht, **KA̲h**.RE̲E̲	
☛ c<u>o</u>me fl<u>oo</u>d (in words spelled with *o* and sometimes *oo*)	ʌ̈ U̟H	ɔ AW	kɔm, flɔd̬ KAWM, FLAWD	
☛ c<u>o</u>nvince c<u>o</u>mpare (*con* and *com* prefixes)	ə uh	o o	ˈkˀon.vi̱ns/ ˈkˀom.pˀəː **KoN**-VE̲E̲NS/ **KoM**-Pe̲	
<u>a</u>bout b<u>a</u>nan<u>a</u>	ə uh	ə̣ uh	ə̣ˈbɛ̣ʊt̬, bɛ.ˈna.nə̣ uh-**BA-UT**, BEH.**NAh**.Nuh	

Back Vowel Shifts

Back Vowel Shifts				
I thought my father would not stop being a bully but the truth is, I was wrong.				
IPA: aɨ θɔt maɨ ˈfɑ.ðə wʊd nɒt stɒp⌐ bɪŋ ə ˈbʊ.lɨ baṭ ðə ṭruθ ɨz aɨ woẕ ɾʊŋ				
SYMBOLS: Ah-EE th>AW<T MAh-EE **FAH**.THuh WŌOD NOT STOP BEENG uh **BŎO**.LEE BAhT THuh TRᴿOOth EEZˢ Ah-EE WoZˢ RᴿONG				
Key Words	*Detailed American English Accent* *IPA* -------------------- *Symbol*	*Shift to Zimbabwean (Shona) Accent of English* *IPA* -------------------- *Symbol*	*Key Words Shifts* *IPA* -------------------- *Symbol*	*Your Key Words*
f<u>oo</u>d gr<u>ew</u>, tr<u>ue</u>, tw<u>o</u>	u -------------------- OO	u -------------------- OO	fuḍ, gɾu, ṭru -------------------- FOOD, GRᴿOO, TRᴿOO	
d<u>u</u>ty t<u>u</u>ne, n<u>ew</u>s	[ɪʊ] when preceded by *t, d, n* in spelling [I-ŌO] when preceded by *t, d, n* in spelling	ju -------------------- YOO	ˈḍʲju.ṭi, ťjun, njuẕ -------------------- **Dᴶ YOO**.TEE, TᶜᴴYOON, NYOOZˢ	
f<u>oo</u>t p<u>u</u>t	ʊ -------------------- U	ʊ̞ -------------------- ŎO	fʊ̞ṭ, p⌐ʊ̞ṭ -------------------- FŎOT, PŎOT	
th<u>ough</u>t t<u>a</u>ll, c<u>au</u>lk, <u>aw</u>ful	ɔ -------------------- AW	ɔ̞ -------------------- >AW<	θɔ̞ṭ, ṭɔ̞ɤ, kɔ̞k -------------------- th>AW<T, T>AW<-<o>, K>AW<K	

Key Words	Detailed American English Accent	Shift to Zimbabwean (Shona) Accent of English	Key Words Shifts	Your Key Words
	IPA	IPA	IPA	
	Symbol	Symbol	Symbol	
☛ cl<u>o</u>th *[ɒ]/[O] d<u>o</u>g, c<u>ou</u>gh, w<u>a</u>sh, h<u>o</u>rrid	ɔ	o	kloθ, d̪og, kof	
	AW	o	KLoth, DoG, KoF	
f<u>a</u>ther	ɑ	a̤	'fɑ̤.ð̪ə	
	AH	AH	**FA̤H.**THuh	
☛ l<u>o</u>t *[ɒ]/[O] sq<u>ua</u>d, w<u>a</u>nder	ɑ	ɒ̤	lɒ̤t, skwɒ̤d, 'wɒ̤n.d̪ə	
	AH	O	LOT, SKWOD, **WON.**Duh	

Diphthong Sound Shifts

Note!

On Diphthongs

Diphthongs that turn into monophthongs tend to replace the dropped phoneme of the diphthong with a lilt.

Example: face → feːs / FēS

Diphthong Shifts				
I'd like to fly away someday and go south to the mountains with the boys.				
IPA: aɨd laik t̪u flai a.weː 'saːm.d̪eˑ and gɔ sauθ t̪u ð̪ə̣ 'maun.t̪ə̣nz̧ wɨθ ð̪ə̣ bɔ̣iz̧				
SYMBOLS: Ah-EED LAh-EEK TOO FLAh-EE Ah-**Wē SĀ̱hM**.Dē AhND G>o< SAH.OOth TOO THuh **MAH-OON**.TuhNZˢ WEƐth THuh Bo-EEZˢ				
Key Words	*Detailed American English Accent* *IPA* ------------------ *Symbol*	*Shift to Zimbabwean (Shona) Accent of English* *IPA* ------------------ *Symbol*	*Key Words Shifts* *IPA* ----------------------- *Symbol*	*Your Key Words*
↦ f<u>a</u>ce p<u>ai</u>n, d<u>ay</u>, w<u>ei</u>ght, st<u>ea</u>k	eɪ̆ ------------------ AY	eː ------------------ ē	feːs, pʰeːn, d̪eː ----------------------- FēS, PēN, Dē	
pr<u>i</u>ce <u>eye</u>s, d<u>ia</u>per, fl<u>y</u>, g<u>uy</u>, h<u>ei</u>ght	aɪ̆ ------------------ EYE	ai ------------------ Ah-EE	pʰrais, aiz̧, 'd̪ai.pʰə̣ ----------------------- PRᴿAh-EES, Ah-EEZˢ, **DAh-EE**.Puh	

Key Words	Detailed American English Accent	Shift to Zimbabwean (Shona) Accent of English	Key Words Shifts	Your Key Words
	IPA ------------------ *Symbol*	*IPA* ------------------ *Symbol*	*IPA* ------------------ *Symbol*	
ch<u>oi</u>ce b<u>oy</u>s	ɔĭ ------------------ OY	ǫ̈i̖ ------------------ o-EE	tʃɔ̰is, bɔi̥z̰ ------------------ CHo-EES, Bo-EEZ[S]	
⊷ g<u>oa</u>t s<u>ew</u>, g<u>o</u>, t<u>oe</u>	oŭ ------------------ OH	ǫ ------------------ >o<	gǫt̪, sǫ, gǫ ------------------ G>o<T, S>o<, G>o<	
m<u>ou</u>th t<u>ow</u>n	aŭ ------------------ OW	ɑu ------------------ AH-OO	mɑuθ, t̪ɑun ------------------ MAH-OOth, TAH-OON	

Diphthongs of R Sound Shifts

Note!

On r-coloration

A Zimbabwean (Shona) accent has no r-coloration in diphthongs and triphthongs of R.

Note!

On Diphthongs of R

The diphthongs of R that turn into monophthongs tend to replace the dropped [ɚ]/[UHR] with a lilt.

Example: hair → heː / He

		Diphthongs and Triphthongs of R Shifts		

***Our* friends st*ar*ted the *fire* n*ear* y*our* n*or*th *or*chard an *hour* bef*ore* we got th*ere*.**

IPA: 'a'we frənẓ 'sṭɑː.ṭịḍ ð̣ə 'fa.ja nị jọ nọːθ 'ọː''ʃ̣ɜḍ an 'a'we 'bị'fọ wị gụṭ ð̣eː

SYMBOLS: **Ah.We** FR^ReNZ^S **STAH**.TE͟E͟D THuh **Fah**.YAh NE͟E͟ Yo NAWth
AW.^TSHUH^RD AhN **Ah.We** BE͟E͟.**FAW** WE͟E͟ GOT THē

Key Words	Detailed American English Accent IPA ------------------ Symbol	Shift to Zimbabwean (Shona) Accent of English IPA ------------------ Symbol	Key Words Shifts IPA ------------------ Symbol	Your Key Words
↜ n<u>ear</u> b<u>eer</u>	ɪɚ ------------ EAR	[ɨ] or [ɨʌ] ------------------ [EE] or [EE-UH]	nɨ, bɨ or nɨʌ, bɨʌ ------------------ NE͟E͟, BE͟E͟ or NE͟E͟-UH, BE͟E͟-UH	
↜ h<u>air</u> st<u>are</u>, p<u>ear</u>, squ<u>are</u>, th<u>ere</u>	ɛɚ ------------ AIR	eː ------------------ ē	heː, sṭeː, pe˞ː ------------------ Hē, STē, Pē	
↜ s<u>ure</u> p<u>oor</u>, y<u>our</u>	ʊɚ ------------ UR	[ɔ] or [ʊʌ] ------------------ [o] or [U-UH]	ʃọ, p˞ọ, jọ or ʃʊʌ, p˞ʊʌ, jʊʌ ------------------ SHo, Po, Yo or SHU-UH, PU-UH, YU-UH	
↜ n<u>or</u>th Ge<u>or</u>ge, p<u>our</u>, w<u>ar</u>p, <u>oar</u>	ɔɚ ------------ AWR	ọː ------------------ A͞W	nọːθ, dʒọːdʒ, p˞ọː ------------------ NA͞Wth, J^SHA͞WJ^SH, PA͞W	
↜ st<u>ar</u>t h<u>ear</u>t	ɑɚ ------------ AHR	ɑː ------------------ A͞H	sṭɑːṭ, hɑːṭ ------------------ STA͞HT, HA͞HT	
f<u>ire</u>	aɪɚ ------------ EYER	a.ja ------------------ Ah-YAh	'fa.ja ------------------ **FAh**-YAh	
h<u>our</u>	aʊɚ ------------ OWR	a.we ------------------ Ah-We	a.we ------------------ **Ah**-We	

Key Sentences for Practice

> **Note!**
> - By practicing the sentences below, you can work through the sound shifts for a Zimbabwean (Shona) accent in the context of a simple thought. I suggest you think, imagine and speak actively from a point of view. As you begin to work with the operative words in the thoughts, the rhythm and melody of the accent will begin to emerge appropriately.
> - Note that less significant words are sometimes less stressed, so articulation of the vowels and diphthongs in these words may 1) move toward the neutral *schwa* [ə]/[uh] in the middle of the mouth and/or 2) be shorter in length.

Consonants:

- **Example:** Pishai Story (Part 2) – 0:43

The school <u>which</u> was <u>pretty</u> new you coul<u>d</u> only go u<u>p</u> <u>to</u>

fi<u>ve</u> year<u>s</u> o<u>f</u> e<u>d</u>ucation.

   IPA: θɨ skul̪ ʍɨʃ wəs ˈprɨ̞'t̪ɨ njuː ju kʊ̬d̪ ʔo̞ˑn.lɨ go̞ ap̚ t̪u faɨ̞ jɨ̞ʌz ə̞v
           ˈə.dˈʒuˈkeːˌʃə̞n

   SYMBOLS: THEE͜ SKUL HWEE͜SH WuhS **PR^REE͜.TEE͜** NYOO YOO
               KŌOD >ō<N.LEE͜ G>o< AhP TOO FAh-EE͜V^F YEE͜-UHZ^S uhV^F
               e̞.D^JYOO.Kē.SHuhN

- *I'<u>ll</u> mee<u>t</u> you a<u>t</u> <u>the</u> fe<u>rr</u>y in an hour wi<u>th</u> <u>the</u> <u>t</u>en <u>children</u>.*

   IPA: aɨ̞ mɨt̪ ju at̪ ð̞ə̞ ˈfə.rɨ ɨn an ˈaˈwe wɨ̞θ ð̞ə̞ t̪ən ˈˈʃɨ̞.d̪rən

   SYMBOLS: Ah-EE͜<o> MEET YOO AhT THuh **Fe̞.R^REE** EE͜N AhN **Ah-We**
               WEE͜.th THuh TeN ^T**SHEE͜E̞R.DR^Re̞N**

Front Vowels: Vowels articulated by arching the front of the tongue up or cupping it down, aiming toward the front of the hard palate.

- *The thief will tell me after we trap him.*

    IPA: ð̥ə̥ θɪf wɪɾ t̪əɫ mɪ 'af.t̪ə wɪ t̪ɾɛp˥ hɪm

    SYMBOLS: THuh thEEF WEE<o> TeL MEE **Ahf**.Tuh WEE TR^REHP HEEM

Middle Vowels: Vowels articulated by arching the middle of the tongue up or cupping it down, aiming toward the middle of the hard palate.

- *In the summer, workers burned the underbrush.*

    IPA: ɪ̥n ð̥ə̥ 'saː.mə 'wə.kəz bənd̥ ð̥ɨ 'aːn.də'braːʃ

    SYMBOLS: EEN THuh S**Ah**.Muh **W>UH**^R<.KuhZ^S BeND THEE **Ah**N.Duh. **BR**^R**Ah**SH

Back Vowels: Vowels articulated by arching the back of the tongue up or cupping it down, aiming toward the back of the hard palate.

- *I thought my father would not stop being a bully but the truth is, I was wrong.*

    IPA: aɪ θ̥ɔt maɪ 'fɑ.ð̥ə wʊd̥ nɒt st̪ɒp˥ bɪŋ ə 'bʊ.li bat̪ ð̥ə̥ t̪ruθ ɪ̥z aɪ woz ɾɒŋ

    SYMBOLS: Ah-EE th>AW<T MAh-EE **FAH**.THuh WOOD NOT STOP BEENG uh **BOO**.LEE BAhT THuh TR^ROOth EEZ^S Ah-EE WoZ^S R^RONG

Diphthongs: When two vowels are combined in one syllable.

- *I'd like to fly away someday and go south to the mountains with the boys.*

    IPA: aɪd̥ laɪk t̪u flaɪ a.weː 'saːm.d̥eˑ and go sauθ t̪u ð̥ə̥ 'maun.t̪ə̥nz wɪθ ð̥ə̥ bɔɪz

    SYMBOLS: Ah-EED LAh-EEK TOO FLAh-EE Ah-**We SAh**M.De AhND G>o< SAH.OOth TOO THuh **MAH-OON**.TuhNZ^S WEEth THuh Bo-EEZ^S

R Diphthongs: A diphthong in which the second vowel is rhotic (e.g., has [R] coloration in the final sound)

Example: near → nɪɚ/NEAR

Triphthongs: A combination of three vowel sounds in which the third vowel is rhotic.

Example: fire → faɪɚ/FEYER

- *Our friends started the fire near your north orchard an hour before we got there.*

    IPA: 'a'we frənz 'st̪ɑː.t̪ɪd̥ ð̥ə 'fa.ja nɪ̥ jɔ nɔːθ 'ɔːˈʃɜd̥ an 'a'we 'bɪ'fɔ̥ wɪ gɒt̪ ð̥eː

    SYMBOLS: **Ah.We** FR^ReNZ^S **STAH**.TEED THuh **FAh**.YAh NEE Yo NAWth **AW**.^T**SHUH**^R**D** AhN **Ah.We** BEE.FAW WEE GOT THe

Making Your Own Map of the Accent

Listen to the Zimbabwean (Shona) accent samples provided and investigate the resources suggested in the *Introduction and Resources* section. Compose (or steal) *Key Phrases* from your listening/viewing that challenge and/or ground you in the accent. Then get more specific and check your sounds against the sounds in the Workbook.

Your take on the sound shifts may be slightly different. That is okay. The breakdown is a tool, not a rule. Recheck what you hear and, if you still stand behind your discoveries, go with them. This will help you to develop **your own** idiolect of the accent.

> *Note!*
> **What is an Idiolect?**
> Each of us speaks differently even if we have the same general accent. The individualized way that each of us speaks is referred to as an idiolect. For the actor, idiolect is part of what creates character. It is the "how" of the accent, and influences the way we craft our thoughts through language.

KEY PHRASES WITH KEY SOUND SHIFTS

Speak your *Key Phrases*, shifting back and forth between your own home *idiolect of English* and the *Zimbabwean (Shona) accent* you are building. **Observe** the shifts ONE by ONE in your Articulators, Focus of Articulation, use of Melody/Pitch/Lilt, Rhythm/Stress/Pace, and Source & Path of Resonance as you shift back and forth between the two accents. Make note of the shifts in the table provided. Putting your understanding of the shifts into your own words will encourage you to develop a more clear and personal idiolect.

ZIMBABWEAN (SHONA) ACCENT *KEY POINTS OF FOCUS: VOCAL POSTURE AND CHARACTERISTICS*

JAW
LIPS
TONGUE
SOFT PALATE
PHARYNX

FOCUS OF ARTICULATION (TOWARDS TEETH, FRONT/MIDDLE/ BACK OF HARD PALATE, SOFT PALATE, ETC.)

MELODY/PITCH/LILT

RHYTHM/STRESS/PACE

SOURCE & PATH OF RESONANCE – Where does the resonance begin and what is the apparent path it travels through your body (chest, hard palate, sinuses, temples, crown, base of skull, etc.)? Refer to the Source & Path of Resonance and Resonators in the *Zimbabwean (Shona) Accent of English: Down & Dirty Warm-Up and Quick Look* on page 88.

OTHER CHARACTERISTICS (What are your observations?)

PERSONAL IMAGES (For many actors personal images can be the most powerful and effective triggers for their transformation into an accent)

Chapter 5

South African (Zulu) Accent of English

Introduction and Resources

The History of the Zulu Language in S.A.

The word *Zulu* means "heaven" or "sky". The language is a Nguni subgroup of the Bantu group of the Benue-Congo subfamily of the Niger-Congo family of languages. It is spoken by around nine million people throughout South Africa, primarily in Zululand, S.A. and Northeastern S.A. Zulu is inclusive of many Afrikaans and English words. Most interestingly, like Xhosa, Zulu uses the unique "click" sounds.

In the 1800s, European missionaries created a Latin script for the Zulu language, which shifted the Zulu oral tradition to include written forms.

The eleven official languages of S.A. include Zulu, Xhosa, Swati, Ndebele, Southern Sotho, Tswana, Northern Sotho, Venda, Tsonga, English and Afrikaans.

Documentaries

Long Night's Journey into Day

Films with Zulu Accents and Zulu Speakers

Bopha, *Power of One* (This film takes place in Alexandra, which is a very multi-ethnic township in Johannesburg. The accents are diverse, but Zulu, Xhosa and Sotho accents are predominant), *Congo, Cry Freedom, A Dry White Season, Ace Ventura: When Nature Calls, Outbreak, The Gods Must Be Crazy 2, The Lion King, Chicken Little, Sarafina* (Leleti Khumalo has a very clear Zulu accent), *Safe House, Cry the Beloved Country, A World Apart, Amandla, Tsotsi* (in Zulu with a few Xhosa and Afrikaans speakers; English subtitles), *Lucky, Nbantwa BAM (With My Children), Cool Runnings*

Television

The following television programs contain a mix of S.A. accents including Zulu: *Shaka Zulu, Yizo Yizo 2, Prime Time South Africa, A Time of Violence*

Plays with Zulu Characters

Asinamal by Mbongeni Ngema, *The Lion King*, *Children of Asazi* by Matsemela Manaka (both Charmaine and Diliza could be played as Zulu), *My Children! My Africa!* by Athol Fugard (the character of Thami could be played as Zulu), *Blood Knot* by Athol Fugard (the character of Zachariah could be played as a Zulu), *Woza Albert*, *The Zulu* by Mbongeni Ngema

Music

Ladysmith Black Mambazo, Thunder Before Dawn: The Indestructible Beat of Soweto, Mahotella Queens, Miriam Makeba (also known as "Mama Africa", was a Grammy-winning South African singer and civil rights activist)

Radio

Radio Khwezi (Isizulu with one hour of English daily), Ukhozi FM (Isizulu)

Personalities

Jacob Zuma (South African president), Mangosuthu Buthelezi (Inkatha Freedom Party Founder and President), Ben Ngubane (former South African Broadcasting Company Chairman and former Minister of Arts & Culture), Njabulo Ndebele (writer and former Chancellor of University of Cape Town), Samkelo Radebe (Paralympic gold medalist), Siphiwe Tshabalala (footballer)

Down & Dirty Warm-up and Quick Look

Note!

On Symbols

- International Phonetic Alphabet Symbols will be listed first and Sound Symbols will be listed second. Example: [i]/[EE]
- Sound Symbol Users: bold-faced letters indicate the syllable is stressed.

1) **The Muscles:** Wake your mouth up so you can more easily discover the physical transformation in speaking the accent.

   a. Scratch the front, middle and back of your tongue with your front top teeth.

   b. Rub the front, middle and back of your hard palate with the tip of your tongue.

   c. Imagine your mouth is numb from being at the dentist and you want to wake it up. Make tongue circles pressing against the back of your lips first clockwise, then counter clockwise (you are waking up your orbicularis muscle).

   d. To get the breath flowing, blow through your lips, getting them to flap together. Travel up and down in pitch on a BBBB and PPP, feeling the vibration as you wiggle up and down your spine.

2) **Vocal Posture for a S.A. (Zulu) Accent:** Imagine wideness in your mouth and throat, like a whale's throat, and say with great wideness and expansiveness: "Jonah's Whale!" This will help you with the laterally-wide, but rounded feel of the mouth needed for the accent. The tongue blade rests forward and down, behind the bottom teeth; and, the articulation is aimed toward the back of the top front teeth. Lips are more forward and pursed than in American English, but very relaxed at the same time. They are ready for sensual action on rounded sounds.

3) **Resonators:** "occupy" the following spaces. This will prepare you to find the Source & Path of Resonance for a S.A. (Zulu) accent. (By "occupy", I

mean just that; be in the space of it and find the pathway and flow of resonance, rather than "putting" the resonance there.)

a.   CHEST – Generously laugh at something – ha ha ha / HAh HAh HAh
b.   HARD PALATE – As if you were discovering something – ho ho ho / Ho Ho Ho
c.   THE BONES AT THE BASE OF YOUR SKULL (THE OCCIPITAL BONE) – Use your hands to scoop the sound from the base of your skull with a Mississippi African-American dialect as if you're flirting with someone nearby – he he he / He He He
d.   FLICK THE SOUND OUT OF YOUR CHEEKBONES with an Italian-American flourish, as if calling to someone across the street – he he he / He He He
e.   WITH YOUR HANDS NEXT TO YOUR TEMPLES, SHAKE THE SOUND OUT WITH LOOSE FISTS – As if you were somewhat crazed – ji̠ ji̠ ji̠ / YE̠E YE̠E YE̠E
f.   IMAGINE A METAL DISK EXTENDING FROM YOUR HANDS THROUGH YOUR SKULL. Bring your hands to the sides of your head just above the temples, with your palms facing the floor, thumbs hooked behind your skull. *Lid* the vibration to create a muted brassy sound. Like a robot saying "Hi" – hai̯ hai̯ hai̯ / Hah-Ĭ Hah-Ĭ Hah-Ĭ
g.   GIGGLE OUT OF THE TOP OF YOUR HEAD – As if you were tickled pink by something – hi̠ hi̠ hi̠ / HE̠E HE̠E HE̠E

4)   Source & Path of Resonance for a S.A. (Zulu) Accent:

•   For men, think of beginning the resonance full bodied in the mouth. Imagine a lateral doming wide in the hard palate. Let the soft palate accommodate this image without consciously lifting it. Next, allow the resonance to move down into the chest and travel up into the cheekbones, directing it out from behind the eyes. There is a bit of nasality. Think of having warm steel wool between the temples.

•   Because women tend to lift more in pitch, they follow the same Path of Resonance as men but allow it to continue up and lid it in the "metal disk" area at the temples (see #3f above). They tend to have less nasality than men.

5)   Get the sound changes into your body and imagination.
Say these phrases occupying the following places in your body, suggesting to yourself the following energetic associations:

•   pubic bone to tail bone – survival instinct

   zʉ / ZO̠O
   I need it – a ni̠d ɪt / Ah NE̠ED E̠ET

•   pubic bone to navel & sacrum in back – sexuality, big feelings

   wo / Wo
   I desire it – a dɪzaĭɾ‿ɪt / Ah DE̠E.**ZAh-ĬRᴿ**‿E̠ET

- rib cage to below heart – will

  ʒ̞ / ZH>AW<
  I want it – a wont̪ ɪt̪ / Ah WoNT EET

- heart – love

  ma / MAh
  I love it – a lʌv ɪt̪ / Ah LAhV EET

- throat – communication (think of talking at a party)

  ba̞ / BAh
  I have to say it – a hɛv tʉ se ɪt̪ / Ah HEHV TOO Se EET

- forehead – intelligence/wisdom

  ke / Ke
  I know it – a no ɪt̪ / Ah No EET

- crown of head – spirituality

  r̝i / R^REE
  I believe it – a 'bɪ'liːv ɪt̪ / Ah **BEE.LEEV EET**

6) **Articulation** – using playful physical actions: punching, flicking, dabbing, slashing

  d̪ʊ d̪ɪ kʊ d̪ʊ d̪ɪ kʊ d̪ʊ d̪ɪ kʊ – d̪ɪ
  d̪ʊ d̪ɪ kʊ d̪ʊ d̪ɪ kʊ d̪ʊ d̪ɪ kʊ – d̪e
  d̪ʊ d̪ɪ kʊ d̪ʊ d̪ɪ kʊ d̪ʊ d̪ɪ kʊ – d̪aɪ̆
  d̪ʊ d̪ɪ kʊ d̪ʊ d̪ɪ kʊ d̪ʊ d̪ɪ kʊ – d̪o
  d̪ʊ d̪ɪ kʊ d̪ʊ d̪ɪ kʊ d̪ʊ d̪ɪ kʊ – d̪ʉ

Repeat as needed, replacing [d̪] with [t̪], [p], [b], [k], [g], [f], [v]

  DOO DEE KOO DOO DEE KOO DOO DEE KOO – DEE
  DOO DEE KOO DOO DEE KOO DOO DEE KOO – De
  DOO DEE KOO DOO DEE KOO DOO DEE KOO – DAh-Ĭ
  DOO DEE KOO DOO DEE KOO DOO DEE KOO – Do
  DOO DEE KOO DOO DEE KOO DOO DEE KOO – DOO

Repeat as needed, replacing [D] with [T], [P], [B], [K], [G], [F], [V]. [D] & [T] are both articulated with the blade of the tongue against the back of the top front teeth (dentalized).

Key Points of Focus

Characteristics and Vocal Posture

S.A. (Zulu) Accent Characteristics

Note!
On Melody/Lilt/Pitch and Rhythm/Stress/Pace
Every accent contains shifts for some, but not necessarily all, of these elements of vocal variety.

Note!
On Use of Musical Notes
Follow the "musical notes" up and down to get a feel for the melody of the accent. The filled-in notes are shorter than the open notes. For those who are musically inclined, think of them as approximating quarter notes and half notes. This distinction will give you a feel for the rhythm of the accent.

Melody/Lilt/Pitch

The melody for a S.A. (Zulu) accent lies within a compact pitch range. Because there is often equal stress in multi-syllabic words, the melody often plays out in a playful patter. There is also a tendency to slightly lift in pitch on the final words of a thought. The S.A. (Zulu) accent is generally pitched slightly higher than American English. Pitch change happens from one syllable to the next, or one word to the next. A word of warning: if you lilt within the lengthened vowels, the accent will become lighter and more contemporary, as in the accents of Thulisile and Thandazile.

Example: Thembi Story – 0:16

So this other day one teacher saw me.

Notice how the final words in Thembi's thought phrases often go up in pitch or stay the same pitch, rather than falling down in pitch, as in American or British English. In this sentence you can hear it on her final word *me.*

Example: Ron Story (Part 1) – 1:08

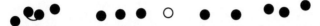

I realized when I got there what was happening.

Ron has a medium-strength accent but still speaks with a playful melody, slightly pitching up for the final words in his thoughts. In this sentence you can hear this on the word, *happening.*

Example: Sifiso Story (Part 2) – 0:08

Our parent used to tell us that don't be a nonsense to yourself.

Sifiso has a medium-strong accent. You can hear the contained pitch range and patter characteristic of a Zulu accent along with the lift in pitch at the end of his thoughts. In this sentence, you can hear the lift in pitch on the second syllable of *yourself.* You can also hear the accent's characteristic of elongating consonants on operative words of a thought, in his lengthening of the second [n]/[N] in *nonsense.*

Rhythm/Stress/Pace

Because unstressed vowels are most often given full stressed value, even in unstressed syllables, there is a syncopated feel to the accent. It is essential not to fall into a robotic, syncopated, staccato quality, but rather link the words into a "swelling" flow in relation to the thought being spoken. There is also, often, a lengthening of consonants in operative words rather than a pitch change.

Example: Poyoyo Story (Part 1) – 0:07

They make eh family unit in in Soweto, Jabilana Hostel.

Note how Poyoyo gives equal stress in each syllable in the multi-syllabic words *family* and *Soweto.*

Example: Sonia Story – 1:09

So that I can try to help my sisters and do something.

Note how Sonia couples length, in selected consonants, with pitch, in order to point out the important words in her thoughts. You can hear this in the words: *si̱sters* and *so̱mething*. She also has the characteristic slight lift in pitch at the end of her thoughts, as you can hear in the second syllable of *some̱thing*.

Source & Path of Resonance

There is a bold buoyancy in this accent's resonance.

- For men, think of beginning the resonance full bodied in the mouth. Imagine a lateral doming wide in the hard palate. Let the soft palate accommodate this image without consciously lifting it. Next, allow the resonance to move down into the chest and travel up into the cheekbones, directing it out from behind the eyes. There is a bit of nasality. Think of having warm steel wool between the temples.

  You can hear this very clearly in Sifiso's, Hamilton's, and Poyoyo's accents. Ron has been in America for a while and has more pharyngeal narrowing and creak in his voice.

- Because women tend to lift more in pitch, they follow the same Path of Resonance as men but allow it to continue up and lid it in the "metal disk" area (see #3f on page 120). They tend to have less nasality than men.

  You can hear this very clearly in Sonia and Thambi. Because Thandazile and Thulisile have lived in America, you will hear this quality to a lesser extent in their audio samples.

S.A. (Zulu) Accent Vocal Posture

> *Note!*
> **On Vocal Posture**
> These adjustments enable you to integrate the accent through physical transformation rather than solely relying on sound shifts.

- **Focus of Articulation:** Because the tongue blade rests forward, articulation is aimed toward the back of the top front teeth.
- **Tongue:** The tongue rests forward and down behind the bottom teeth and rises in the middle, falling lower at the back.

- **Lips:** The lips are more forward and pursed than in American English, but very relaxed at the same time. They are ready for playful rounding on rounded sounds.
- **Jaw:** The jaw has a relaxed quality similar to American English.
- **Mouth, Soft Palate, and Pharynx:** Imagine wideness in your mouth and throat, like a whale's throat, and say with great wideness and expansiveness: "Jonah's Whale!" This will help you with the latterly wide, but rounded feel of the mouth needed for the accent. The more round and wide, the stronger the accent.

Note!

On Pharynx

Ways to open into the roundness in the pharynx:

- Think of going into a sob and feel how your throat widens.
- Technically speaking, there is somewhat less twang in this accent than in American English. A way to diminish twang is to sing in the voice of an 8-year-old English choir boy: "Laudamus Te, Adoramus Te" (or any sort of gibberish Latin); then bring the pitch to your range and speak with that kind of openness in your throat. The choir boy before puberty has a very pure tone made with a very open throat: just what you need for this.
- Start with this kind of openness. Add just a little creakiness around your glottis (vocal folds) if you want to work with a weaker accent.

Distinct Sounds of the Language and/or Accent

Note!

On Distinct Sounds

These are some of the sounds that South African (Zulu) speakers use and American speakers do not. In speaking the sounds and/or the words that contain them, you can heighten your physical understanding of the S.A. (Zulu) accent's *Vocal Posture* as compared to your own. This frame of reference will both inform and strengthen your accent.

Consonants

1. *IPA:* [ɓ] → Bilabial implosive. Instead of blowing air out to make a [b], you suck it in.
   Symbol: [Bh] → Bilabial implosive. Instead of blowing air out to make a [B], you suck it in.
   This sound is used in speaking S.A. (Zulu).
2. *IPA:* [ɾ] → tapped [ɹ].
   Symbol: [R^R] → tapped [R]. This is made by lightly tapping the top of the tip of the tongue on the alveolar ridge.
   Used in place of [ɹ]/[R]: *ran, ferry*
   This sound is used in speaking both the language and accent of S.A. (Zulu).
3. *IPA:* [ɲ] → palatal nasal.
   Symbol: [NG] → [NG]. Made on the hard palate rather than the soft palate.
   Used in place of [ŋ]/[NG]: *sing*
   This sound is used in speaking both the language and accent of S.A. (Zulu).

Consonant Clicks

4. *IPA:* [|] → Dental click. Press the tip of the tongue against the back of the front teeth, withdraw it quickly while at the same time dropping the back of the tongue from the soft palate. It is sort of like sucking something

from the front teeth. It sounds a little like when you are scolding someone: *tsk tsk tsk.*

Symbol: [tsk] → Dental click. Press the tip of the tongue against the back of the front teeth, withdraw it quickly while at the same time dropping the back of the tongue from the soft palate. It is sort of like sucking something from the top front teeth. It sounds a little like when you are scolding someone: *tsk tsk tsk.*

This sound is used in speaking S.A. (Zulu).

5. *IPA:* [!] → Post Alveolar click. Press the front of the tongue against the post alveolar ridge, withdraw it quickly while at the same time dropping the back of the tongue from the soft palate. It is sort of like quickly sucking peanut butter off the post alveolar ridge. It sounds a bit like a cork coming out of a bottle.

Symbol: Post Alveolar click. Press the front of the tongue against the post alveolar ridge, withdraw it quickly while at the same time dropping the back of the tongue from the soft palate. It is sort of like quickly sucking peanut butter off the post alveolar ridge. It sounds a bit like a cork coming out of a bottle.

This sound is used in speaking the S.A. (Zulu) language.

6. *IPA:* [‖] → Lateral click. Press the sides of the tongue against the molars and suck them off. This is like the sound you might make to get a horse walking.

Symbol: Lateral click. Press the sides of the tongue against the molars and suck it away. It sounds a bit like the sound you would make to get a horse walking.

This sound is used in speaking the S.A. (Zulu) language.

Vowels

The vowels of S.A. (Zulu) include:

IPA: [i], [e], [ɛ], [a], [u], [o], [ɔ]
Symbol: [EE], [e], [EH], [Ah], [OO], [o], [AW]

Knowing the vowels for the Zulu language will provide clues for the vowel shifts in the accent.

7. *IPA:* [e]
Symbol: [e] → This is the first sound in the D.A.E. diphthong [AY] as in *face.*
Used in place of [ɛ]/[Eh]: *dress, bed*
This sound is used in speaking both the language and accent of S.A. (Zulu).

8. *IPA:* [a]
Symbol: [Ah] → This is the first sound in the D.A.E. diphthong [EYE].
Used in place of [æ]/[A]: *trap, bath*
This sound is used in speaking both the language and accent of S.A. (Zulu).

9. *IPA:* [ʉ] → centralized [u].
  Symbol: [O͜O] → [OO] articulated in the middle rather than the back, of the mouth.
  Used in place of [u]/[OO]: *food, grew*
  This sound is used in speaking both the language and accent of S.A. (Zulu).

10. *IPA:* [o]
  Symbol: [o]. This is the first sound in the D.A.E. diphthong [OH].
  Used in place of [oŏ]/[OH]: *goat, sew*
  This sound is used in speaking both the language and accent of S.A. (Zulu).

11. *IPA:* [ɐ]
  Symbol: [UH] → articulated with the middle tongue dipping deeply down in the mouth.
  Sometime used in place of [ə]/[uh]: *about, banana* and [ɚ]/[er]: *sister, traitor*
  This sound is used in speaking a S.A. (Zulu) accent of English.

Consonant Sound Shifts

- ⌐ indicates that this sound is a key sound shift
- You can begin to fold melody and rhythm with the sound changes by speaking the sample sentences that are before each section of sound changes.

Note!

On Consonants

Double consonants do not exist at the ends of words in Bantu languages, so double consonants at the ends of words in English are sometimes reduced to a single consonant, or dropped:

Example: stand → stan   shelf → she

Consonant Shifts

Example: Hamilton Story – 0:04

And <u>the</u> el<u>ders</u> <u>they</u> were al<u>so</u> <u>chillin</u> there a<u>t</u> a sepa<u>rate</u> <u>room</u>.

IPA: and də ˈelˑdəz̧ de wɜɹ‿al.so ˈˈʃɪˌliːɪ̞n deː aṯ ə̧ ˈseˌpa̧ˈɾɪ̞ṯ rɐm·

SYMBOLS: AhND DUH eL̄.DUHZ^S De WUH^RR‿AhL.So ^TSHEĒ.LEĒN Dē A̱hT UH Se.PA̱h.R^REĒT R^ROO̱M̄

I'll meet you a̱t the ferry in an hour wi̱th the te̱n children.

IPA: aɤ mi̱t jʉ ɛt̞ də ˈfe.ɾiː ɪn an ˈa.wə̧ wɪt̞ də ten ˈˈʃɪl.dɾen

SYMBOLS: Ah-<o> ME̱ĒT YO̱O EHT DUH Fe. R^REĒ EĒN AhN A̱h.WUH WEĒT DUH TeN ^TSHEĒL.DR^eN

Key Words	Detailed American English Accent IPA ——————— Symbol	Shift to S.A. (Zulu) Accent of English IPA ——————— Symbol	Key Words Shifts IPA ——————— Symbol	Your Key Words
☛ team de<u>b</u>t, di<u>d</u>	[t]/[d] ————— [T], [D]	[t̪]/[d̪] ————— [T] and [D] are dentalized	t̪im, d̪et̪, d̪ɪd̪ ————— TEEM, DeT, DĔED	
☛ <u>th</u>ese <u>th</u>ere, brea<u>th</u>e	ð ————— TH	[d̪] or [z] ————— [D] (dentalized) or [Z]	d̪iz, d̪e, brɪd̪ or zɪz, ze, brɪz ————— DEEZ, De, BRᴿEED or ZEEZ, Ze, BRᴿEEZ	
☛ <u>th</u>in <u>th</u>ick, mou<u>th</u>	θ ————— th	[t̪] or [s] ————— [T] (dentalized) or [S]	t̪ɪn, t̪ɪk, maʊ̆t̪ or sɪn, sɪk, maʊ̆s ————— TEEN, TEEK, MOWT or SEEN, SEEK, MOWS	
☛ <u>r</u>ed d<u>r</u>ess, me<u>rr</u>y, so<u>rr</u>y	ɹ ————— R	[ɾ] or [ɻ] ————— [Rᴿ]	red, d̪res, ˈmɛ.ɾiː, ˈsɒ.ɾi̯ or ɻed̪, d̪ɻes, ˈmɛ.ɻi̯ː, ˈsɒ.ɻi̯ː ————— RᴿeD, DRᴿeS, **MEH.**Rᴿ**EE**, **SO.**Rᴿ**EE** or RᴿeD, DRᴿeS, **MEH.**Rᴿ**EE**, **SO.**Rᴿ**EE**	
exce<u>l</u> fa<u>ll</u>, tab<u>le</u> (final *l* in spelling)	l ————— L	sometimes ɤ ————— sometimes <o>	ˈekˈseɤ ————— **eK.Se-<o>**	
☛ ju<u>dg</u>e	dʒ ————— J	d̥ʒ̊ ————— Jˢᴴ	d̥ʒ̊ad̥ʒ̊ ————— JˢᴴAhJˢᴴ	
☛ <u>ch</u>ur<u>ch</u>	tʃ ————— CH	ˈʃ ————— ᵀSH	ˈʃɜˈʃ ————— ᵀSHUHᴿᵀSH	
boy<u>s</u> (final *s* in spelling when pronounced [z])	z ————— Z	z̥ ————— Zˢ	boɪz̥ ————— Bo-ɪZˢ	
si<u>ng</u>	ŋ ————— NG	ɲ̊ ————— NG̊	sɪɲ̊ ————— SEENG̊	

Front Vowel Sound Shifts

Note!
On Vowels
The vowels of the S.A. (Zulu) language include:

IPA: [i], [e], [ɛ], [a], [u], [o], [ɔ]
Symbol: [EE], [e], [EH], [Ah], [OO], [o], [AW]

Knowing the vowels of the S.A. (Zulu) language will provide clues for the
vowel shifts in the accent.

	Front Vowel Shifts			
The thief will tell me after we trap him.				
IPA: ðə tif wɪl tel mi ˈaf.tə wi trɛp hɪm				
SYMBOLS: DUH TEEF WEEL TeL MEE **AhF**.TUH WEE TR^REHP HEEM				
Key Words	*Detailed American English Accent* *IPA* ------------------- *Symbol*	*Shift to S.A. (Zulu) Accent of English* *IPA* ------------------- *Symbol*	*Key Words Shifts* *IPA* ------------------- *Symbol*	*Your Key Words*
fleece sneeze, plead	i ------------------- EE	i̧ ------------------- [EE]	flis, sniz, plid ------------------- FLEES, SNEEZ^s, PLEED	
☛ kit pitch, dim, lip	ɪ ------------------- I	I̧ ------------------- [EE] ([I] made more like an [EE])	kɪt, pɪtʃ, dɪm, lɪp ------------------- KEET, PEE^TSH, DEEM, LEEP	

Key Words	Detailed American English Accent IPA Symbol	Shift to S.A. (Zulu) Accent of English IPA Symbol	Key Words Shifts IPA Symbol	Your Key Words
☛ country (*y* in final position of spelling)	ɪ ──── EE	iː ──── EE	ˈkɔn.t̠riː ──── KAWN.TRᴿEE	
☛ berated	[ɪ] in prefix ──── [EE] in prefix	i̠ ──── [EE]	ˌbi̠ˈre.t̠id BEE.Rᴿe.TEED	
dress bed, feather, send	ɛ ──── EH	[e] or [ɛ] ──── [e] or [EH]	d̠res, bed̠, ˈfe.d̠ə, send or d̠rɛs, bɛd̠, ˈfɛ.d̠ə, sɛnd ──── DRᴿeS, BeD, Fe.Duh, SeND or DRᴿEHS, BEHD, FEH.Duh, SEHND	
☛ trap mad, rat, candle	æ ──── A	[ɛ] or [a] ──── [EH] or [Ah]	t̠rɛp, mɛd̠, rɛt̠, ˈkɛn.d̠əl or t̠rap, mad̠, rat̠, ˈkan.d̠əl ──── TRᴿEHP, MEHD, RᴿEHT, KEHN.DUHL or TRᴿAhP, MAhD, Rᴿ AhT, KAhN.DUHL	
☛ bath *[a]/[Ah] ask, after, dance, example, half, mask, rascal, transfer In Chapter 1, there is a list of these words called the BATH or ASK list of words.	æ ──── A	a̠ ──── [Ah] ([Ah] articulated more in the middle-back of the mouth)	ba̠t̠, ˈa̠f ˈt̠ə, da̠ns, ˈekˈsa̠m.pəl ──── BAhT, AhF.TUH, DAhNS ek.SAhM.PUHL	

Middle Vowel Sound Shifts

Middle Vowel Shifts				
In the summer, workers burned the underbrush.				
IPA: ɪn də 'sɐ'mə 'wɜ.kəz bɜnd dɪ 'ɐn'dəbraʃ				
SYMBOLS: ĔEN DUH **SAh.MUH WUH**ᴿ.KUHZˢ BUHᴿND DĔE **AhN.Duh.**BRᴿAhSH				
Key Words	*Detailed American English Accent* IPA -------------------- *Symbol*	*Shift to S.A. (Zulu) Accent of English* IPA -------------------- *Symbol*	*Key Words Shifts* IPA -------------------- *Symbol*	*Your Key Words*
☞ n<u>ur</u>se b<u>ir</u>d, w<u>or</u>k, s<u>er</u>vice, l<u>ear</u>n	ɝ ------------------- ER	[ʒ] or [ɛ] ---------------------- [UHᴿ] or [EH] ([EH] articulated more in the middle of the mouth)	nʒs, bʒd, wʒk, 'sʒ.vɪs or nɛs, bɛd, wɛk, 'sɛ.vɪs ---------------------- NUHᴿS, BUHᴿD, WUHᴿK, **SUH**ᴿ.VĔES or NEHS, BEHD, WEHK, **SEH**.VĔES	
sist<u>er</u> trait<u>or</u>, hang<u>ar</u>	ɚ ------------------- er	[ə] or [ɐ] ---------------------- [uh] or [UH]	'sɪs'tə, 'tre'tə, 'hɛn'ə or 'sɪs'tɐ, 'tre'tɐ, 'hɛn'ɐ ---------------------- **SĔES**.Tuh, **TR**ᴿ**e**.Tuh, **HEHNG**.uh or **SĔES.TUH**, **TR**ᴿ**e.TUH**, **HEHNG.UH**	
str<u>u</u>t c<u>u</u>rry	ʌ̈ ------------------- UH	ɐ ---------------------- Ah	strɐt, kɐ.rɪ: ---------------------- STRᴿAhT, **KAh**.Rᴿ**ĔE**	

Key Words	Detailed American English Accent IPA	Shift to S.A. (Zulu) Accent of English IPA	Key Words Shifts IPA	Your Key Words
	Symbol	Symbol	Symbol	
☞ c**o**me fl**oo**d, c**ou**ntry (in words spelled with *o, oo, ou*)	ʌ̈	[ɔ] or [o]	kɔm, flɔḓ, 'kɔn.t̗riː or kom, flod, 'kon.t̗riː	
	[UH] (made on the middle of the tongue)	[AW] or [o]	KAWM, FLAWD, **KAWN**.TR^RĒ̈Ē̈ or K*o*M, FL*o*D, K*o*N.TR^RĒ̈Ē̈	
about b**a**n**a**n**a**	ə	[ə̗] or [ɐ]	ə̗'baʊ̠t̗, 'bə̗'na.nə̗ or ɐ'baʊ̠t̗, 'bɐ'na.nɐ	
	uh	[uh] or [UH] ([UH] made in the middle of the mouth with the tongue pushed down very low)	uh.**BOWT**, **BUH.NAh**.Nuh or UH.**BOWT**, **BUH.NAh**.NUH	
☞ c**o**nsider c**o**mpare	[ə] (in *com* and *com* prefixes)	o	'kon'sɪ̗.d̗ə̗, 'kom'pe	
	[uh] (in *com* and *com* prefixes)	o	K*o*N.SĒ̈Ē̈.DUH, K*o*M.Pe	

Back Vowel Sound Shifts

Back Vowel Shifts				
I thought my father would not stop being a bully but the truth is, I was wrong.				
IPA: a tɔt maĭ 'fa'də wʊd nɒt stɒp bin̞ ə̞ 'bʊ'liː bat də trʉt ɪz aĭ woz̞ r̞ɔn̞				
SYMBOLS: Ah T>AW<T MAh-Ĭ **FAh.DUH** WŌOD NOT STOP BEĘNG UH **BŎO.LĘE** BAhT DUH TRᴿOOT ĘEZˢ Ah-Ĭ WoZˢ Rᴿ>AW<NG				
Key Words	*Detailed American English Accent* <hr> *IPA* <hr> *Symbol*	*Shift to S.A. (Zulu) Accent of English* <hr> *IPA* <hr> *Symbol*	*Key Words Shifts* <hr> *IPA* <hr> *Symbol*	*Your Key Words*
☛ f<u>oo</u>d gr<u>ew</u>, tr<u>ue</u>, tw<u>o</u>	u <hr> OO	ʉ <hr> [OO] ([OO] articulated more in the middle of the mouth)	fʉd, grʉ, trʉ, tʉ <hr> FOOD, GRᴿOO, TRᴿOO, TOO	
☛ d<u>u</u>ty t<u>u</u>ne, n<u>ew</u>s *u* or *ew* preceded by *t, d, n* in spelling	ɪʊ <hr> I-ŌO	jʉ <hr> YOO	'djʉ.tị, tjʉn, njʉz <hr> **DYOO**.TĔE, TYOON, NYOOZˢ	
☛ f<u>oo</u>t p<u>u</u>t	ʊ <hr> U	ʊ̞ <hr> ŎO	fʊ̞t, pʊ̞t <hr> FŎOT, PŎOT	
th<u>ou</u>ght t<u>a</u>ll, c<u>au</u>lk, <u>a</u>wful	ɔ <hr> AW	ɔ̞ <hr> [>AW<] ([AW] made with very round lips)	tɔt, tɔl, kɔk <hr> T>AW<K, T>AW<L, K>AW<K	

Key Words	Detailed American English Accent	Shift to S.A. (Zulu) Accent of English	Key Words Shifts	Your Key Words
	IPA	*IPA*	*IPA*	
	Symbol	*Symbol*	*Symbol*	
☛ cl<u>o</u>th *[ɒ]/[O] d<u>o</u>g, c<u>ou</u>gh, w<u>a</u>sh, h<u>o</u>rrid	ɔ	o	klot̪, dog, kof	
	AW	o	KLoT, DoG, KoF	
f<u>a</u>ther	ɑ	a	ˈfaˈd̪ə̰	
	AH	Ah	**FAh.DUH**	
☛ l<u>o</u>t *[ɒ]/[O] sq<u>ua</u>d, w<u>a</u>nder	ɑ	ɒ	lɒt̪, skwɒd̪, ˈwɒn.d̪ə̰	
	AH	O	LOT, SKWOD, **WON**.DUH	

Diphthong Sound Shifts

		Diphthong Shifts		

I'd like to fly away someday and go south to the mountains with the boys.

IPA: ad lak tʉ fla·ĭ 'a'we 'sạm'de ɛnḍ gəʊ saʊ̝t tʉ ḍə 'maʊn'tɔnẓ wɪ̞t ḍə boĭẓ

SYMBOLS: AhD LAhK TQO FLAh-Ĭ **Ah.We SAhM.De** EHND Guh-Ŭ SOWT TQO DUH **MOWN.TUHNZ**ˢ WĔET DUH Bo-EĔZˢ

Key Words	Detailed American English Accent IPA ---- Symbol	Shift to S.A. (Zulu) Accent of English IPA ---- Symbol	Key Words Shifts IPA ---- Symbol	Your Key Words
face pain, day, weight, steak	eĭ ---- AY	[e] or [eĭ] ---- [e] or [e-Ĭ]	fes, pen, ḍe or feĭs, peĭn, ḍeĭ ---- FeS, PeN, De or Fe-ĬS, Pe-ĬN, De-Ĭ	
price eyes, diaper, fly, guy, height	aĭ ---- EYE	[a] or [a·ĭ] ---- [Ah] or [Āh-Ĭ]	pɾas, aẓ, 'ḍa.pə or pɾa·ĭs, a·ĭẓ, 'ḍa·ĭ.pə ---- PRᴿAhS, AhZˢ, **DAh**.PUH or PRᴿĀh-ĬS, Āh-Ĭẓˢ, **DĀh-Ĭ**.PUH	
choice boys	ɔĭ ---- OY	oĭ ---- o-EE	'ʃoĭs, boĭẓ ---- ᵀSHo-EĔS, Bo-EĔZˢ	
↦ goat sew, go	oʊ ---- OH	[əʊ] or [o] ---- [uh-Ŭ] or [o]	gəʊ̝t, səʊ, gəʊ or goṭ, so, go ---- Guh-ŬT, Suh-Ŭ, Guh-Ŭ or GoT, So, Go	
mouth town	aʊ ---- OW	aʊ ---- OW	maʊ̝t, ṭaʊn ---- MOWT/TOWN	

Diphthongs of R Sound Shifts

> *Note!*
> **On r-coloration**
> A S.A. (Zulu) accent has no r-coloration in diphthongs and triphthongs of R.

Diphthongs and Triphthongs of R Shifts				
***Our** friends st**ar**ted the **fi**re n**ear** **your** n**or**th **or**chard an h**our** bef**ore** we got th**ere**.*				
IPA: ˈaˈwə frenʒ ˈstaˈtɪd də faɪə nɪɜ jɔ nɒt ˈɔˈʃəd an ˈaˈwə bɪˈfɔ wɪ gɒt də				
SYMBOLS: **Ah.WUH** FR^ReNZ^S **STAh.TĒED** DUH FEYE-UH NI-uh Y>AW< N>AW<T >AW<.^T**SHUHD** AhN **Ah.WUH** BĒE.F>**AW**< WEE GOT De				
Key Words	*Detailed American English Accent* IPA ------------------------ *Symbol*	*Shift to S.A. (Zulu) Accent of English* IPA ------------------------ *Symbol*	*Key Words Shifts* IPA ------------------------ *Symbol*	*Your Key Words*
n**ear** b**ee**r	ɪɜ˞ ------------------ EAR	[ɪɜ̰] or [ɪɐ] --------------------- [I-ŨH] or [I-A̰H]	nɪɜ, bɪɜ or nɪɐ, bɪɐ ----------------------- NI-ŨH, BI-ŨH or NI-A̰H, BI-A̰H	
⌐ h**air** st**are**, p**ear**, squ**are**, th**ere**	ɛɜ˞ ------------------ AIR	e --------------------- e	he, s**te**, pe, skwe ----------------------- He, STe, Pe, SKWe	
s**ure** p**oor**, y**our**	ʊɜ˞ ------------------ UR	ʊɜ̰ --------------------- OO-ŨH	ʃʊɜ̰, pʊɜ̰, jʊɜ̰ ----------------------- SHŌO-ŨH, PŌO-ŨH, YŌO-ŨH	

Key Words	Detailed American English Accent IPA	Shift to S.A. (Zulu) Accent of English IPA	Key Words Shifts IPA	Your Key Words
	Symbol	Symbol	Symbol	
⊶ north George, pour, warp, oar	ɔɝ AWR	ɔ̣ [>AW<] ([AW] made with very round lips)	nɔ̣t, dʒɔ̣dʒ, pɔ̣, wɔ̣p N>AW<T, Jˢᴴ>AW<Jˢᴴ, P>AW<, W>AW<P	
⊶ start heart	ɑɝ AHR	a Ah	sṭat, haṭ STAhT, HAhT	
fire	aɪɝ EYER	aɪə̣ EYE-UH	faɪə̣ FEYE-UH	
hour	aʊɝ OWR	a.wə̣ Ah.WUH	ˈaˈwə̣ **Ah.WUH**	

Key Sentences for Practice

Note!
- By practicing the sentences below, you can work through the sound shifts for a S.A. (Zulu) accent in the context of a simple thought. I suggest you think, imagine and speak actively from a point of view. As you begin to work with the operative words in the thoughts, the rhythm and melody of the accent will begin to emerge appropriately.

Consonants:

- **Example:** Hamilton Story – 0:04

And <u>the</u> <u>elders</u> <u>they</u> were <u>also</u> <u>chillin</u> <u>there</u> <u>at</u> a <u>separate</u>

<u>room.</u>

    IPA: and d̪ə ˈel·.d̪əz̪ d̪e wɜɹ_al.so ˈˈʃɪ.lːɪn d̪eː at̪ ə ˈse.pə̜ˈrɪt rɐm·

    SYMBOLS: AhND DUH e̱L̄.DUHZᔆ De WUHᴿR̲_AhL.So ᵀSHĒE.LĒEN

                 Dē A̱hT UH Se.PAh.RᴿĒET RᴿO̞ŌM

- *I'<u>ll</u> mee<u>t</u> you a<u>t</u> <u>the</u> <u>ferry</u> in an hour wi<u>th</u> <u>the</u> <u>ten</u> <u>children</u>.*

    IPA: aɣ mɪt̪ jʉ ɛt̪ d̪ə ˈfe.ɾiː ɪn an ˈa.wə̜ wɪt̪ d̪ə ten ˈˈʃɪl.dɾen

    SYMBOLS: Ah-<o> ME̱ET YO̱O EHT DUH **Fe.** Rᴿ̄EE ĒEN AhN **Ah.**WUH

                 WĒET DUH TeN ᵀSHĒEL.DRheN

Front Vowels: Vowels made by arching or cupping the front of the tongue toward the front of the hard palate.

- *The thi<u>ef</u> w<u>ill</u> t<u>e</u>ll m<u>e</u> <u>a</u>fter w<u>e</u> tr<u>a</u>p h<u>i</u>m.*

    IPA: d̪ə t̪if wɪl t̪el mɪ̈ ˈaf.t̪ə̜ wɪ̈ t̪rep hɪm

    SYMBOLS: DUH TE̱EF WĒEL TeL MĒE **AhF.**TUH WE̱E TRᴿEHP HĒEM

Middle Vowels: Vowels made by arching or cupping the middle of the tongue toward the middle of the hard palate.

- *In th<u>e</u> s<u>u</u>mm<u>e</u>r, w<u>o</u>rk<u>e</u>rs b<u>u</u>rned the <u>u</u>nd<u>e</u>rbr<u>u</u>sh.*

  IPA: ɪn də ˈsʌ.mə ˈwɜ.kəz bɜnd di ˈʌnˈdəbrəʃ

  SYMBOLS: ĒEN DUH **SAh.MUH WUH**ᴿ.KUHZˢ BUHᴿND DE̱E̱
  AhN.Duh.BRᴿAhSH

Back Vowels: Vowels made by arching or cupping the back of the tongue toward the back of the hard palate.

- *I th<u>ou</u>ght my f<u>a</u>ther w<u>ou</u>ld n<u>o</u>t st<u>o</u>p being a b<u>u</u>lly but the tr<u>u</u>th is, I w<u>a</u>s wr<u>o</u>ng.*

  IPA: a tɔt maɪ ˈfaˈdə wʊd nɒt stɒp bɪŋ ə ˈbʊˈliː bət də trʊt ɪz aɪ wɒz
  rɔŋ

  SYMBOLS: Ah T>AW<T MAh-Ĭ **Fah.DUH** WŎOD NOT STOP BE̱E̱NG
  UH **BŎO.LE̱E̱** BAhT DUH TRᴿOO̥T E̱E̱Zˢ Ah-Ĭ WoZˢ
  Rᴿ>AW<NG

Diphthongs: When two vowels are combined in one syllable.

- *I'd l<u>i</u>ke to fl<u>y</u> aw<u>ay</u> somed<u>ay</u> and g<u>o</u> s<u>ou</u>th to the m<u>ou</u>ntains with the b<u>oy</u>s.*

  IPA: ad lak tʉ flaˈĭ ˈaˈwe ˈsʌmˈde ɛnd gəʊ saʊ̯t tʉ də ˈmaʊnˈtənz wɪt
  də boɪ̯z

  SYMBOLS: AhD LAhK TOO̥ FLAh-Ĭ **Ah.We SAhM.De** EHND Guh-Ŭ
  SOWT TOO̥ DUH **MOWN.TUHNZ**ˢ WE̱E̱T DUH Bo-E̱E̱Zˢ

Diphthongs of R: A diphthong in which the second vowel is rhotic (e.g., has r-coloration in the final sound)

Example: near → nɪɚ/NEAR

Triphthongs of R: A combination of three vowel sounds, in which the third vowel is rhotic.

Example: fire → faɪɚ/FEYER

- *<u>Our</u> friends st<u>a</u>rted the f<u>ire</u> n<u>ear</u> y<u>our</u> n<u>o</u>rth <u>o</u>rchard an h<u>our</u> bef<u>o</u>re we got th<u>ere</u>.*

  IPA: ˈaˈwə frenz ˈstaˈtɪd də faɪə nɪɚ jɔ nɒt ˈɔ.ˈʃəd an ˈaˈwə bɪˈfɔ wɪ
  gɒt de

  SYMBOLS: **Ah.WUH** FRᴿeNZˢ **STAh.TE̱E̱D** DUH FEYE-UH NI-u̱h
  Y>AW< N>AW<T >AW<.ᵀSHUHD AhN **Ah.WUH**
  BE̱E̱.F>AW< WE̱E̱ GOT De

Making Your Own Map of the Accent

Listen to the S.A. (Zulu) accent samples provided and investigate the resources suggested in the *Introduction and Resources* section. Compose (or steal) *Key Phrases* from your listening/viewing that challenge and/or ground you in the accent. Then get more specific and check your sounds against the sounds in the Workbook.

Your take on the sound shifts may be slightly different. That is okay. The breakdown is a tool, not a rule. Recheck what you hear and, if you still stand behind your discoveries, go with them. This will help you to develop **your own** idiolect of the accent.

> *Note!*
> **What is an Idiolect?**
> Each of us speaks differently even if we have the same general accent. The individualized way that each of us speaks is referred to as an idiolect. For the actor, idiolect is part of what creates character. It is the "how" of the accent, and influences the way we craft our thoughts through language.

KEY PHRASES WITH KEY SOUND SHIFTS

Speak your *Key Phrases*, shifting back and forth between your own home *idiolect of English* and the *S.A. (Zulu) accent* you are building. **Observe** the shifts ONE by ONE in your Articulators, Focus of Articulation, use of Melody/Pitch/Lilt, Rhythm/Stress/Pace, and Source & Path of Resonance as you shift back and forth between the two accents. Make note of the shifts in the table provided. Putting your understanding of the shifts into your own words will encourage you to develop a more clear and personal idiolect.

S.A. (ZULU) ACCENT *KEY POINTS OF FOCUS: VOCAL POSTURE AND CHARACTERISTICS*

JAW
LIPS
TONGUE
SOFT PALATE
PHARYNX

FOCUS OF ARTICULATION (TOWARDS TEETH, FRONT/MIDDLE/ BACK OF HARD PALATE, SOFT PALATE, ETC.)

MELODY/PITCH/LILT

RHYTHM/STRESS/PACE

SOURCE & AND PATH OF RESONANCE – Where does the resonance begin and what is the apparent path it travels through your body (chest, hard palate, sinuses, temples, crown, base of skull, etc.)? Refer to the Source & Path of Resonance and Resonators in the *S.A. (Zulu) Accent of English: Down & Dirty Warm-Up and Quick Look* on page 119.

OTHER CHARACTERISTICS (What are your observations?)

PERSONAL IMAGES (For many actors personal images can be the most powerful and effective triggers for their transformation into an accent)

Chapter 6

South African (Afrikaans) Accent of English

Introduction and Resources

The Afrikaans Language in South Africa

The eleven official languages of S.A. include Zulu, Xhosa, SiSwati, Ndebele, Southern Sotho, Tswana, Northern Sotho, Venda, Tsonga, English and Afrikaans. Although English is a minority language in South Africa, 45% of the South African population can speak it.

The Afrikaans language is a Western Germanic subgroup of the Indo-European family language group. Afrikaans means "African" in Dutch. The language began as pidgin spoken between the 16th century Dutch colonizers of the Dutch East India Company, the Malay and the S.A. Khoi and San. Interestingly, the Khosian language group, which includes Khoi and San, is one of the few non-Bantu languages in South Africa. Khosian "clicks" were absorbed by the Bantu languages of Xhosa, Sotho and Zulu. Afrikaans spread throughout S.A., developed into a creole and then into a language and was influenced along the way by English, German, Portuguese, French, Belgian, and many of the Bantu languages of S.A.

The first major British immigration to the Eastern Cape in 1820 was made up primarily of middle and lower middle class families from Southern England. The next immigration in 1850 brought middle and upper middle class families from Northern England. Both of these waves of immigration brought distinct dialects of English with them.

English was declared the official language in 1822. From 1910–1925, Dutch and English were the official languages; Afrikaans replaced Dutch in 1925. In 1994, the new constitution chose Afrikaans as one of the eleven official languages of S.A. In 1948 when the Afrikaans National Party took control and pushed its apartheid policy on the country, Afrikaans became the ruling language of the whites even though there were more Cape Coloured speakers at the time. Afrikaans became associated with this white supremacy and many of the Cape Coloured speakers switched to English as their language of choice.

There are two dialects of English in South Africa that have been influenced by Afrikaans: 1) *WUESA*: a dialect spoken by *White urban English speakers*; 2) Cape Coloured: a dialect of English spoken by non-Caucasians whose traditional language is Afrikaans.

Documentaries

The Struggle for South Africa: documentary with Nelson Mandela (Xhosa), President de Klerk (Afrikaans), Chief Buthelezi (Zulu) and Eugene Terreblanche (Afrikaans)

Films

A Dry White Season; *The Power of One*; *Cry Freedom*; *Master Harold and the Boys*; The Market Place Theatre's production of *Othello* with John Kani; *Sarafina*; *Amandla!: A Revolution in Four Part Harmony*; *Red Dust*; *Invictus*; Daniel Craig (British Actor) in *Munich*; *The Color of Freedom*; *The Guest* (character: Eugene Marais); *District 9*; *Yankee Zulu*

Television

Egoli, Generations, Backstage

Plays with Afrikaans Characters

Zinnie Harris' *Further than the Furthest Thing* (character: Mr. Hansen), Athol Fugard's: *Exits & Entrances* (all characters), *Hello & Goodbye* (all characters), *A Lesson from Aloes* (characters: Piet, Gladys; Gladys' Afrikaans accent would have some British influence), *People Are Living There* (all characters), *Playland* (character: Gideon), *Road to Mecca* (character: Elsa), *Valley Song* (character: Author), and *The Painted Rocks at Revolver Creek* (character: Elmarie)

Music

John Klegg, Die Antwoord

Radio

KFM, 567 CapeTalk

Personalities

Trevor Noah, Alan Committie, Nik Rabinowitz, Marc Lottering, F.W. DeKlerk, Athol Fugard, Gary Player, Ernie Els, Minki Vander Westhuizen, Andrea Brink, Johann Rupert, Dr. Christian Barnard, Oscar Pistorius

Down & Dirty Warm-up and Quick Look

Note!

On Symbols

- International Phonetic Alphabet Symbols will be listed first and Sound Symbols will be listed second. Example: [i]/[EE]
- Sound Symbol Users: bold-faced letters indicate the syllable is stressed.

1) **The Muscles:** Wake your mouth up so you can more easily discover the physical transformation in speaking the accent.

   a. Scratch the front, middle and back of your tongue with your front top teeth.

   b. Rub the front, middle and back of your hard palate with the tip of your tongue.

   c. Imagine your mouth is numb from being at the dentist and you want to wake it up. Make tongue circles pressing against the back of your lips first clockwise, then counter clockwise (you are waking up your orbicularis muscle).

   d. To get the breath flowing, blow through your lips, getting them to flap together. Travel up and down in pitch on a BBBB and PPP, feeling the vibration as you wiggle up and down your spine.

2) **Vocal Posture for an Afrikaans Accent:** Focus of articulation is key in speaking an Afrikaans accent. The tongue is slightly bunched and pitched forward, with the front of the tongue resting behind the lower front teeth. The middle of the tongue is raised (high) towards the middle back of the hard palate. *This is key in speaking an Afrikaans accent!* The back of the tongue is very ready to dip for the low back vowels as in words like: *thought*, *father*, *cloth* and *lot*. The lip corners tend to pull back slightly and are only slightly rounded for the rounded vowels in words like: *bird*, *food*, *foot*, *thought*, *cloth*, *lot*. The jaw is fairly closed and can be a little more held for a stronger accent. The soft palate is lifted, creating a bit of hypo-nasality, and the pharynx actively narrows, resulting in a bit of pharyngeal twang.

3) **Resonators:** "occupy" the following spaces. This will prepare you to find the Source & Path of Resonance for an Afrikaans accent. (By "occupy", I mean just that; be in the space of it and find the pathway and flow of resonance, rather than "putting" the resonance there.)

    a.   CHEST – Generously laugh at something – hɑ̞ hɑ̞ hɑ̞ / HAH HAH HAH

    b.   HARD PALATE – As if you were discovering something – hʌŭ hʌŭ hʌŭ / HUH-Ṳ HUH-Ṳ HUH-Ṳ

    c.   THE BONES AT THE BASE OF YOUR SKULL (THE OCCIPITAL BONE) – Use your hands to scoop the sound from the base of your skull with a Mississippi African-American dialect as if you're flirting with someone nearby – he̞ĭ he̞ĭ he̞ĭ / He̲-Ĭ He̲-Ĭ He̲-Ĭ (The second half of the diphthong is very short)

    d.   FLICK THE SOUND OUT OF YOUR CHEEKBONES with an Italian-American flourish, as if calling to someone across the street – he̞ĭ he̞ĭ he̞ĭ / He̲-Ĭ He̲-Ĭ He̲-Ĭ

    e.   WITH YOUR HANDS NEXT TO YOUR TEMPLES, SHAKE THE SOUND OUT WITH LOOSE FISTS – As if you were somewhat crazed – jɨ jɨ jɨ / YEE YEE YEE

    f.   IMAGINE A METAL DISK EXTENDING FROM YOUR HANDS THROUGH YOUR SKULL. Bring your hands to the sides of your head just above the temples, with your palms facing the floor, thumbs hooked behind your skull. *Lid* the vibration to create a muted brassy sound. Like a robot say "Hi" – haĭ̈ haĭ̈ haĭ̈ / HAh-EĒ̈ HAh-EĒ̈ HAh-EĒ̈

    g.   GIGGLE OUT OF THE TOP OF YOUR HEAD – As if you were tickled pink by something – hɨ hɨ hɨ / HEE HEE HEE

4) **Source & Path of Resonance for an Afrikaans Accent:** Because of the lift in the middle of the tongue, the resonance is focused toward the middle of the hard palate and into the cheekbones. There is a degree of hyponasality which also contributes in focusing the resonance toward the cheekbones. From the cheekbones, there is a sense of it traveling out of the eyes. Both men and women have a bit of pharangeal twang in their voice. Men have pretty full chest resonance. Because women tend to speak at a higher pitch than men, their resonance tends to rise up from the cheekbones and is lidded at the "metal disk" area at the temples (see #3f above).

5) **Get the sound changes into your body and imagination.**
Say these phrases occupying the following places in your body, suggesting to yourself the following energetic associations:

    ●   pubic bone to tail bone – survival instinct

        zʉ / ZOO
        I need it – ä nɨd ɨ̠t˺ / Ah NEED IT

- pubic bone to navel & sacrum in back – sexuality, big feeling

  wʌ̆ / WUH-Ų̆
  I desire it – ä ˈdə̞ːza.ɾ_ï̦t̚ / A̱h **Du̱h**-ZAh.Rᴿ_IT̲

- rib cage to below heart – will

  ʒɔ̞ / ZH<AW>
  I want it – ä wɒ̞n̹t̹ ï̦t̚ / A̱h W<O>NT I̲T̲

- heart – love

  mɑ̞ / MAH
  I love it – ä lä̈v ï̦t̚ / A̱h LU̱HV I̲T

- throat – communication (think of talking at a party)

  bä̈ / BU̱H
  I have to say it – ä e̱y̥ t̚ö seː ï̦t̚ / A̱h e̱Vꟳ TŲ S̱e̱ IT̲

- forehead – intelligence/wisdom

  k̚e̱ï / Kᴳe̱-Ĭ
  I know it – ä nʌ̆ ï̦t̚ / A̱h NUH-Ų̆ I̲T

- crown of head – spirituality

  ɾï / RᴿE̱E̱
  I believe it – ä ˈbə̞.ɬˈïv ï̦t̚ / A̱h **Bu̱h**-LE̱E̱V I̲T

6) **Articulation** – using playful physical actions: punching, flicking, dabbing, slashing

  d̦ö d̦ï k̚ö d̦ö d̦ï k̚ö d̦ö d̦ï k̚ö – d̦ɨ
  d̦ö d̦ï k̚ö d̦ö d̦ï k̚ö d̦ö d̦ï k̚ö – d̦e̱ï̆
  d̦ö d̦ï k̚ö d̦ö d̦ï k̚ö d̦ö d̦ï k̚ö – d̦aï̩̩̆
  d̦ö d̦ï k̚ö d̦ö d̦ï k̚ö d̦ö d̦ï k̚ö – d̦ʌ̆
  d̦ö d̦ï k̚ö d̦ö d̦ï k̚ö d̦ö d̦ï k̚ö – d̦ʉ

Repeat as needed, replacing [d̦] with [ț], [p̚], [b], [k̚], [g], [f], [v]

  DŲ DI̲ KŲ DŲ DI̲ KŲ DŲ DI̲ KŲ – DE̱E̱
  DŲ DI̲ KŲ DŲ DI̲ KŲ DŲ DI̲ KŲ – De̱-Ĭ
  DŲ DI̲ KŲ DŲ DI̲ KŲ DŲ DI̲ KŲ – DAh-E̱E̱
  DŲ DI̲ KŲ DŲ DI̲ KŲ DŲ DI̲ KŲ – DUH-Ų̆
  DŲ DI̲ KŲ DŲ DI̲ KŲ DŲ DI̲ KŲ – DO̱O

Repeat as needed, replacing [D] with [Tᴰ], [Pᴮ], [B], [K], [G], [F], [V]. [D] & [T] are made with the blade (rather than the tip) of the tongue on the alveolar ridge.

Key Points of Focus

Characteristics and Vocal Posture

Afrikaans Accent Characteristics

> *Note!*
> **On Melody/Lilt/Pitch and Rhythm/Stress/Pace**
> Every accent contains shifts for some, but not necessarily all, of these elements of vocal variety.

> *Note!*
> **On Use of Musical Notes**
> Follow the "musical notes" up and down to get a feel for the melody of the accent. The filled-in notes are shorter than the open notes. For those who are musically inclined, think of them as approximating quarter notes and half notes. This distinction will give you a feel for the rhythm of the accent.

Melody/Lilt/Pitch

The melody has a more expanded pitch range than American English and women with strong accents tend to speak at a higher pitch.

1. There is often a pitched uplift and lengthening of the vowel or diphthong in the last syllable of the final word in a thought. Lighter accents will do this on the syllable that is most normally stressed in the word. (See Yvonne's final use of _childhood_ on p. 153)
2. There are minor sounding lifts and falls from syllable to syllable, but most often not within a syllable.
3. The melodic phrasing is short within long thoughts and often slightly lifts in pitch at the end of each phrase.

Example: Jakob Story (Part 1) – 1:24

Until eventually one night he waited for us

and opened the door literally with a shotgun.

Notice how in this sentence, Jakob's long thought has clearly defined short phrases and slight lifts in pitch. At the end of each phrase, he tends to slightly lift in pitch and lengthen the stressed syllable of the word: *night, door, shotgun* (#1 and #3, p. 152). His pitch resolve has a minor feel on both *door* and *night* (#2, p. 152).

Example: Yvonne Story – 0:18

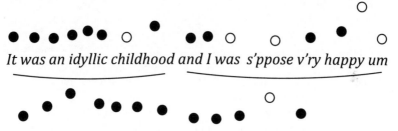

It was an idyllic childhood and I was s'ppose v'ry happy um

and I'm still really happy cause of my childhood.

Notice Yvonne's clearly defined short phrases within this longer thought (#3, p. 152). She lifts in pitch on the final word and syllable at the end of her first two phrases: *child<u>hood</u>, ha<u>pp</u>y* (#1, p. 152). She also lifts in pitch and lengthens on the first syllable at the end of her long thought, *<u>child</u>hood* (#1, p. 152). You can hear a somewhat minor resolve in the second syllable in her first use of *child<u>hood</u>* and *ha<u>pp</u>y*.

Rhythm/Stress/Pace

1. The pace is more brisk than American English.
2. The accent can be a little more clipped than American English because [p]/[P], [t]/[T], and [k]/[K] are either non-aspirated, or are slightly clipped.
3. The lengthening of vowels in stressed syllables of operative words gives the rhythm a kind of, "hop, hop, hop, leap" feel. As mentioned in the Melody section, this lengthening of vowels is often accompanied by a lift in pitch.

The "leap" can sound like a leap up, on that syllable. In younger speakers, this "leap" can also be a lowering in pitch.

Example: Bianca Story (Part 1) – 0:32

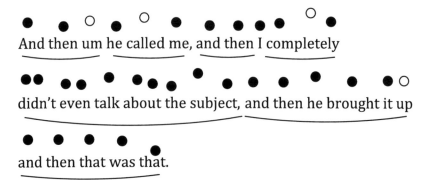

And then um he called me, and then I completely

didn't even talk about the subject, and then he brought it up

and then that was that.

Bianca's accent is an excellent example of contemporary twenty-something Afrikaans speakers. She has a briskness in her speech as in the phrases: *didn't even talk about the subject* & *and that was that,* but she also paces herself in the phrases: *and then um,* & *he called me* (#1, p. 152). Her p's, t's and k's are aspirated very gently in c̠alled, c̠ompletely, talk, subjec̠t, up̠, which makes her accent sound slightly clipped (#2, p. 153). Her t's are dentalized to a degree that make them sound like a [tˢ]/[Tˢ], which smooths her speech. A variation of the "hop, hop, hop, leap" characteristic is present in her accent. In the words *called* and *completely,* Bianca classically lifts in pitch on the vowel in operative words. In the word *up,* the "leap" is characterized by lengthening the vowel only. In the words *subject* and *that,* she goes against the classic pattern and lowers her pitch at the end of her thought. Bianca's pattern of speaking illustrates the tendency of twenty-somethings to break away from the more classic lift in pitch and lengthening of the vowel at the end of a thought. This is, of course, due to the fact that they have been more exposed to English at early ages than most of their parents were when they grew up in apartheid S.A. (#3, p. 152).

Example: Greg Story (Part 1) – 1:02

So you'd go and find a stick, put a bit of clay on it

and you'd swipe it at somebody to hit them with a

little blob of clay.

Greg speaks with a brisk pace (#1, p. 153). His p's, t's and k's are not fully aspirated in words like *stick*, *put*, *bit*, *clay*, *it*, *swipe*, *hit*, which make his speech sound somewhat clipped and also contributes to the brisk pace (#2, p. 153). In his phrasing, the characteristic "hop, hop, hop, leap" is apparent as he briskly moves to his lengthened operative words. In the case of *stick*, *clay*, and *swipe*, he also lifts in pitch (#3, p. 153).

Source & Path of Resonance

Because of the lift in the middle of the tongue, the resonance is focused toward the middle of the hard palate and into the cheekbones. There is a degree of hypo-nasality which also contributes in focusing the resonance toward the cheekbones. From the cheekbones, there is a sense of it traveling out of the eyes. Both men and women have a bit of pharyngeal twang in their voice. Men have pretty full chest resonance.

Greg's resonance is quite clearly along these lines, while Jakob's resonance is not quite as brightly focused. This is due, in part, to the fact that Greg is older than Jakob, and from Johannesburg, where resonance tends to be a little brighter for men. Wilhelm from the Western Cape has the strongest of the accents and the Path of Resonance described above is very clear.

Because women tend to speak at a higher pitch than men, their resonance rises up from the cheekbones and is lidded at the "metal disk" area at the temples (see #3f on page 150). This is apparent in Yvonne and Elize, who both have higher pitch ranges than the younger female speakers, Bianca and Mieke. The path of resonance is much the same, however, for both sets of women, except that Bianca and Mieke cap their resonance in the cheekbone area rather than the "metal disk" area of the skull.

Afrikaans Accent Vocal Posture

> *Note!*
> **On Vocal Posture**
> These adjustments enable you to integrate the accent through physical transformation rather than solely relying on sound shifts.

> *Note!*
> 1.   All front vowels [ɨ]/[EE], [ɪ̃]/[I], [e̞]/[e], [ɛ]/[EH] are made more toward the middle of the mouth than in the front of the mouth, as they would be in D.A.E.
> 2.   Rounded sounds [ʉ]/[OO], [ö]/[U], [ɔ]/[<AW>], [ŋ]/[Q] use very little lip rounding.

- **Focus of Articulation:** Because the tongue is pitched forward and the middle of the tongue is raised, the articulation is focused on the middle and front of the hard palate.
- **Tongue:** The tongue is slightly bunched and pitched forward, with the front of the tongue resting behind the lower front teeth. The middle of the tongue is raised (high) towards the middle back of the hard palate. *This is key in speaking an Afrikaans accent!* The back of the tongue is very ready to dip for the low back vowels: [ɔ]/[<AW>], [ŋ]/[ǫ], [ɑ]/[AH].
- **Lips:** The lip corners tend to pull back slightly and are only slightly rounded for the rounded vowels, as mentioned in the *Note!* above.
- **Jaw:** The jaw is fairly closed and can be a little more held for a stronger accent.
- **Soft Palate:** The soft palate is very lifted to make space for the raised middle-back of the tongue.
- **Pharynx:** The pharynx actively narrows, resulting in a bit of pharyngeal twang.

Distinct Sounds of the Language and/or Accent

> *Note!*
> **On Distinct Sounds**
> These are some of the sounds that South African (Afrikaans) speakers use and American speakers do not. In speaking the sounds and/or words that contain them, you can heighten your physical understanding of the Afrikaans accent's *Vocal Posture* as compared to your own. This frame of reference will both inform and strengthen your accent.

Consonants

1. *IPA:* [r] → alveolar trill.
   Symbol: [RR] → trilled [R].
   Used in place of [ɹ]/[R]: r̲ed, dr̲ess
   This sound is used in speaking both the language and accent of Afrikaans.
2. *IPA:* [ɾ] → alveolar tap.
   Symbol: [R^R] → tapped [R].
   Used in place of [ɹ]/[R]: r̲ed, dr̲ess
   This sound is used in speaking both the language and accent of Afrikaans.
3. *IPA:* [x] → voiceless velar fricative.
   Symbol: [XX] → Rather like the sound of a cat with a furball.
   This sound is used in speaking the Afrikaans language.

Vowels

The vowels of the Afrikaans language include:

IPA: [i], [y], [ɪ], [e], [ɛ], [a], [ə], [ɵ], [u], [ʊ], [o], [ɔ], [ɑ]
Symbol: [EE], [>EE<], [I], [e], [EH], [Ah], [uh], [o̦], [OO], [U], [o], [AW], [AH]

Knowing the vowels for the Afrikaans language will provide clues for the vowel shifts in the accent.

4. *IPA:* [y] → [i] with rounded lips.
   Symbol: [>EE<] → [EE] with rounded lips.
   This sound is used in speaking the Afrikaans language.

5. *IPA:* [e]
   Symbol: [e] → This is the first sound in the D.A.E. diphthong [AY] as in
   face.
   [e̞]/[e̞] used in place of [ɛ]/[EH]: *dre̞ss, be̞d*
   This sound is used in speaking both the language and accent of Afrikaans.

6. *IPA:* [a]
   Symbol: [Ah] → This is the first sound in the D.A.E. diphthong [EYE].
   Used in place of [æ]/[A]: *trap, bath*
   This sound is used in speaking both the language and accent of Afrikaans.

7. *IPA:* [ɨ] → centralized [i].
   Symbol: [EE] → [EE] made in the middle of the mouth.
   Used in place of [i]/[EE]: *fleece, sneeze, plead*
   This sound is used in an Afrikaans accent of English.

8. *IPA:* [ʉ] → centralized [u].
   Symbol: [OO] → [OO] made in the middle of the mouth.
   Used in place of [u]/[OO]: *food, grew, true*
   This sound is used in speaking an Afrikaans accent of English.

9. *IPA:* [ɵ] → centralized [o].
   Symbol: [o̞] → [o] made in the middle of the mouth.
   This sound is used in speaking both the language and accent of Afrikaans.
   *** This sound is the physical epicenter for articulation in both the language
   and the accent.***

10. *IPA:* [o]
    Symbol: [o] → This is the first sound in the D.A.E. diphthong [OH].
    Used in place of [oŏ]/[OH]: *goat, sew*
    This sound is used in speaking both the language and accent of Afrikaans.

11. *IPA:* [ɒ]
    Symbol: [O] → This is the British *hot, copper, coffee, pot* sound.
    [ɒ̞]/[<O>] often used in place of [ɔ]/[AW] in the *cloth, dog, cough* set of
       words
    [ɒ̞]/[<O>] often used in place of [ɑ]/[AH] in the *lot, squad, wander* set of
       words
    This sound is used in speaking an Afrikaans accent of English.

Consonant Sound Shifts

- ☞ indicates that this sound is a key sound shift
- You can begin to fold melody and rhythm with the sound changes by speaking the sample sentences that are before each section of sound changes.

Consonant Shifts

Example: Elize Story – 0:02

He was one eh very special person for me, he started off in

eh the forestry.

IPA: ɨ wəz wʌn ʔe̞ ˈʋe̞.ɹi ˈspʰe̞.ʃɤ ˈpʰe̞.sən fə mɨ, hɨ ˈstɑː.təd ɔf ïn ʔe̞ ˈðə̞ ˈfɔ.rïs.t̞ɨi

SYMBOLS: EE WuhZ^S WUHN ʔe̞ **V^We̞.REE SP^Be̞.**SH<o> **P^Bo̞.**SuhN FUH MEE, HEE **STĀH.**TuhD <AW>F IN ʔe̞ THuh **F<A̞W>.**R^RIS.TREE

Elize illustrates significant shifts in the underlined consonants above.

I'll meet you at the ferry in an hour with the ten children.

IPA: ał mit̚ʲ‿jʉ et̞ ðə̞ ˈfe̞.ɾi ïn ən aə wïθ ðə̞ t̚ʰen ˈtʃəɤ.dɹə̞n

SYMBOLS: AhL MEET^{CH}‿YOO eT THuh **Fe̞.**R^REE IN AhN Ah-uh WIth THuh T^DeN **CHuh-<o>.**DR^RuhN

Key Words	Detailed American English Accent IPA	Shift to Afrikaans Accent of English IPA	Key Words Shifts IPA	Your Key Words
	Symbol	Symbol	Symbol	
☛ team <u>d</u>eb<u>t</u>, <u>d</u>i<u>d</u>	[t]/[d] ------- [T]/[D]	[tʰ] or [t̪ʰ]/ [d̪] or [d] ------- [T] and [D] are both made with the blade of the tongue on the back of the front top teeth or on the post alveolar ridge. There is often no explosion of air after the [t] '	tʰim, d̪et̪, d̪ïd or tʰim, d̪et̪, d̪ïd ------- TᴰEEM, DeTᴰ, DID	
<u>th</u>ese <u>th</u>ere, brea<u>the</u>	[ð] ------- [TH voiced]	[ð̪] or [d̪] ------- [TH] or [D] made with the blade of the tongue on the back of the top front teeth (dentalized)	ð̪is, ð̪eː, brið̪ or d̪is, d̪eː, brid̪ ------- THEES, THe, BRᴿEETH or DEES, De, BRᴿEED	
<u>th</u>in <u>th</u>ick, mou<u>th</u>	[θ] ------- [th] (no voice)	[θ̪] or [t̪] ------- [th] or [T] made with the blade of the tongue on the back of the top front teeth (dentalized)	θ̪ïn, θ̪ïkˈ, mæ̆ŭθ̪ or t̪ïn, t̪ïkˈ, mæ̆ŭt̪ ------- thIN, thIK, MA-Ŭth or TIN, TIK, MA-ŬT	
☛ <u>r</u>ed d<u>r</u>ess, me<u>rr</u>y, so<u>rr</u>y	ɹ ------- R	[ɾ] or [r] or [ɻ] ------- [Rᴿ] tapped, or [RR] trilled, or [R̟]	red, dres, 'me.ri or red, dres, 'me.ri or ɻed, dɻes, 'me.ɻi ------- RᴿeD, DRᴿeS, Me.RᴿEE or RReD, DRReS, Me.RREE or R̟eD, DR̟eS, Me.R̟EE	
☛ exce<u>l</u> fa<u>ll</u>, tab<u>le</u> (final *l* in spelling)	l ------- L	ɫ ------- [L] ([L] made with raised back of tongue. This is called a dark [L])	ek'seɫ, fɔɫ, teːbəɫ ------- eK.SeL, F<AW>L, Te.BuhL	

Key Words	Detailed American English Accent IPA ---- Symbol	Shift to Afrikaans Accent of English IPA ---- Symbol	Key Words Shifts IPA ---- Symbol	Your Key Words
↦ bui<u>l</u>t *l* before another consonant	[l] ---- [L]	ɤɬ ---- <o>L̲ [<o>] is an [o] with lip corners pulled back rather than rounded	bïɤ̇ɬ̪ ---- BI̱<o>L̲T	
↦ <u>p</u>ut <u>c</u>an, <u>top</u> (initial and sometimes final *p, k, t*)	[p], [k], [t] ---- [P], [K], [T]	often [pˀ], [kˀ], [tˀ] ---- often [Pᴮ], [Kᴳ], [Tᴰ]	pˀöt̪ˀ, kˀɛn, t̪ˀp̪p̪ˀ ---- PᴮU̱Tᴰ, KᴳEHN, Tᴰ<O>Pᴮ	
lo<u>v</u>e (final *v* in spelling)	v ---- V	v̥ ---- Vꟳ	läv̥ ---- LU̱HVꟳ	
↦ boy<u>s</u> (final *s* when pronounced [z])	z ---- Z	z̥ ---- Zˢ	boïz̥ ---- Bo-E̱E̱Zˢ	
readi<u>ng</u> (final *ing* in spelling)	[ŋ] ---- [NG]	ɲ ---- [N̪G]	ˈɾi.d̪ɲ ---- RᴿEE.DE̱E̱N̪G	
<u>h</u>ome (initial *h* in spelling)	h ---- H	sometimes dropped ---- sometimes dropped	ʌŭm ---- UH-Ŭ̯M	
<u>con</u>vince <u>com</u>pare (*con* and *com* prefixes)	ə ---- uh	sometimes [o] with the prefix stressed ---- sometimes [o] with the prefix stressed	ˈkˀon.vïns ---- KᴳoN.VI̱NS	

Front Vowel Sound Shifts

Front Vowel Shifts				
The th*ie*f w*i*ll t*e*ll m*e* *a*fter w*e* tr*a*p h*i*m.				
IPA: ð̥ə θ̥if wïɹɬ tɛɤ mɨ ˈɑf.t̠ˀə̥ wɨ t̠rɛp ïm				
SYMBOLS: THu̲h thEEF WI̲-<o>L̲ Te̲<o> ME̲E **AHF**.TUH WE̲E TRᴿEHP I̲M				
Key Words	*Detailed American English Accent* *IPA* ------------------ *Symbol*	*Shift to Afrikaans Accent of English* *IPA* ------------------ *Symbol*	*Key Words Shifts* *IPA* ------------------ *Symbol*	*Your Key Words*
☞ fl*ee*ce sn*ee*ze, pl*ea*d	i ------------------ EE	ɨ ------------------ E̲E̲	flis, sniz̲, pˀli̲d̲ ------------------ FLE̲ES, SNE̲EZˢ, PᴮLE̲ED	
☞ k*i*t p*i*tch, d*i*m, l*i*p	ɪ ------------------ I	ï ------------------ I̲	kˀït̠ˀ, pˀïtʃ, d̠ïm ------------------ KᴳI̲T, PᴮI̲CH, DI̲M	
country (*y* in final position of spelling)	I̠ ------------------ E̲E̲	ɨ ------------------ E̲E̲	ˈkˀʌ̈n.t̠r̠i̠ ------------------ **KᴳU̲HN**.TRᴿE̲E̲	
b*e*rated	[ɪ̠] in prefix ------------------ [E̲E̲] in prefix	[ə̥] often with this prefix stressed ------------------ [u̲h] often with this prefix stressed	ˈbə̥ˌre̠ː.t̠əd̠ ------------------ **Bu̲h**.Rᴿe̲.Tᴰu̲hD	

Key Words	Detailed American English Accent *IPA* Symbol	Shift to Afrikaans Accent of English *IPA* Symbol	Key Words Shifts *IPA* Symbol	Your Key Words
⊷ dr<u>e</u>ss b<u>e</u>d, f<u>ea</u>ther, s<u>e</u>nd	ɛ	[ị] or [e̱]	d̯rïs, bïd̚, ˈfï.ð̬ə or d̯re̱s, be̱d̚, ˈfe̱.ð̬ə	
	EH	[I] or [e] [I]/[e] both made more in the middle of the mouth	DRᴿIs, BID, FI.THUH or DRᴿe̱s, BeD, Fe̱.THUH	
⊷ tr<u>a</u>p m<u>a</u>d, r<u>a</u>t, c<u>a</u>ndle	æ	[ɛ] or [a]	t̯rɛp, mɛd̯, rɛt̯̚, ˈkˀen.d̯ɫ or t̯rap, mad̯, rat̯̚, ˈkˀan.d̯ɫ	
	A	[EH] or [Ah]	TRᴿEHP, MEHD, RᴿEHT, KᴳEHN.D<u>L</u> or TRᴿAhP, MAhD, Rᴿ AhT, KᴳAhN.D<u>L</u>	
⊷ b<u>a</u>th *[a]/[Ah] <u>a</u>sk, <u>a</u>fter, d<u>a</u>nce, ex<u>a</u>mple, h<u>a</u>lf, m<u>a</u>sk, r<u>a</u>scal, tr<u>a</u>nsfer In Chapter 1, there is a list of these words called the BATH or ASK list of words.	æ A	[ɑ] or [ɔ] [AH] or [<AW>]	bɑθ, ɑsk or bɔ̬θ, ɔsk BAHth, AHSK or B<AW>th, <AW>SK	

Middle Vowel Sound Shifts

Middle Vowel Shifts				
In the summer, workers burned the underbrush.				
IPA: ïn ð̞ə̣ ˈsʌ.mə̣ ˈwə.kə̣ẓ bənd̞ ð̞ɨ ˈʌn.d̞ə̣ˌbɾʌʃ				
SYMBOLS: IN THuh **SUH**.MUH **W>ǫ<**.KUHZ^S BǫND TH**EE UHN**.DUH.BR^RU̧HSH				
Key Words	*Detailed American English Accent* *IPA* --------------------- *Symbol*	*Shift to Afrikaans Accent of English* *IPA* --------------------- *Symbol*	*Key Words Shifts* *IPA* --------------------- *Symbol*	*Your Key Words*
⟝ nurse bird, work, service, learn	ɝ --------------------- UHR	θ --------------------- ǫ̧	nəs, bəd̞, wək, ˈsə.vïs, lən --------------------- N>ǫ<S, B>ǫ<D, W>ǫ<K, S>ǫ<.VIS, L>ǫ<N	
sister traitor, hangar	ɚ --------------------- er	ə̧ --------------------- UH	ˈsïs.tə̣, ˈtɾɛˑ.tə̣, ˈɛŋ.gə̣ --------------------- **SIS**.TUH, **TR^RĘ̄.TUH, EHNG.GUH**	
strut curry, come	ʌ --------------------- U̧H	ʌ̈ --------------------- U̧H	sṯ̣ɾʌ̈ṭ, ˈkˀʌ̈.ɾɨ, kˀʌ̈m --------------------- STR^RU̧HT, K^GU̧H.R^REE, K^GU̧HM	
about banana	ə --------------------- uh	ə̧ --------------------- u̱h	ə̧ˈba̭ṷ̌ṭ, ˌbə̣ˈna.nə̣ --------------------- u̱h.**BAh-Ṷ̌T**, Bu̱h.**NAH**.Nu̱h	

Back Vowel Sound Shifts

Back Vowel Shifts				
I thought my father would not stop being a bully but the truth is, I was wrong.				
IPA: aɪ̃ θɔt̪ maɪ̃ 'fɑ.ðə wöd n̪ɒt̪ st˥ɒp bïŋ ə 'bö.łi bət̪_ðə t̪rʉθ ïz aɪ̃ wəz ɾɒɲ				
SYMBOLS: Ah-EE̱ th<AW>T MAh-EE̱ **FAH.**THUH WU̱D N<O>T ST^D<O>P BI̱NG uh **BU̱.**LEE BuhT_THu̱h TR^ROOth I̱Z^S Ah-EE̱ Wu̱hZ^S R^R<O>N̪G				
Key Words	*Detailed American English Accent* *IPA* ---------------------- *Symbol*	*Shift to Afrikaans Accent of English* *IPA* ---------------------- *Symbol*	*Key Words Shifts* *IPA* ---------------------- *Symbol*	*Your Key Words*
↳ f<u>oo</u>d gr<u>ew</u>, tr<u>ue</u>, tw<u>o</u>	u ---------------------- OO	ʉ ---------------------- [O̱O] [OO] made in the middle of the mouth	fʉd̪, grʉ, t̪rʉ ---------------------- FOO̱D, GR^ROO̱, TR^ROO̱	
↳ d<u>u</u>ty t<u>u</u>ne, <u>news</u>	[ɪʊ̯] when preceded by *t, d, n* in spelling ---------------------- [I-O͡O] when preceded by *t, d, n* in spelling	d̪jʉ, t̪jʉ, njʉ ---------------------- DYO̱O, TYO̱O, NYO̱O	'd̪jʉ.t̪i, t̪jʉn, njʉ ---------------------- **DYOO̱.**TEE̱, TYOO̱N, NYOO̱	
↳ f<u>oo</u>t p<u>u</u>t	ʊ ---------------------- U	[ö] or [ɜ] ---------------------- [U̱] or [UH^R] [U] is made in the middle of the mouth	föt̪, p˥öt̪ or fɜt̪, p˥ɜt̪ ---------------------- FU̱T, P^BU̱T or FUH^RT, P^BUH^RT	

Key Words	Detailed American English Accent IPA	Shift to Afrikaans Accent of English IPA	Key Words Shifts IPA	Your Key Words
	Symbol	Symbol	Symbol	
thought tall, caulk, awful	ɔ	ɔ̞	θɔ̞t, tɔ̞ɫ, kˀɔk, ˈɔ.fə̞ɫ	
	AW	[<AW>] internally rounded in the mouth but not with the lips	th<AW>T, T<AW>L, Kᴳ<AW>K, <AW>.FuhL	
☛ cloth *[ɒ]/[O] dog, cough, wash, horrid	ɔ	ɒ̞	kˀɫɒ̞θ, dɒ̞g, kˀɒ̞f, wɒ̞ʃ,	
	AW	<O̞> internally rounded in the mouth but not with the lips	KᴳL<O̞>th, D<O̞>G, Kᴳ<O̞>F, W<O̞>SH	
father	ɑ	ɑ̞	ˈfɑ.ð̞ə̞	
	AH	AH	**FAH**.THUH	
☛ lot *[ɒ]/[O] squad, wander	ɑ	ɒ̞	ɫɒ̞t, skwɒ̞d, ˈwɒn.də̞	
	AH	<O> internally rounded in the mouth but not with the lips	L<O>T, SKW<O>D, **W<O>N**.DUH	

Diphthong Sound Shifts

	Diphthong Shifts			
I'd like to fly away someday and go south to the mountains with the boys.				
IPA: aĭd laĭkˀ t̚ˀə ﬂaĭ ə'weː 'sʌ̈m.də ən gʌʊ̆ sæŏ̆θ t̚ˀə ð̬ə 'mæŏ̆n.tˀnẓ wïθ ð̬ə boĭẓ				
SYMBOLS: Ah-E̲E̲D LAh-E̲E̲KᴳTᴰu̲h FLAh-E̲E̲ u̲h.We̲̲ SU̲HM.De̲ u̲hN GUH-Ų̆ SA-Ų̆th Tu̲h THu̲h **MA-Ų̆N**.TᵘʰNZˢ WI̲th THu̲h Bo-E̲E̲Zˢ				
Key Words	Detailed American English Accent — IPA — Symbol	Shift to Afrikaans Accent of English — IPA — Symbol	Key Words Shifts — IPA — Symbol	Your Key Words
👉 f̲a̲ce pa̲i̲n, da̲y̲, we̲i̲ght, ste̲a̲k	eĭ ------ AY	[eː] or [eĭ] or [æĭ] ------ [e̲̲] or [e-Ĭ] or [A-Ĭ]	feːs, pˀeːn, d̲e̲ː or feĭs, pˀeĭn, d̲e̲ĭ or fæĭs, pˀæĭn, d̲æĭ ------ Fe̲̲S, Pᴮe̲̲N, D̲e̲̲ or Fe̲-Ĭ̲S, Pᴮe̲-Ĭ̲N, D̲e̲-Ĭ or FA-Ĭ̲S, PᴮA-Ĭ̲N, DA-Ĭ̲	
pr̲i̲ce e̲y̲es, di̲a̲per, fl̲y̲, gu̲y̲, he̲i̲ght	aĭ ------ EYE	a̲ĭ ------ Ah-E̲E̲	pˀra̲ĭs, a̲ĭẓ, d̲a̲ĭ.pˀə̲ ------ PRᴿAh-E̲E̲S, Ah-E̲E̲Zˢ, **DAh-E̲E̲**.PᴮUH	
cho̲i̲ce bo̲y̲s	ɔĭ ------ OY	oĭ̲ ------ o-E̲E̲	tˀʃoĭs, boĭẓ ------ CHo-E̲E̲S, Bo-E̲E̲Zˢ	
👉 g̲o̲at s̲e̲w, g̲o̲, t̲o̲e	oŏ̆ ------ OH	ʌŏ̆ ------ UH-Ų̆	gʌŏ̆t̲, sʌŏ̆, gʌʊ̆ ------ GUH-Ų̆T, SUH-Ų̆, GUH-Ų̆	
mo̲u̲th to̲w̲n	aŏ̆ ------ OW	[æŏ̆] or [a̲ŏ̆] ------ [A-Ų̆] or [Ah-Ų̆]	mæŏ̆θ, tˀæŏ̆n or m̲a̲ŏ̆θ, tˀa̲ŏ̆n ------ MA-Ų̆th, TᴰA-Ų̆N or MAh-Ų̆th, TᴰAh-Ų̆N	

Diphthongs of R Sound Shifts

> **Note!**
> **On r-coloration**
> r-coloration is dropped in diphthongs and triphthongs of R, and replaced by either length or lilt.

Diphthongs and Triphthongs of R Shifts				
Our friends started the fire near your north orchard an hour before we got there.				
IPA: aː frɛnz ˈstɑːtəd ðə faə niə̯ jʉ̈ noːθ ˈoːtʃəd ən aə̯ ˈbïfo wɨ gɒt ðeː				
SYMBOLS: Āh FRᴿenZˢ **STĀH**.TuhD THuh FAh-uh NEE-UH YU Nōth ō.CH>UHᴿ<D uhN Ah-uh̄ **BĪ**.Fo WEE G<O>T THē				
Key Words	Detailed American English Accent IPA ----- Symbol	Shift to Afrikaans Accent of English IPA ----- Symbol	Key Words Shifts IPA ----- Symbol	Your Key Words
n<u>ear</u> b<u>ee</u>r	ɪɚ ----- EAR	iə̯ ----- EE-UH	niə̯, biə̯ ----- NEE-UH, BEE-UH	
⊷ h<u>air</u> st<u>are</u>, p<u>ear</u>, sq<u>uare</u>, th<u>ere</u>	ɛɚ ----- AIR	eː ----- ē	heː, steː, pˀeː, skweː, ðeː ----- Hē, STē, Pē, SKWē, THē	
s<u>ure</u> p<u>oor</u>, y<u>our</u>	ʊɚ ----- UR	[ö̯ə̯] or [ʏ̈] ----- [ʉ-UH] or [O͡O]	ʃö̯ə̯, pö̯ə̯, jö̯ə̯ or ʃʏ̈, pʏ̈, jʏ̈ ----- SHʉ-UH, Pʉ-UH, Yʉ-UH or SHO͡O, PO͡O, YO͡O	

Key Words	Detailed American English Accent *IPA*	Shift to Afrikaans Accent of English *IPA*	Key Words Shifts *IPA*	Your Key Words
	Symbol	*Symbol*	*Symbol*	
↤ n<u>or</u>th G<u>eor</u>ge, p<u>our</u>, w<u>arp</u>, <u>oar</u>	ɔɝ	oː	noːθ, dʒoːdʒ, pˀoː, woːp	
	AWR	ō	Nōth, JōJ^{CH}, P^Bō, WōP	
↤ st<u>art</u> h<u>eart</u>	ɑɝ	ɑː	sta̟ːt̯, ʰɑːt̯	
	AHR	ĀH	STĀHT, ^HĀHT	
f<u>ire</u>	aɪɝ	aə̯	faə̯	
	EYER	Ah-UH	FAh-UH	
h<u>our</u>	aʊɝ	[a] or [aə̯]	a or aə̯	
	OWR	[Ah] or [Ah-<u>uh</u>]	Ah or Ah-<u>uh</u>	

170

Key Sentences for Practice

> **Note!**
> - By practicing the sentences below, you can work through the sound shifts for an Afrikaans accent in the context of a simple thought. I suggest you think, imagine and speak actively from a point of view. As you begin to work with the operative words in the thoughts, the rhythm and melody of the accent will begin to emerge appropriately.
> - Note that less significant words are often unstressed, and articulation of vowels and diphthongs in these words may move toward the neutral *schwa* [ə]/[uh].

Consonants:

- **Example:** Elize Story – 0:02

He was one eh very special person for me, he started off

in eh the forestry.

IPA: i wǒz wän ʔe̝ ˈʋe̝.ɹi ˈspʔe̝.ʃr ˈpʔɵ.sən fǒ mi, hi ˈstɑː.tǒd ǒf ïn ʔe̝ ˈðǒ ˈfɔ.rïs̪.t̪ɥi

SYMBOLS: EE W̲u̲h̲Zˢ WU̲HN ʔe̝ Vᵂe̝.REE SPᴮe̝.SH<o> Pᴮǫ.Su̲h̲N FUH ME̲E̲, HE̲E̲ STA̅H̲.Tu̲h̲D <AW>F I̲N ʔe̝ THuh F<A̲W>.RᴿI̲S.TRE̲E̲

- *I'll meet you at the ferry in an hour with the ten children.*

    IPA: a̠ɫ mit̚ʲ‿ju et̠ ð̠ə 'fe̠.ɾi ïn a̠n a̠ə wïθ ð̠ə t̚ʲen 't̠ʃəɤ.d̠ɾən

    SYMBOLS: AhL MEET^CH‿YO̠O eT THu̠h Fe̠.R^REE IN AhN Ah-u̠h WIth
              THu̠h T^De̠N CHuh-<o>.DR^RuhN

Front Vowels: Vowels articulated by arching the front of the tongue up or cupping it down, aiming toward the front of the hard palate.

- *The thief will tell me after we trap him.*

    IPA: ð̠ə θif wïɫ te̠ɤ mi 'af.t̚ʲə wɨ t̠ɾɛp ïm

    SYMBOLS: THu̠h thEEF WI-<o>L Te̠<o> MEE AHF.TUH WEE TR^REHP
              IM

Middle Vowels: Vowels articulated by arching the middle of the tongue up or cupping it down, aiming toward the middle of the hard palate.

- *In the summer, workers burned the underbrush.*

    IPA: ïn ð̠ə 'sʌ̈.mə 'wə.kə̠ɤ̠ bənd ð̠ɨ 'ʌ̈n.d̠ə,bɾʌ̈ʃ

    SYMBOLS: IN THu̠h SU̠H.MUH W>o̠<.KUHZ^S Bo̠ND THEE
              U̠HN.DUH.BR^RU̠HSH

Back Vowels: Vowels articulated by arching the back of the tongue up or cupping it down, aiming toward the back of the hard palate.

- *I thought my father would not stop being a bully but the truth is, I was wrong.*

    IPA: a̠ï θɔt ma̠ï 'fɑ.ð̠ə wöd̠ nɒt̠ st̚ʲpp bïɲ ə 'bö.ɬi bət̠‿ð̠ə t̠ɾuθ ïz a̠ï
           wə̠z ɾɒɲ

    SYMBOLS: Ah-E̠E th<AW>T MAh-E̠E FAH.THUH WU̠D N<O>T
              ST^D<O>P BI̠NG u̠h BU̠.LEE BuhT‿THu̠h TR^ROOth IZ^S Ah-E̠E
              WuhZ^S R^R<O̠>N̠G

Diphthongs: When two vowels are combined in one syllable.

- *I'd like to fly away someday and go south to the mountains with the boys.*

    IPA: a̠ïd la̠ïk̚ʲ t̚ʲə fɬa̠ï ə'we̠ː 'sʌ̈m.de ən gʌŏ sæ̆ŏθ t̚ʲə ð̠ə 'mæŏn.t̚ʲ°nz
           wïθ ð̠ə bo̠ïz

    SYMBOLS: Ah-E̠ED LAh-E̠EK^G T^Du̠h FLAh-E̠E u̠h.We̠ SUHM.De u̠hN
              GUH-Ŭ̠ SA-Ŭ̠th Tu̠h THu̠h MA-Ŭ̠N.T^uhNZ^S WIth THu̠h
              Bo-E̠EZ^S

Diphthongs of R: A diphthong in which the second vowel is rhotic (e.g., has r-coloration in the final sound)

Example: near → nɪɚ/NEAR

Triphthongs of R: A combination of three vowel sounds, in which the third vowel is rhotic.

Example: fire → faɪɚ/FEYER

- ***<u>Our</u> friends st<u>a</u>rted the f<u>i</u>re n<u>ear</u> <u>your</u> n<u>or</u>th <u>or</u>chard an h<u>our</u> bef<u>ore</u> we got th<u>ere</u>.***

  IPA: aː frenz̥ ˈstɑː.təd̥ ð̥ə faə̯ nɪɚ̯ jö noːθ ˈoː.t̠ʃəd̥ ən aɚ̯ ˈbï.fo wɨ gʊt̥ ð̥eː

  SYMBOLS: Āh FRᴿenZˢ **STĀH**.TuhD THu̠h FAh-u̠h NEE-UH̄ YU̠ Nōth ō.CH>UHᴿ<D u̠hN Ah-u̠h̄ **BI̱**.Fo WEE G<O>T THē

Extra Sentences:

- ***Who would have thought that little bit of a dress would make the girl so happy.***

  IPA: ʉ wöd̥ hɛɣ θɔt̚ ð̥et̚ lï.tl̩ bït̚ əɣ ə dres̠ wöd̥ meːk̚ ð̥ə gəl sʌö̆ ˈɛ.pʰ̩ɨ

  SYMBOLS: O̱O WU̱D HEHVᶠ th<AW>T THeT LI̱TL BI̱T_uhVᶠ uh DRᴿes̠ WU̱D MēKᴳ_THu̠h G>UHᴿ<L SUH-Ŭ̥ **EH**.PᴮEE

- ***I cut the shape of our house out of rough old boards.***

  IPA: aɪ̆ kʰʌt̚ ð̥ə ʃeːpʰ_əɣ_aː æös æŏ̆t̚ əɣ rʌ̈f ʌŏ̆ɫd̥ boːd̥z̥

  SYMBOLS: Ah-EĒ KᴳU̱HT_THu̠h SHēPᴮ_uhVᶠ_Āh A-Ŭ̥S A-Ŭ̥T uhVᶠ RᴿU̱HF UH-Ŭ̥LD BōDZˢ

Making Your Own Map of the Accent

Listen to the Afrikaans accent samples provided and investigate the resources suggested in the *Introduction and Resources* section. Compose (or steal) *Key Phrases* from your listening/viewing that challenge and/or ground you in the accent. Then get more specific and check your sounds against the sounds in the Workbook.

Your take on the sound shifts may be slightly different. That is okay. The breakdown is a tool, not a rule. Recheck what you hear and, if you still stand behind your discoveries, go with them. This will help you to develop **your own** idiolect of the accent.

> *Note!*
> **What is an Idiolect?**
> Each of us speaks differently even if we have the same general accent. The individualized way that each of us speaks is referred to as an idiolect. For the actor, idiolect is part of what creates character. It is the "how" of the accent, and influences the way we craft our thoughts through language.

KEY PHRASES WITH KEY SOUND SHIFTS

Speak your *Key Phrases*, shifting back and forth between your own home *idiolect of English* and the *Afrikaans accent* you are building. **Observe** the shifts ONE by ONE in your Articulators, Focus of Articulation, use of Melody/Pitch/Lilt, Rhythm/Stress/Pace, and Source & Path of Resonance as you shift back and forth between the two accents. Make note of the shifts in the table provided. Putting your understanding of the shifts into your own words will encourage you to develop a more clear and personal idiolect.

AFRIKAANS ACCENT *KEY POINTS OF FOCUS: VOCAL POSTURE AND CHARACTERISTICS*

JAW
LIPS
TONGUE
SOFT PALATE
PHARYNX

FOCUS OF ARTICULATION (TOWARDS TEETH, FRONT/MIDDLE/ BACK OF HARD PALATE, SOFT PALATE, ETC.)

MELODY/PITCH/LILT

RHYTHM/STRESS/PACE

SOURCE & PATH OF RESONANCE – Where does the resonance begin and what is the apparent path it travels through your body (chest, hard palate, sinuses, temples, crown, base of skull, etc.)? Refer to the Source & Path of Resonance and Resonators in the *Afrikaans Accent of English: Down & Dirty Warm-Up and Quick Look* on page 149.

OTHER CHARACTERISTICS (What are your observations?)

PERSONAL IMAGES (For many actors personal images can be the most powerful and effective triggers for their transformation into an accent)

Chapter 7

Rwandan (Kinyarwanda) Accent of English

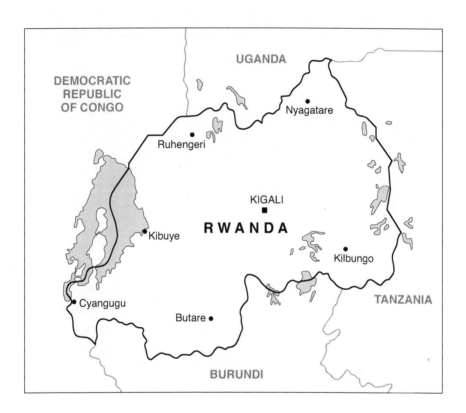

Introduction and Resources

The Kinyarwanda Language in Rwanda

Rwanda is a former colony of both Germany and Belgium. Kinyarwanda, French and English are all official languages. Kinyarwanda is spoken by all three of the main ethnic groups in Rwanda – the Hutu, Twa and Tutsi – and is also spoken in eastern DR Congo and southern Uganda. It is a Bantu language from the Niger-Congo language group.

Documentaries

PBS Frontline: *Ghosts of Rwanda*; *Shake Hands with the Devil: The Journey of Roméo Dallaire*; *Sweet Dreams*; *Coexist*; *6954 Kilometers to Home*; *Life After Death*; *Flower in the Gun Barrel*; *Keepers of Memory*; *In Rwanda We Say…The Family That Does Not Speak Dies*; *Behind This Convent*

Films

Beyond the Gates, *Sometimes in April*, *100 Days*, *In My Country*, *Hotel Rwanda* (look at the secondary actors in this film), *Kinyarwanda*

Television

Primus Guma Guma Super Star (Igihe TV)

Plays with Rwandanese Characters

The Overwhelming by J.T. Rogers; *Sky Like Sky* by Emily Mendelsohn and Elizabeth Spackman; *The Theatre of Genocide: Four Plays about Mass Murder in Rwanda, Bosnia, Cambodia, and Armenia* by Robert Skloot (editor); *Unexplored Territory* by Jay O. Sanders; *I Have Before Me a Remarkable Document Given to Me by a Young Lady from Rwanda* by Sonja Linden; *Maria Kizito* by Erik Ehn

Music

Jean Samputu, Mani Martin, Alpha Rwirangira

Radio

Radiyoyacu VOA (Voice of America)

Personalities

Paul Kagame (President), Anastase Murekezi (Prime Minister), Juvénal Habya-
rimana (ex-President), Agathe Uwilingiyimana (Rwanda's first and only female
Prime Minister), Olivier Karekezi (footballer), Honorine Uwera (model), Alexis
Kagame (literary figure)

Down & Dirty Warm-up and Quick Look

Note!

On Symbols

- International Phonetic Alphabet Symbols will be listed first and Sound Symbols will be listed second. Example: [i]/[EE]
- Sound Symbol Users: bold-faced letters indicate the syllable is stressed.

1) **The Muscles:** Wake your mouth up so you can more easily discover the physical transformation in speaking the accent.

   a. Scratch the front, middle and back of your tongue with your front top teeth.

   b. Rub the front, middle and back of your hard palate with the tip of your tongue.

   c. Imagine your mouth is numb from being at the dentist and you want to wake it up. Make tongue circles pressing against the back of your lips first clockwise, then counter clockwise (you are waking up your orbicularis muscle).

   d. To get the breath flowing, blow through your lips, getting them to flap together. Travel up and down in pitch on a BBBB and PPP, feeling the vibration as you wiggle up and down your spine.

2) **Vocal Posture for a Rwandan (Kinyarwanda) Accent:** The focus of articulation is largely in the middle front of the mouth with the middle of the tongue very active in making vowels. The blade of the tongue is active towards the top front teeth and post alveolar ridge. The blade of the tongue relaxes behind the lower front teeth. There is a slight bunching up in the middle of the tongue. The lips 1) are full of ease, 2) actively lead in articulation, and 3) round actively for the rounded vowels. The jaw is easy and follows the tongue and lips in articulation. The soft palate is lifted which is instrumental in creating the light hypo-nasal quality of the accent (like when you have a cold and you can't resonate in your nasal sinuses). There is a slight narrowing of the pharynx which gives the accent a pharyngeal twang.

3) **Resonators:** "occupy" the following spaces. This will prepare you to find the Source & Path of Resonance for a Rwandan (Kinyarwanda) accent. (By "occupy", I mean just that: be in the space of it and find the pathway and flow of resonance, rather than "putting" the resonance there.)

    a.   CHEST – Generously laugh at something – hạ hạ hạ / HAH HAH HAH

    b.   HARD PALATE – As if you were discovering something – ho ho ho / Ho Ho Ho

    c.   THE BONES AT THE BASE OF YOUR SKULL (THE OCCIPITAL BONE) – Use your hands to scoop the sound from the base of your skull with a Mississippi African-American dialect as if you're flirting with someone nearby – heị heị heị / He-EE He-EE He-EE

    d.   FLICK THE SOUND OUT OF YOUR CHEEKBONES with an Italian-American flourish, as if calling to someone across the street – heị heị heị / He-EE He-EE He-EE

    e.   WITH YOUR HANDS NEXT TO YOUR TEMPLES, SHAKE THE SOUND OUT WITH LOOSE FISTS – As if you were somewhat crazed – jị jị jị / YEE YEE YEE

    f.   IMAGINE A METAL DISK EXTENDING FROM YOUR HANDS THROUGH YOUR SKULL. Bring your hands to the sides of your head just above the temples, with your palms facing the floor, thumbs hooked behind your skull. *Lid* the vibration to create a muted brassy sound. Like a robot saying "Hi" – haɪ̌ haɪ̌ haɪ̌ / HAh-EE HAh-EE HAh-EE

    g.   GIGGLE OUT OF THE TOP OF YOUR HEAD – As if you were tickled pink by something – hị hị hị / HEE HEE HEE

4) **Source & Path of Resonance for a Rwandan (Kinyarwanda) Accent:** Both men and women begin with warm chest resonance. The sound comes up through a slightly narrowed pharynx, creating pharyngeal twang. Because of the raised soft palate the sound travels quite fully into the mouth. Think of focusing it to a small dome in the middle of the hard palate with the middle of the tongue slightly lifted. Nasal consonants [n]/[N], [m]/[M], [ŋ]/[NG] and the vowels next to them do get nasalized. The sound rattles a little as it is lidded just below the temples.

5) **Get the sound changes into your body and imagination.**
Say these phrases occupying the following places in your body, suggesting to yourself the following energetic associations:

    ● pubic bone to tail bone – survival instinct

         zụː / Z>OO<
         I need it – a nịd ịt / Ah NEED EET

    ● pubic bone to navel & sacrum in back – sexuality, big feelings

         wo / Wo
         I desire it – a dị'za.jəɹ̣ ịt / Ah DEE.**ZAh**-YuhR̲ EET

- rib cage to below heart – will

  ʒɔ / ZH>AW<
  I want it – a wɒnt it / Ah WAHNT EET

- heart – love

  mɑ / MAH
  I love it – a lɜv it / Ah LUHᴿV EET

- throat – communication (think of talking at a party)

  bɜ / BUHᴿ
  I have to say it – a hɒv tu seː it / Ah HAHV T>OO< Sē EET

- forehead – intelligence/wisdom

  kei / Ke-EE
  I know it – a no it / Ah No EET

- crown of head – spirituality

  ɾi / RᴿEE
  I believe it – a biˈɾiv it / Ah BEE.RᴿEEV EET

6) **Articulation** – using playful physical actions: punching, flicking, dabbing, slashing

  du di ku du di ku du di ku – di
  du di ku du di ku du di ku – deː
  du di ku du di ku du di ku – daɨ
  du di ku du di ku du di ku – do
  du di ku du di ku du di ku – du

Repeat as needed, replacing [d] with [t], [p], [b], [k], [g], [f], [v]

D>OO< DEE K>OO< D>OO< DEE K>OO< D>OO< DEE K>OO< – DEE
D>OO< DEE K>OO< D>OO< DEE K>OO< D>OO< DEE K>OO< – Dē
D>OO< DEE K>OO< D>OO< DEE K>OO< D>OO< DEE K>OO< – DAh-EE
D>OO< DEE K>OO< D>OO< DEE K>OO< D>OO< DEE K>OO< – Do
D>OO< DEE K>OO< D>OO< DEE K>OO< D>OO< DEE K>OO< – D>OO<

Repeat as needed, replacing [D] with [T], [P], [B], [K], [G], [F], [V].
[D] & [T] are both articulated with the blade of the tongue against the front of the hard palate at the alveolar ridge.

Key Points of Focus
Characteristics and Vocal Posture

Rwandan (Kinyarwanda) Accent Characteristics

> *Note!*
> **On Melody/Lilt/Pitch and Rhythm/Stress/Pace**
> Every accent contains shifts for some, but not necessarily all, of these elements of vocal variety.

> *Note!*
> **On Use of Musical Notes**
> Follow the "musical notes" up and down to get a feel for the melody of the accent. The filled-in notes are shorter than the open notes. For those who are musically inclined, think of them as approximating quarter notes and half notes. This distinction will give you a feel for the rhythm of the accent.

Melody/Lilt/Pitch

Kinyarwanda is a tonal language with high and low tones. This, along with the influence of the French language, has determined factors in creating the accent's pitch-confined melodic patter. It has the ease and sometimes unexpected tumble of a gurgling brook.

1. There is often a lift in pitch in the second to the last syllable in multi-syllabic words. This originates in the language's Bantu roots.
2. There is very little lengthening of vowels. When there is a need to stress a word, the word may rise in pitch or contain a lilt. The pitch change within lilts is not dramatic. This is due, in part, to the influence of the French language, which tends not to have large leaps in pitch within a word.

3. Note the occasional nasalized lilts that occur on vowels that are preceded or followed by a nasal consonant ([n]/[N], [m]/[M], [ŋ]/[NG]), just as in a French accent.
4. The end of a thought is most often accompanied by a slight drop in pitch on either the last word or the last syllable of the last word, in multi-syllabic words.
5. Sometimes there is a wild card hurling up on a pitch for a word. Upon examination of the French language, this may not seem random, since the French, at the end of mini-thoughts, often hurl a word up in pitch. You can hear this in a number of the speakers; it is an expressive element you might include in your own idiolect of the accent.

Notice, when you listen to Natasha, Mutiniz and George speak in Kinyarwanda, that the lilts in their speech are quite pronounced and create a lot of musical variety. Speaking English seems to inhibit this melodic play.

Example: Belize Story (Part 1) – 0:25

So when I get home and she's not there I feel like I am missing

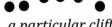

something big, like I'm always afraid.

Belize raises pitch very slightly on operative words *home, there, feel, something* (#2, p. 184). She lilts on two of them: *home* (which also contains a nasal consonant) and *there* (#2, p. 184 & #3 above). The final word of her thought, *afraid*, comes to a gentle conclusion with a slight drop in pitch (#4 above). Because of the steady rhythm of her speech, notice how her lilting in *so*, *home* and *there* pop out. Although the pitch range is narrow and words do not often lengthen, there is an expressive quality in her gentle melodic patter (#2, p. 184).

Example: Mutiniz Story (Part 1) – 0:08

I was sitting in the passenger seat but we reached

a particular cliff.

The most outstanding characteristics in Mutiniz's short thought above are: 1) how the vowels in the multi-syllabic words *passenger* and *particular* do not lengthen or exhibit much change in pitch (#2, p. 184); 2) the very slight lift in pitch in the second to the last syllable of both words (#1, p. 184); 3) the end of Mutiniz's thought falls slightly in pitch on the final word *cliff* (#4, p. 185); 4) the wild card in this sentence is the fly away rise in pitch on *seat* (#5, p. 185).

Rhythm/Stress/Pace

Note that because most of the syllables are the same length, lilts and change in pitch become quite expressive. This consistency in length is because the accent rarely uses weak forms of vowels. This is also a characteristic of the French language. Instead, vowels remain in a strong form and the syllables sound equal in stress.

Example: Janvier Story (Part 1) – 0:01

I remember when I was young I went to tell my father that

I am his child, but he denied me.

In this first sentence, which begins the telling of her moving story, Janvier lilts on three of her operative words: *young, child,* and *denied*. In *young* and *denied*, a nasal consonant either ends or begins (respectively) the lilt, much like in a French accent. Because of the equal length of most of the syllables, notice how the lilts call your attention to the words. Also note that in the multi-syllabic word <u>remember</u> the syllables are equal in length. This is a distinct characteristic and worth folding into your idiolect of the accent.

Example: George Story (Part 1) – 1:48

He forgot totally the good work that I'd done in cleaning up

the compound.

As you can hear and see, George's rhythm is consistent in syllable length except for in the nasalized lilt in *com<u>pound</u>*. The syllables in the multi-syllabic words *forgot, totally* and *cleaning* remain equal in length because the vowels all remain in strong form.

Source & Path of Resonance

Both men and women begin with warm chest resonance. The sound comes up through a slightly narrowed pharynx, creating a pharyngeal twang. Because of the raised soft palate the sound travels quite fully into the mouth. Think of focusing it to a small dome in the middle of the hard palate with the middle of the tongue slightly lifted. Nasal consonants [n]/[N], [m]/[M], [ŋ]/[NG] and the vowels next to them do get nasalized. The sound rattles a little as it is lidded just below the temples.

The Path of Resonance as described above can be heard in all of the speakers – even in Isaac, who has the weakest of the recorded accents. The women tend to speak in a higher pitch range than men. Belize almost sings on her higher pitched segments of speech.

Rwandan (Kinyarwanda) Accent Vocal Posture

Note!
On Vocal Posture
These adjustments enable you to integrate the accent through physical transformation rather than solely relying on sound shifts.

- **Focus of Articulation:** The focus of articulation is largely in the middle front of the mouth with the middle of the tongue very active in making vowels. The blade of the tongue is active towards the top front teeth and post alveolar ridge.
- **Tongue:** The tongue rests forward. The blade relaxes behind the lower front teeth. There is a slight bunching up in the middle of the tongue.
- **Lips:** The lips are full of ease and actively lead in articulation. They round actively on the accent's rounded vowels: [ə]/[>UH^R<], [o]/[o], [ʉ]/[>O͡O<], [u̞]/[>OO<], [ɔ̝]/[>AW<], [ɔ]/[>AW<]
- **Jaw:** The jaw is easy and follows the tongue and lips in articulation.
- **Soft Palate:** The soft palate is lifted which is instrumental in creating the light hypo-nasal quality of the accent (like when you have a cold and you can't resonate in your nasal sinuses).
- **Pharynx:** There is a slight narrowing creating a pharyngeal twang.

188

Distinct Sounds of the Language and/or Accent

> *Note!*
> **On Distinct Sounds**
> These are some of the sounds that Rwandans use and American speakers do not. In speaking the sounds and/or the words that contain them, you can heighten your physical understanding of the Rwandan (Kinyarwanda) accent's *Vocal Posture* as compared to your own. This frame of reference will both inform and strengthen your accent.

Consonants

1. *IPA:* [ɟ] → Voiced palatal plosive.
   Symbol: [G̟ᵞ] → [G] made more forward in the mouth with a little [ᵞ] following.
   This sound is used in speaking the Kinyarwanda language.
2. *IPA:* [ɲ] → Palatal nasal.
   Symbol: [N̟Gᵞ] → [NG] made on the hard palate with a little [ᵞ] following.
   Used in place of [ŋ]/[NG]: *si<u>ng</u>*
   This sound is used in speaking both the language and accent of Kinyarwanda.
3. *IPA:* [ɾ] → alveolar tap.
   Symbol: [Rᴿ] → Tapped [R].
   Sometimes used in place of [ɹ]/[R]: <u>r</u>ed, *fe<u>rr</u>y*
   This sound is used in speaking both the language and accent of Kinyarwanda.
4. *IPA:* [β] → voiced bilabial fricative. This is made by flapping the lips lightly on a [b].
   Symbol: [Bᴴ] → This is made by flapping the lips lightly on a [B].
   This sound is used in speaking the Kinyarwanda language.
5. *IPA:* [ç] → Voiceless palatal fricative.
   Symbol: [SHᵞ] → [SH] articulated in the middle of the mouth with a little [ᵞ] following.

Pre-nasalized and Post-nasalized Consonants

6. *IPA:* [ᵐp], [ᵐb], [ⁿt], [dᵐ]
   Symbol: [ᵐP], [ᵐB], [ᴺT], [Dᵐ]
   These sounds are used in speaking the Kinyarwandan language.
   Kinyarwanda has three pre-nasalized and one post-nasalized consonant.
   Although these consonants are not used in the accent, there is a slight
   nasality that carries over.

Vowels

The vowels of the Kinyarwanda language include:

   IPA: [i], [e], [u], [o], [ɑ]
   Symbol: [EE], [e], [OO], [o], [AH]

Knowing the vowels for the Kinyarwanda language will provide clues for the
vowel shifts in the accent.

7. *IPA:* [e]
   Symbol: [e] → This is the first sound in the D.A.E. diphthong [AY] as in
   fa̲ce.
   Used in place of [ɛ]/[EH]: *dre̲ss, be̲d*
   This sound is used in speaking both the language and accent of Kinyarwanda.
8. *IPA:* [o]
   Symbol: [o]. This is the first sound in the D.A.E. diphthong [OH].
   Used in place of [oʊ]/[OH]: *goa̲t, se̲w*
   This sound is used in speaking both the language and accent of Kinyarwanda.

Consonant Sound Shifts

- ⊶ indicates that this sound is a key sound shift
- You can begin to fold melody and rhythm with the sound changes by speaking the sample sentences that are before each section of sound changes.

> *Note!*
> **On End of Word Consonant Clusters *nt* and *nd***
> Sometimes in words ending in *nt* or *nd*, the *t* and *d* are dropped.
>
> Example: pla̲n̲t̲ → pla̲n̲, sta̲n̲d̲ → sta̲n̲.

Consonant Shifts
Example: Belize (Part 3) – 0:04

I al̲ways̲ l̲ov̲e kid̲s̲.
IPA: aɪ̆ ˈɔ̰ɤ.wez̥ ɾɜv̥ ki̞d̪z̥
SYMBOLS: Ah-E̲E̲ >**AW**<-<**o**>.WeZ^{S} R^{R}UH^{R}V^{F} KE̲E̲DZ^{S}
Example: Belize (Part 3) – 3:14

Ever̲ybod̲y I give ever̲yth̲ing th̲ey want̲.
IPA: ˈev.ɾɪ̆.bo.d̪i̠ a gi̞v ev.ɾɪ̆.t̪i̞ŋ d̪eⁱ wɑ̟̃nt̪
SYMBOLS: **e**V.R^{R}E̲E̲.Bo.DE̲E̲ Ah GE̲E̲V **e**V.R^{R}E̲E̲.TE̲E̲NG De^{EE} W*A̟H*NT
I'l̲l̲ meet you at̲ th̲e fer̲r̲y in an hour with̲ th̲e t̲en chil̲dr̲en.
IPA: aˈɤ mit̪ʃ‿ju̹ ɑ̟t d̪a ˈfe.ɾi̠ i̞n an ˈa.wə wi̞t̪ d̪a t̪en tʃi̞ɹ.d̪ɾen
SYMBOLS: Ah<oo> ME̲E̲T^{CH}‿Y>OO< A̟HT DAh **Fe**.R^{R}E̲E̲ E̲E̲N AhN **Ah**.Wuh WE̲E̲T DAh TeN **CHE̲E̲R**.DR^{R}eN

Key Words	Detailed American English Accent	Shift to Rwandan (Kinyarwanda) Accent of English	Key Words Shifts	Your Key Words
	IPA	*IPA*	*IPA*	
	Symbol	Symbol	Symbol	
team deb<u>t</u>, <u>did</u>	[t]/[d] ------------ [T], [D]	[t̪]/[d̪] ------------ [T]/[D] both made on the front of the hard palate with the blade of the tongue rather than the tip of the tongue	tim, det, did ------------ TEEM, DeT, DEED	
↤ <u>th</u>ese <u>th</u>ere, brea<u>th</u>e	ð ------------ TH	[ð̪] or [d̪] ------------ [T] or [D] both dentalized	ð̪iz, ð̪eə, b̪ɹið̪ or d̪iz, d̪eə, b̪ɹid̪ ------------ THEEZ, THe-UH, BREETH or DEEZ, De-UH, BREED	
↤ <u>th</u>in <u>th</u>ick	θ ------------ [th]	[θ̪] or [t̪] ------------ [Th] or [T] (both dentalized)	θ̪in, θ̪ik or t̪in, t̪ik ------------ ThEEN, ThEEK or TEEN, TEEK	
mou<u>th</u> (final *th*)	θ ------------ [th]	sometimes [f] ------------ sometimes [F]	maʊf ------------ MAh-ŬF	
<u>s</u>ee gue<u>ss</u>, <u>z</u>oo	[s]/[z] ------------ [S]/[Z]	[s̪]/[z̪] ------------ [S]/[Z] both dentalized	s̪i, ges̪ / z̪u ------------ SEE, GeS / Z>OO<	
boy<u>s</u> (final *s* when prounounced [z])	z ------------ Z	z̪ ------------ [Zˢ] dentalized	beiz̪ ------------ Bọ-EEZˢ	
↤ <u>r</u>ed d<u>r</u>ess, me<u>rr</u>y, so<u>rr</u>y	ɹ ------------ R	[ɹ̪] or [ɾ] (in stronger accents) ------------ [R̪] or [Rᴿ] (in stronger accents)	ɹ̪ed, d̪ɹ̪es, 'me.ɹ̪i or ɾed, d̪ɾes, 'me.ɾi ------------ ReD, DReS, **Me.REE** or Rᴿed, DRᴿeS, **Me.RᴿEE**	

Key Words	Detailed American English Accent	Shift to Rwandan (Kinyarwanda) Accent of English	Key Words Shifts	Your Key Words
	IPA	IPA	IPA	
	Symbol	Symbol	Symbol	
☙ exce**l** fa**ll**, tab**l**e (final *l*)	l	[ɫ] or [ɤ] or [ɹ]	ek'sɛ̱ɫ, fɔ̱ɫ, 'tɛː.bə̱ɫ' or ek'sɛɤ, fɔ̱ɤ, 'tɛː.bəɤ or ek'sɛɹ, fɔ̱ɹ, 'tɛː.bə̱ɹ	
	L	[L] or [<o>] or [R]	eK.Se**L**, F>AW<**L**, T**ẽ**.Buh**L** or eK.**Se**<o>, F>AW<-<o>, T**ẽ**.Buh<o> or eK.**SeR**, F>AW<R, T**ẽ**.BuhR	
☙ sti**lt** bui**lt**, chi**ld**ren (*l* in consonant clusters *lt* or *ld*)	[lt]/[ld]	ɤ̱t/ɤ̱d	sti̱ɤ̱t / 'tʃi̱ɤ.d̥rẽn	
	[LT]/[LD]	<o>T/<o>D	ST**EE̱**<o>T / CH**EE̱**.<o>.DR^ReN	
☙ deve**l**op g**l**obe, friend**ly** ([l]/[L] between vowels, in consonant clusters, and in *ly* endings)	l	sometimes [ɹ] or [ɾ]	di̱'ve.ɹɜp, gɹob, 'frend̥.ɹi̱ or di̱'ve.ɾɜp, gɾob, 'frend̥.ɾi̱	
	L	sometimes [R] or [R^R]	D**EE̱**.**Ve**.RUH^RP, GRoB, **FR**^R**enD**.REE or D**EE̱**.**Ve**.R^RUH^RP, GR^RoB, **FR**^R**enD**.R^R**EE̱**	
ju**dge** (final [dʒ]/[J])	dʒ	often dʒ	dʒ̥3d̥ʒ	
	J	often J^{CH}	JUH^RJ^{CH}	
si**ng**ing (penultimate *ng* in spelling)	ŋ	sometimes ŋ.g	'si̱ŋ'gin	
	NG	sometimes NG.G	S**EE̱**NG.G**EE̱**N	

Front Vowel Sound Shifts

Note!
On Vowels
The vowels of the Kinyarwanda language include:

IPA: [i], [e], [u], [o], [ɑ]
Symbol: [EE], [e], [OO], [o], [AH]

Knowing the vowels for the Kinyarwanda language will provide clues for the vowel shifts in the accent.

Note!
For Symbol Users
When vowels are italicized, it means they are nasalized.

Example: no → N*o*

Front Vowel Shifts				

The thief will tell me after we trap him.

IPA: ða θif wɪ̈ tel̃ mi 'ɑf.ta wï trɑp hɪ̈m

SYMBOLS: THAh thEEF WEE-<OO> TeL MEE **AHF**.TAh WEE TRᴿAHP HEEM

Key Words	Detailed American English Accent IPA ———— Symbol	Shift to Rwandan (Kinyarwanda) Accent of English IPA ———— Symbol	Key Words Shifts IPA ———— Symbol	Your Key Words
fleece sneeze, plead	i ———— EE	i̠ ———— EE	fɹis, sniz, plid ———— FREES, SNEEZˢ, PLEED	
☛ kit pitch, dim, lip	ɪ ———— I	i̠ ———— EE	kɪt, pɪtʃ, dɪm ———— KEET, PEECH, DEEM	
☛ country (*y* in final position of spelling)	ɪ̠ ———— EE	i ———— EE	'kɜn.tɹi ———— KUHᴿN.TRᴿEE	
☛ berated	[ɪ] in prefix ———— [EE] in prefix	i ———— EE	bi're.tɪd ———— BEE.Rᴿe.TID	
dress bed, feather, send	ɛ ———— EH	e ———— e	dɹes, bed, 'fe.ða ———— DRᴿes, BeD, **Fe**.DAh	
☛ trap mad, rat, candle	æ ———— A	ɑ ———— AH	trɑp, mɑd, rɑt ———— TRᴿAHP, MAHD, RᴿAHT	
☛ bath *[a]/[Ah] ask, after, dance, example, half, mask, rascal, transfer In Chapter 1, there is a list of these words called the BATH or ASK list of words.	æ ———— A	ɑ ———— AH	bɑf, ɑsk, 'ɑf.ta, dɑns ———— bAHF, AHSK, **AHF**.TAh, DAHNS	

Middle Vowel Sound Shifts

Middle Vowel Shifts				
In the summer, workers burned the underbrush.				
IPA: ɪ̰n ð̪a 'sɜ.ma 'wə.kaz̪ bənd̪ ð̪ɪ̰̃ 'ɜn.'d̪a.brɜʃ				
SYMBOLS: ḚEN THAh **SUH^R.MAh W>UH^R<.KAhZ^S B>UH^R<ND** THḚ̄E **UH^RN.DAh**.BR^RUH^RSH				
Key Words	*Detailed American English Accent* *IPA* ------------------------ *Symbol*	*Shift to Rwandan (Kinyarwanda) Accent of English* *IPA* ------------------------ *Symbol*	*Key Words Shifts* *IPA* ------------------------ *Symbol*	*Your Key Words*
↤ bird service, learn, nurse, work (*ir, er, ear, ur, or* in spelling)	ɝ ------------------------ ER	[ə] or [ɜ] ------------------------ [>UH^R<] or [UH^R]	bəd̪, 'sə.vḭs, lə̃n, nəs̪, wək or bɜd̪, 'sɜ.vḭs, lɜ̃n, nɜs̪, wɜk ------------------------ B>UH^R<D, **S>UH^R<.VḚ̄ES**, L>*UH^R*<N, N>UH^R<S, W>UH^R<K or BUH^RD, **SUH^R.VḚ̄ES**, L*UH^R*N, NUH^RS, WUH^RK	
↤ sister traitor, hangar	ɚ ------------------------ er	a ------------------------ Ah	'sḭs.t̪a ------------------------ **SḚ̄ES**-TAh	
strut curry, come, flood	Ʌ̈ ------------------------ U̞H	ɜ ------------------------ UH^R	st̪rɜt̪, kɜ.ɾḭ, kɜ̃m, flɜd̪ ------------------------ STR^RUH^RT, KUH^R.RḚE, K*UH^R*M, FLUH^RD	

Key Words	Detailed American English Accent	Shift to Rwandan (Kinyarwanda) Accent of English	Key Words Shifts	Your Key Words
	IPA	*IPA*	*IPA*	
	Symbol	*Symbol*	*Symbol*	
<u>a</u>bout <u>ba</u>nan<u>a</u>	ə	a	aˈb<u>aʊ̆</u>ṭ	
	uh	Ah	Ah.**BA<u>h</u>UT**	
<u>con</u>sider <u>com</u>pare	[ə] in *con* and *com* prefixes	o	kõn.s̬i̬da kõm.peə̬	
	[uh] in *con* and *com* prefixes	o	K*o*N.S*EE̱*.DAh, K*o*M.Pe-UH	

Back Vowel Sound Shifts

Back Vowel Shifts				
I thought my father would not stop being a bully but the truth is, I was wrong.				
IPA: aɪ̆ tɔt maɪ̆ ˈfɑ.da wʊd nɔt stɔp bɪŋ a ˈbʊ.li bɜt da tɾut ɪz aɪ̆ wɑz ɾɔŋ				
SYMBOLS: Ah-E͜E T>AW<T MAh-E͜E **FAH**.DAh W>O͞O<D NoT SToP BEENG Ah **B>O͞O**<.LEE BUHᴿT DAh TR̬>OO<T E͜EZˢ Ah-E͜E WAHZˢ R̬>AW<NG				
Key Words	Detailed American English Accent *IPA* ------------------- *Symbol*	Shift to Rwandan (Kinyarwanda) Accent of English *IPA* ------------------- *Symbol*	Key Words Shifts *IPA* ------------------- *Symbol*	Your Key Words
f<u>oo</u>d gr<u>ew</u>, tr<u>ue</u>, tw<u>o</u>	u ------------------- OO	u̬ ------------------- >OO<	fu̬d, gɾu̬, tɾu̬ ------------------- F>OO<D, GR̬>OO<, TR̬>OO<	
☛ <u>du</u>ty <u>tu</u>ne, <u>new</u>s	[ɪʊ̬] when preceded by *t, d, n* in spelling ------------------- [I-O͞O] when preceded by *t, d, n* in spelling	ju̬ ------------------- Y>OO<	ˈdju̬.ti̬, tju̬n, nju̬z ------------------- **DY>OO**<.TEE, TY>OO<N, NY>OO<Zˢ	
☛ f<u>oo</u>t p<u>u</u>t	ʊ ------------------- U	u̬ ------------------- >O͞O<	fu̬t, pu̬t ------------------- F>O͞O<T, P>O͞O<T	
th<u>ou</u>ght t<u>a</u>ll, c<u>au</u>lk, <u>aw</u>ful	ɔ ------------------- AW	ɔ̬ ------------------- >AW<	tɔ̬t, tɔ̬ł, kɔk ------------------- T>AW<T, T>AW<<u>L</u>, K>AW<K	

Key Words	Detailed American English Accent IPA ---- Symbol	Shift to Rwandan (Kinyarwanda) Accent of English IPA ---- Symbol	Key Words Shifts IPA ---- Symbol	Your Key Words
cl<u>o</u>th *[ɒ]/[O] d<u>o</u>g, c<u>ou</u>gh, w<u>a</u>sh, h<u>o</u>rrid	ɔ ---- AW	ǫ̰ ---- >AW<	krǫ̰θ, dǫ̰g, kǫ̰f, wǫ̰ʃ ---- KRᴿ>AW<th, D>AW<G, K>AW<F, W>AW<SH	
f<u>a</u>ther	ɑ ---- AH	ą̰ ---- A̰H	'fą̰.ḏa ---- **FA̰H**-DAh	
☛ l<u>o</u>t *[ɒ]/[O] squ<u>a</u>d, w<u>a</u>nder	ɑ ---- AH	[o] or [ą̰] ---- [o] or [A̰H]	lǫ̰ṯ, ṣkwǫ̰ḏ, 'wǫ̰n.ḏa or lą̰ṯ, ṣkwą̰ḏ, 'wą̰n.ḏa ---- LoT, SKWoD, **Wo**N.DAh or LA̰HT, SKWA̰HD, **WA̰HN**.DAh	

Diphthong Sound Shifts

		Diphthong Shifts		

I'd like to fly away someday and go south to the mountains with the boys.

IPA: aɪ laɪk tu fɹaɪ a'weɪ 'sɜm.deː ãn go saʊ̃θ tu ða 'maʊ̃n.tɪnz wɪθ ða boɪz

SYMBOLS: AhD LAh-EĔK T>OO< FRАh-EĔ Ah-**We-EE** SUHᴿM.Dē *Ah*N Go SAh-Ŭth T>ŌŌ< THAh ***MAh-ŬN***.TɪNZˢ WEEth THAh Bǫ-EEZˢ

Key Words	Detailed American English Accent	Shift to Rwandan (Kinyarwanda) Accent of English	Key Words Shifts	Your Key Words
	IPA	IPA	IPA	
	---------------	---------------	---------------	
	Symbol	Symbol	Symbol	
f<u>a</u>ce p<u>ai</u>n, d<u>ay</u>, w<u>eigh</u>t, st<u>ea</u>k	eɪ	[eː] or [eɪ̞]	feːs̬, pẽːn, d̪eː, weːt̬, st̬eːk or feɪs̬, pẽɪn, d̪eɪ, weɪt̪, st̬eɪk	
	---------------	---------------	---------------	
	AY	[ē] or [e-EE]	Fēs, Pēn, Dē, WēT, STēK or Fe-EES, Pe-*EE*N, De-EE, We-EET, STe-EEK	
pr<u>i</u>ce <u>eye</u>s, d<u>ia</u>per, fl<u>y</u>, g<u>uy</u>, h<u>eigh</u>t	aɪ	[aɪ] or [a]	pɾaɪs̬, aɪ̯z̬, 'd̪aɪ.pa, fɹaɪ, gaɪ or pɾas̬, az̬, 'd̪a.pa, fɹa, ga	
	---------------	---------------	---------------	
	EYE	[Ah-EE] or [Ah]	PRᴿAh-EES, Ah-EEZˢ, **DAh-EE**.PAh, FRАh-EE, GAh-EE or PRᴿAhs, AHZˢ, **DAh**.PAh, FRАh, GAh	

Key Words	Detailed American English Accent IPA	Shift to Rwandan (Kinyarwanda) Accent of English IPA	Key Words Shifts IPA	Your Key Words
	Symbol	Symbol	Symbol	
☞ ch**oi**ce b**oy**s	ɔɪ	ɵi̞	tʃɵi̞s, bɵi̞z	
	OY	ǫ-E̱E̱	CHǫ-E̱E̱S, Bǫ-E̱E̱Zˢ	
☞ g**oa**t s**ew**, g**o**, t**oe**	oʊ̆	o	got̪	
	OH	o	GoT	
m**ou**th t**ow**n	aʊ̆	a̱ʊ̆	ma̱ʊ̆θ, t̪a̱ʊ̆n	
	OW	A̱h-U	MA̱h-Ŭ̱T, TA̱h-Ŭ̱N	

Diphthongs of R Sound Shifts

Note!

On r-coloration

A Rwandan (Kinyarwanda) accent has no r-coloration in diphthongs or triphthongs of R.

Diphthongs and Triphthongs of R Shifts				
<u>Our</u> friends st<u>a</u>rted the <u>fi</u>re n<u>ear</u> <u>your</u> n<u>or</u>th <u>or</u>chard an h<u>our</u> bef<u>ore</u> we got th<u>ere</u>.				
IPA:	a fɹenz 'sta.tɪd ða 'fa.jə niːə jɔ nɔːθ 'ɔ.tʃɜd an 'a.wə bɪ'fɔː wi got ðeə			
SYMBOLS:	Ah FReNZˢ STAh.TĬD THAh **Fah**.Yuh NĒE-UH Y>AW< N>ĀW<th >AW<.CHUHᴿD AhN **Ah**.Wuh BEE.**F>AW<** WEE GoT THe-UH			
Key Words	Detailed American English Accent IPA Symbol	Shift to Rwandan (Kinyarwanda) Accent of English IPA Symbol	Key Words Shifts IPA Symbol	Your Key Words
⊷ n<u>ear</u> b<u>ee</u>r	ɪɝ EAR	iːə ĒE-UH	niːə, biːə NĒE-UH, BĒE-UH	
h<u>air</u> st<u>are</u>, p<u>ear</u>, squ<u>are</u>, th<u>ere</u>	ɛɝ AIR	eə e-UH	skweə SKWe-UH	
s<u>ure</u> p<u>oor</u>, y<u>our</u>	ʊɝ UR	ʊə OŎ-uh	ʃʊə SHOŎ-uh	

Key Words	Detailed American English Accent	Shift to Rwandan (Kinyarwanda) Accent of English	Key Words Shifts	Your Key Words
	IPA	*IPA*	*IPA*	
	Symbol	*Symbol*	*Symbol*	
↦ n<u>or</u>th G<u>eor</u>ge, p<u>our</u>, w<u>ar</u>p, <u>oar</u>	ɔ˞	ɔː	nɔ̰ːθ, dʒɔːdʒ, pɔ̥ː, wɔːp̥	
	AWR	>A͞W<	N>A͞W<th, J>A͞W<Jᶜᴴ, P>A͞W<, W>A͞W<P	
↦ st<u>art</u> h<u>ear</u>t	ɑ˞	<u>a</u>	s̰t<u>a</u>t̰, h<u>a</u>t̰	
	AHR	A͟h	STA͟hT, HA͟hT	
f<u>ire</u>	aɪ˞	[a.jə] or [aɪə]	ˈfa.jə, faɪə	
	EYER	[Ah.Yuh] or [EYE-uh]	**FA͟h**.Yuh, FEYE-uh	
h<u>our</u>	aʊ˞	[a.wə] or [a]	a.wə or <u>a</u>	
	OWR	[Ah.Wuh] or [A͟h]	**Ah**-Wuh, A͟h	

Key Sentences for Practice

Note!
- By practicing the sentences below, you can work through the sound shifts for a Rwandan (Kinyarwanda) accent in the context of a simple thought. I suggest you think, imagine and speak actively from a point of view. As you begin to work with the operative words in the thoughts, the rhythm and melody of the accent will begin to emerge appropriately.
- Note that less significant words are often unstressed, and articulation of vowels and diphthongs in these words may move toward the neutral *schwa* [ə]/[uh].

Consonants:

- **Example:** Belize (Part 3) – 0:04

I always love kids.

IPA: aɪ ˈɔ-ɤ.weẓ ɾɜy kɪḏẓ

SYMBOLS: Ah-EE̱ >**AW**<-<**o**>.WeZ^S R^RUH^RV^F KE̱E̱DZ^S

- **Example:** Belize (Part 3) – 3:14

Everybody I give everything they want.

IPA: ˈev.rɪ̱.bo.ḏi a gi̱v ev.rɪ̱.tin̯ ḏe^i wą̱nṯ

SYMBOLS: e**V**.R^RE̱E̱.Bo.DE̱E̱ Ah GE̱E̱V e**V**.R^RE̱E̱.TE̱E̱NG De^EE WA̱ɟNT

- *I'll meet you at the ferry in an hour with the ten children.*

  IPA: a'ɤ miʧ‿jʉ ɑt ḓa 'fe.ɾi i̱n an 'a.wə wi̱t ḓa ten tʃi̱ɹ.dɾen

  SYMBOLS: Ah<oo> MEET^{CH}‿Y>OO< A̱HT DAh Fe.R^{R}EE E̱EN AhN
  Ah.Wuh WE̱ET DAh TeN **CHE̱ER**.DR^{R}eN

Front Vowels: Vowels made by arching or cupping the front of the tongue toward the front of the hard palate.

- *The thief will tell me after we trap him.*

  IPA: ḓa θif wi̱ɤ teɫ mi 'ɑf.ta wi tɾɑp hi̱m

  SYMBOLS: THAh thE̱EF WEE-<OO> TeḺ MEE̱ A̱HF.TAh WEE̱ TR^{R}A̱HP
  HE̱EM

Middle Vowels: Vowels made by arching or cupping the middle of the tongue toward the middle of the hard palate.

- *In the summer, workers burned the underbrush.*

  IPA: i̱n ḓa 'sɜ.ma 'wə.kaẕ bənḓ ḓi̱ 'ɜn.'ḓa.bɾɜʃ

  SYMBOLS: E̱EN THAh **SUH^{R}**.MAh **W>UH^{R}**<.KAhZ^{S} B>UH^{R}<ND THE̱E
  UH^{R}N.DAh.BR^{R}UH^{R}SH

Back Vowels: Vowels made by arching or cupping the back of the tongue toward the back of the hard palate.

- *I thought my father would not stop being a bully but the truth is, I was wrong.*

  IPA: ai̱ tɔ̱t mai̱ 'fɑ̱.da wu̱ḓ noṯ stop bi̱ŋ a 'bu̱.li bɜṯ da tɹ̱ut i̱z ai̱ wɑ̱z
  ɹ̱ɔŋ

  SYMBOLS: Ah-E̱E T>AW<T MAh-E̱E **FA̱H**.DAh W>O͞O<D NoT SToP
  BEENG Ah **B>O͞O**<.LEE̱ BUH^{R}T DAh TṞ>OO<T E̱EZ^{S} Ah-E̱E
  WA̱HZ^{S} R>AW<NG

Diphthongs: When two vowels are combined in one syllable.

- *I'd like to fly away someday and go south to the mountains with the boys.*

  IPA: aḓ lai̱k tʉ fɹ̱ai̱ a'wei̱ 'sɜm.deː ãn go saʊ̯θ tʉ ḓa 'maʊ̯n.ti̱nz wi̱θ
  ḓa bei̱ẕ

  SYMBOLS: AhD LAh-E̱EK T>OO< FṞAh-E̱E Ah-**We-E̱E SUH^{R}**M.Dē *Ah*N
  Go SA̱h-Ŭth T>O͞O< THAh **MA̱h-ŬN**.TI̱NZ^{S} WE̱Eth THAh
  Bǫ-E̱EZ^{S}

Diphthongs of R: A diphthong in which the second vowel is rhotic (e.g., has r-coloration in the final sound).

Example: near → nɪɚ/NEAR

Triphthongs of R: A combination of three vowel sounds, in which the third vowel is rhotic.

Example: fire → faɪɚ/FEYER

- ***O͟ur friends sta͟rted the fi͟re ne͟ar y͟our no͟rth o͟rchard an ho͟ur befo͟re we got th͟ere.***

  IPA: a̠ f̪ɹenz̠ ˈsta̠.tɪ̠d ð̠a ˈfa.jə niːə̠ jɔ̜ nɔ̜ːθ ˈɔ.t̠ʃɜd an ˈa.wə bɪ̠ˈfɔː wi̠
             got̠ ð̠eə̠

  SYMBOLS: A͟h FR̠eNZˢ **STAh.TɪD** THAh **FAh**.Yuh NE͞E-U͟H Y>AW<
             N>A͞W<th >**AW<**.CHUHᴿD AhN **Ah**.Wuh BE͟E.**F>AW<** WE͟E
             GoT̠ THe-U͟H

206

Making Your Own Map of the Accent

Listen to the Rwandan (Kinyarwanda) accent samples provided and investigate the resources suggested in the *Introduction and Resources* section. Compose (or steal) *Key Phrases* from your listening/viewing that challenge and/or ground you in the accent. Then get more specific and check your sounds against the sounds in the Workbook.

Your take on the sound shifts may be slightly different. That is okay. The breakdown is a tool, not a rule. Recheck what you hear and, if you still stand behind your discoveries, go with them. This will help you to develop **your own** idiolect of the accent.

> *Note!*
> **What is an Idiolect?**
> Each of us speaks differently even if we have the same general accent. The individualized way that each of us speaks is referred to as an idiolect. For the actor, idiolect is part of what creates character. It is the "how" of the accent, and influences the way we craft our thoughts through language.

KEY PHRASES

Speak your *Key Phrases*, shifting back and forth between your own home *idiolect of English* and the *Rwandan (Kinyarwanda) accent* you are building. **Observe** the shifts <u>ONE by ONE</u> in your Articulators, Focus of Articulation, use of Melody/Pitch/Lilt, Rhythm/Stress/Pace, and Source & Path of Resonance as you shift back and forth between the two accents. Make note of the shifts in the table provided. Putting your understanding of the shifts into your <u>own words</u> will encourage you to develop a more clear and personal idiolect.

RWANDAN (KINYARWANDA) ACCENT *KEY POINTS OF FOCUS: VOCAL POSTURE AND CHARACTERISTICS*

JAW
LIPS
TONGUE
SOFT PALATE
PHARYNX

FOCUS OF ARTICULATION (TOWARDS TEETH, FRONT/MIDDLE/ BACK OF HARD PALATE, SOFT PALATE, ETC.)

MELODY/PITCH/LILT

RHYTHM/STRESS/PACE

SOURCE & PATH OF RESONANCE – Where does the resonance begin and what is the apparent path it travels through your body (chest, hard palate, sinuses, temples, crown, base of skull, etc.)? Refer to the Source & Path of Resonance and Resonators in the *Rwandan (Kinyarwanda) Accent of English: Down & Dirty Warm-Up and Quick Look* on page 181.

OTHER CHARACTERISTICS (What are your observations?)

PERSONAL IMAGES (For many actors personal images can be the most powerful and effective triggers for their transformation into an accent)

Chapter 8

DR Congolese (Lingala) Accent of English

Introduction and Resources

The Lingala Language in DR Congo

The word 'Lingala' means *language of the Bangala* (people of the river). Its mother language is Bobangi, a Bantu language of the Benue-Congo branch of the Niger-Congo family.

Lingala began as a creole language of necessity for the Belgian colonizers and missionaries in the 19th century, and quickly developed into a full blown language with basic Bantu language structure. It is a tonal language which, along with the French language spoken in DR Congo, results in an accent that is rich in musical variety.

Although French is the official language of DR Congo, over ten million people speak Lingala. It is considered the language of culture and urban life.

Documentaries

Kinshasa Symphony, The Forgotten Children of Congo (English documentary with Lingala speakers), *On the Rumba River, The Importance of Being Elegant, Benda Bilili!, Victoire Terminus Kinshasa, Back to the South, 35 Cows and a Kalashnikov, Pygmée Blues, Le Voyage de Lomama*

Films

Kinshasa Kids, Lopango, War Witch, Vivi Riva, Lumumba (English with Lingala-speaking characters)

Plays with DR Congolese (Lingala) Characters

Ruined by Lynn Nottage

Music

Lopango Ya Banka, Franco Makiadi and TPOK Jazz

Radio

Radio Bendele

Personalities

Faidam Mitifu (Ambassador DRC), Zacharie Babaswé (journalist), Dikembe Mutombo (NBA basketball player), Muteba Kidiaba (footballer), Faustin Linyekula (dancer and choreographer), Modeste Mutinga (Senator of the DR Congo and journalist)

Down & Dirty Warm-up and Quick Look

> *Note!*
>
> **On Symbols**
> - International Phonetic Alphabet Symbols will be listed first and Sound Symbols will be listed second. Example: [i]/[EE]
> - Sound Symbol Users: bold-faced letters indicate the syllable is stressed.

1) **The Muscles:** Wake your mouth up so you can more easily discover the physical transformation in speaking the accent.

   a. Scratch the front, middle and back of your tongue with your front top teeth.

   b. Rub the front, middle and back of your hard palate with the tip of your tongue.

   c. Imagine your mouth is numb from being at the dentist and you want to wake it up. Make tongue circles pressing against the back of your lips first clockwise, then counter clockwise (you are waking up your orbicularis muscle).

   d. To get the breath flowing, blow through your lips, getting them to flap together. Travel up and down in pitch on a BBBB and PPP, feeling the vibration as you wiggle up and down your spine.

2) **Vocal Posture for a DR Congolese (Lingala) Accent:** The jaw is easy in its action but does not open very widely; this leaves the tongue and lips to lead in articulation. The lips are gently active in rounding both consonant and vowel sounds. The front of the tongue rests low and the blade rests behind the bottom front teeth. The middle of the tongue is slightly lifted and bunched. The root is gently retracted and the back of the tongue feels as if it falls down and back toward the throat. The pharynx is somewhat narrowed which creates pharyngeal twang in the accent. The soft palate is raised, which contributes in making the accent hypo-nasal. The focus of articulation is on the middle front of the hard palate.

3) **Resonators:** "occupy" the following spaces. This will prepare you to find the Source & Path of Resonance for a DR Congolese (Lingala) accent. (By "occupy", I mean just that; be in the space of it and find the pathway and flow of resonance, rather than "putting" the resonance there.)

    a.   CHEST – Generously laugh at something – hɑ hɑ hɑ / HAH HAH HAH

    b.   HARD PALATE – As if you were discovering something – ho ho ho / Ho Ho Ho

    c.   THE BONES AT THE BASE OF YOUR SKULL (THE OCCIPITAL BONE) – Use your hands to scoop the sound from the base of your skull with a Mississippi African-American dialect as if you're flirting with someone nearby – he^i he^i he^i / He^{EE} He^{EE} He^{EE}

    d.   FLICK THE SOUND OUT OF YOUR CHEEKBONES with an Italian-American flourish, as if calling to someone across the street – he^i he^i he^i / He^{EE} He^{EE} He^{EE}

    e.   WITH YOUR HANDS NEXT TO YOUR TEMPLES, SHAKE THE SOUND OUT WITH LOOSE FISTS – As if you were somewhat crazed – ji̱ ji̱ ji̱ / YEE YEE YEE

    f.   IMAGINE A METAL DISK EXTENDING FROM YOUR HANDS THROUGH YOUR SKULL. Bring your hands to the sides of your head just above the temples, with your palms facing the floor, thumbs hooked behind your skull. *Lid* the vibration to create a muted brassy sound. Like a robot saying "Hi" – hai hai hai / HAh-EE HAh-EE HAh-EE

    g.   GIGGLE OUT OF THE TOP OF YOUR HEAD – As if you were tickled pink by something – hi̱ hi̱ hi̱ / HEE HEE HEE

4) **Source & Path of Resonance for a DR Congolese (Lingala) Accent:**
Starting with strong vibration in the chest, the resonance comes up through a slightly narrowed pharynx. The soft palate can be more or less lifted, depending on the speaker, but normally the sound travels fully into the middle of the hard palate, and then comes up into the sinuses and is lidded at the *metal disk* area at the temples (#3f above). For some speakers, the resonance will be lidded in the sinuses. The accent has a fair amount of hypo-nasality.

5) **Get the sound changes into your body and imagination.**
Say these phrases occupying the following places in your body, suggesting to yourself the following energetic associations:

• pubic bone to tail bone – survival instinct

    zu̱ / Z>OO<
    I need it – ai ni̯d ɪt / Ah-EE N*EE*D E̱̱ET

• pubic bone to navel & sacrum in back – sexuality, big feelings

    wo / Wo
    I desire it – ai di'za.ju̯ɟ_ɪt / Ah-EE DEE.**ZAh**.YR^W_E̱̱ET

- rib cage to below heart – will

  ʒɔ / ZHAW
  I want it – ai wãnt ɪt̪ / Ah-EE W*AH*NT E͜ET

- heart – love

  mɑ / MAH
  I love it – ai lɜv ɪt̪ / Ah-EE LUH^RV E͜ET

- throat – communication (think of talking at a party)

  bɑ̟ / BA̱H
  I have to say it – ai haɤ t̪u se^i ɪt̪ / Ah-EE HAV^F T>OO< Se^EE E͜ET

- forehead – intelligence/wisdom

  ke^i / Ke^EE
  I know it – ai no ɪt̪ / Ah-EE NO E͜ET

- crown of head – spirituality

  ɹi: / R͟E͜E
  I believe it – ai bi.lïv ɪt̪ / Ah-EE BEE.LEEV E͜ET

6) **Articulation** – using playful physical actions: punching, flicking, dabbing, slashing

  d̪u d̪ɪ ku d̪u d̪ɪ ku d̪u d̪ɪ ku – d̪i
  d̪u d̪ɪ ku d̪u d̪ɪ ku d̪u d̪ɪ ku – d̪e^i
  d̪u d̪ɪ ku d̪u d̪ɪ ku d̪u d̪ɪ ku – d̪ai
  d̪u d̪ɪ ku d̪u d̪ɪ ku d̪u d̪ɪ ku – d̪o
  d̪u d̪ɪ ku d̪u d̪ɪ ku d̪u d̪ɪ ku – d̪u

  Repeat as needed, replacing [d̪] with [t̪], [p], [b], [k], [g], [f], [v]

D>OO< DE͟E K>OO< D>OO< DE͟E K>OO< D>OO< DE͟E K>OO< – DEE
D>OO< DE͟E K>OO< D>OO< DE͟E K>OO< D>OO< DE͟E K>OO< – De^EE
D>OO< DE͟E K>OO< D>OO< DE͟E K>OO< D>OO< DE͟E K>OO< – DAh-EE
D>OO< DE͟E K>OO< D>OO< DE͟E K>OO< D>OO< DE͟E K>OO< – Do
D>OO< DE͟E K>OO< D>OO< DE͟E K>OO< D>OO< DE͟E K>OO< – D>OO<

Repeat as needed, replacing [D] with [T], [P], [B], [K], [G], [F], [V].
[D] & [T] are both articulated with the blade of the tongue against the back
of the top front teeth (dentalized).

Key Points of Focus
Characteristics and Vocal Posture

DR Congolese (Lingala) Accent Characteristics

Note!
On Melody/Lilt/Pitch and Rhythm/Stress/Pace
Every accent contains shifts for some, but not necessarily all, of these
elements of vocal variety.

Note!
On Use of Musical Notes
Follow the "musical notes" up and down to get a feel for the melody of
the accent. The filled-in notes are shorter than the open notes. For those
who are musically inclined, think of them as approximating quarter notes
and half notes. This distinction will give you a feel for the rhythm of the
accent.

Melody/Lilt/Pitch

1. Lingala has two tones: high and low. This manifests in a significant amount
    of up and down pitch variation in the accent.
2. In two-syllable words, the first syllable is raised or dropped in pitch and
    often the interval in pitch change is minor. This is a carryover from the
    French language, which is full of minor intervals between syllables as well
    as between words. When the first syllable is lifted, the second syllable
    is often dropped in pitch and sometimes the drop is quite dramatic. DR
    Congolese (Lingala) speakers who speak a lot of French will reflect this
    characteristic most clearly.
3. Operative words are lengthened, lilted, and either lifted or dropped in pitch.
4. The words at the ends of thoughts normally drop in pitch.

Example: Mimi Story (Part 2) – 1:30

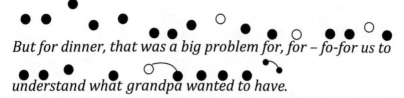

But for dinner, that was a big problem for, for – fo-for us to

understand what grandpa wanted to have.

Notice the lovely little bounces in pitch, which create a lively melody in Mimi's thought above. In her two-syllable operative words *dinner*, *problem*, and *grandpa*, she lifts the pitch on a minor interval in the first syllable of each word (#2, p. 216). In *grandpa* and *problem* she also lengthens the first syllable (#3, p. 216). Mimi lifts her pitch on the final word *have* and lilts down in conclusion of her thought (#3 and #4, p. 216).

Example: Faustin Story (Part 1) – 0:02

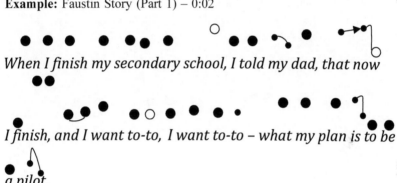

When I finish my secondary school, I told my dad, that now

I finish, and I want to-to, I want to-to – what my plan is to be

a pilot.

You can hear the careful positioning of words Faustin used to speak to his father as a young man, still present in his speech now as a grown man. He emphasizes the operative word *school* through pitch and length, and the operative word *finish*, through pitch (#3, p. 216). His lilts in *now*, *is*, and *pilot* have a significant up and down bounce (#1, p. 216). He concludes his thought with a drop in pitch in the final syllable of *pilot* (#4, p. 216).

Rhythm/Stress/Pace

1. This accent has a quick, light, flicking quality with little jagged bounces in pitch.
2. Because there is a pretty steady, even rhythm, the pace can become quite rapid.
3. When pitch change does not stress the operative words, there is a change in the length of words or syllables. But often, when words or syllables are lengthened, there is a pitch change as well. Ultimately, change in pitch is more frequently used as the expressive element. In Lingala, the rhythm is

pretty steady and even, with only occasional lengthening of a syllable or word. You will hear this when you listen to Bibiche, Mimi, Rose and Pierre speak in Lingala in the accent library.

Example: Bibiche Story (Part 1) – 2:42

So we had to cross the whole compound, running like crazy,

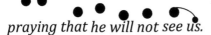

praying that he will not see us.

Bibiche lengthens the first syllables of her operative words _compound_, _running_, _crazy_, and like many speakers, links the lengthening to a lift in pitch. Her operative word _cross_ is also lengthened (#3, p. 217). You can hear the influence of her living in America because her pace is not as rapid as some of the other speakers and the slowing down mutes some of the light, flicking quality of the accent (#1 and #2, p. 217).

Example: Herman Story – 0:31

Suddenly, somebody came out of this forest, wearing

only a shirt.

The quick, light, flicking rhythm of this accent lends itself to Herman's suspenseful little story (#1, p. 217). His steadiness in rhythm makes his pace become quite rapid (#2, p. 217). The only operative word he lengthens – the ominous word, _forest_ – he lengthens in French fashion, on the second syllable (#3, p. 217). He uses melody and pitch in telling his story much more than he does stress, lilt or rhythm.

Source & Path of Resonance

Starting with strong vibration in the chest, the resonance comes up through a slightly narrowed pharynx. The soft palate can be more or less lifted, depending on the speaker, but normally the sound travels fully into the middle of the hard palate, comes up into the sinuses and is lidded at the *metal disk* area at the temples (#3f on page 214). You can hear this very clearly in Rose, Mimi, Johan, Herman and Pierre. Faustin, Bibiche and Mimi have less "brassiness" in their voices; their resonance lids more consistently in the sinuses. All of the speakers have a fair amount of hypo-nasality.

DR Congolese (Lingala) Accent Vocal Posture

> *Note!*
> **On Vocal Posture**
> These adjustments enable you to integrate the accent through physical transformation rather than solely relying on sound shifts.

- **Focus of Articulation:** The tongue and lips lead in articulation. The focus of the articulation is on the middle front of the hard palate.
- **Tongue:** The front of the tongue rests low and the blade rests behind the bottom front teeth. The middle of the tongue is slightly lifted and bunched. The root is gently retracted and the back of the tongue feels as if it falls down and back toward the throat.
- **Lips:** The lips are gently active in rounding both consonant and vowel sounds.
- **Jaw:** The jaw is easy in its action, but does not open very widely.
- **Soft Palate:** The soft palate is raised, which contributes in making the accent hypo-nasal.
- **Pharynx:** The pharynx is somewhat narrowed, which creates the pharyngeal twang in the accent.

Distinct Sounds of the Language and/or Accent

> *Note!*
>
> **On Distinct Sounds**
>
> These are some of the sounds that DR Congolese (Lingala) speakers use and American speakers do not. In speaking the sounds and/or the words that contain them, you can heighten your physical understanding of the DR Congolese (Lingala) accent's *Vocal Posture* as compared to your own. This frame of reference will both inform and strengthen your accent.

Consonants

1. *IPA:* [ɲ] → Palatal nasal.
   Symbol: [NGʸ] → [NG]. Made on the hard palate with a little [ʸ] following. Used in place of [ŋ]/[NG]: *sing*
   This sound is used in speaking both the language and accent of DR Congolese (Lingala).
2. *IPA:* [ɰ] → velar approximant.
   Symbol: [Rᵂ] → [R] made on the soft palate.
   Used in place of [ɹ]/[R] in the middle of a word: *merry, sorry* or in a diphthong of R: *hear*
   This sound is used in speaking a DR Congolese (Lingala) accent of English.
3. *IPA:* [ɣ]: voiced velar fricative.
   Symbol: [Rᴳᴴᴴ] made by vibrating the back of the tongue against the soft palate.
   Used in diphthongs of R: *near*
   This sound is used in speaking both the language and accent of DR Congolese (Lingala).
4. *IPA:* [gb] → labio-velar plosive.
   Symbol: [GB] → Make a [G] with your lips ready to make a [B] and release the sound.
   This sound is used in speaking the DR Congolese (Lingala) language.

Pre-nasalized Consonants

5. *IPA:* [^{m}b], [^{n}k], [^{n}g], [^{n}ʒ]
    Symbol: [^{M}B], [^{NG}K], [^{N}G], [^{N}ZH]
    Although these consonants are used only in the Lingala language, there is
      a slight nasality that carries over into the vowels of the accent when they
      precede or follow a nasal consonant.
    These sounds are used in speaking the DR Congolese (Lingala) language.

Vowels

The vowels of the Lingala language include:

  IPA: [i], [e], [ɛ], [a], [u], [o], [ɔ]
  Symbol: [EE], [e], [EH], [Ah], [u], [o], [AW]

Knowing the vowels for the Lingala language will provide clues for the vowel
shifts in the DR Congolese (Lingala) accent.

6. *IPA:* [e]
    Symbol: [e] → This is the first sound in the D.A.E. diphthong [AY] as in *face*.
    Used in place of [ɛ]/[Eh]: *dr<u>e</u>ss*, *b<u>e</u>d*
    This sound is used in speaking both the language and accent of DR Congo-
      lese (Lingala).
7. *IPA:* [a]
    Symbol: [Ah] → This is the first sound in the D.A.E. diphthong [EYE].
    Used in place of [æ]/[A]: *tr<u>a</u>p*, *b<u>a</u>th*
    This sound is used in speaking both the language and accent of DR Congo-
      lese (Lingala).
8. *IPA:* [o]
    Symbol: [o]. This is the first sound in the D.A.E. diphthong [OH].
    Used in place of [oʊ]/[OH]: *g<u>o</u>at*, *s<u>ew</u>*
    This sound is used in speaking both the language and accent of DR Congo-
      lese (Lingala).

Consonant Sound Shifts

- ↤ indicates that this sound is a key sound shift
- You can begin to fold melody and rhythm with the sound changes by speaking the sample sentences that are before each section of sound changes.

> **Note!**
> **On Consonant Clusters**
> Often when a consonant cluster ends a word, the final consonant is dropped.
>
> Example: stand → stan

Consonant Shifts

Example: Mimi Story (Part 2) – 0:52

For lu*nch* you ha*v*e you*r* fufu your *r*i*c*e you*r* mea*ts* your

v*eg*etab*l*e.

IPA: fɔɰ lə̃ʃ jʉ haɣ jɔ fʉfʉ jɔ‿ɰais jɔ mĩ̪ts jɔ veʒ.tə.bə̪ɫ

SYMBOLS: FA*WR*ᵂ L>*UH*ᴿ<SH Y>OO< HAhVᶠ YAW F>OO<.F>OO<
         YAW_RᵂAh-EES YAW M*EE*TS YAW VeZH.Tuh.B*uh*L

And *th*en a*r*ound *s*even P. M. you will ha*v*e you*r r*i*c*e and bean*s* or

you wi*ll* ha*v*e again mi*l*k a*nd* b*r*ead.

IPA: ẽn ðẽːn eⁱ.ɰaũnd̪ ˈse.ven pi̪ ẽm jʉ wi̪ɫ haɣ jɔ‿ɰais ãn bĩ̪nz oɰ jʉ haɣ
         e.gẽn mɪɾk ãn bʉɰed̪

SYMBOLS: *e*N Th*e*N *e*ᴱᴱ.RᵂAh-*OO*ND Se.VeN PEE *em* Y>OO< W*EE*L HAhVᶠ
         YAW_RᵂAh-EES *Ah*N B*EE*NZˢ oRᵂ Y>OO< HAhVᶠ e.G*EH*N
         M*EE*-<o>K *Ah*N BRᵂEHD

I'*ll* mee*t*_you at *th*e *f*erry in an hour wi*th* *th*e *t*en *ch*il*dr*en.

IPA: aɪ mĩ̪t̚‿ʉ at̪ ðə fe.ɰi ĩn ãɣ wi̪θ ðə t̪ẽn ˈtʃĩɾ.d̪i̪ẽⁿ

SYMBOLS: Ah-EE-<o> MEETᶜᴴ_>OO< AhT THuh Fe.RᵂEE *EEN Ah*N AHRᴳᴴᴴ
         W*EE*th THuh Te*N* **CH*EE*-<o>**.DR*e*ᴺ

Key Words	Detailed American English Accent IPA ------------------ Symbol	Shift to DR Congolese (Lingala) Accent of English IPA ------------------ Symbol	Key Words Shifts IPA ------------------ Symbol	Your Key Words
⊷ team debt, did	[t]/[d] ------------------ [T]/[D]	[t̪]/[d̪] ------------------ [T]/[D] both dentalized	t̪im, det̪, d̪id̪ ------------------ TEEM, DeT, DĒED	
⊷ these there, breathe	ð ------------------ TH	[ð̪] or [d̪] ------------------ [TH] or [D] both dentalized	ð̪iz, ð̪eə, bɹu̯ið̪ or d̪iz, d̪eə, bɹu̯id̪ ------------------ THEEZˢ, THe-uh, BRᵂEETH or DEEZˢ, De-uh, BRᵂEED	
⊷ thin thick, mouth	θ ------------------ th	[θ̪] or [t̪] ------------------ [th] or [T] both dentalized	θ̪in, θ̪ɪk, mau̯θ̪ or t̪in, t̪ɪk, mau̯t̪ ------------------ thEEN, thĒEK, MAh-OOth or TEEN, TĒEK, MAh-OOT	
mouth (final *th* in spelling)	θ ------------------ th	sometimes [f] ------------------ sometimes [F]	mau̯f ------------------ MAh-OOF	
⊷ red dress (*r* at the beginning of a word)	ɹ ------------------ R	[ɹ̪] or [u̯] ------------------ [R̪] or [R̪ᵂ]	ɹ̪ed, dɹ̪es or u̯ed̪, du̯es ------------------ R̪eD, DR̪eS or R̪ᵂeD, DR̪ᵂeS	
⊷ merry sorry (*r* in the middle of a word)	ɹ ------------------ R	[u̯] or [ɹ̪] ------------------ [R̪ᵂ] or [R̪]	me.u̯i, sa.u̯i or me.ɹ̪i, sa.ɹ̪i ------------------ Me.R̪ᵂEE, SAH.R̪ᵂEE or Me.R̪EE, SAH.R̪EE	
⊷ excel fall, table (final *l* in spelling)	l ------------------ L	[ɤ] or [ɫ] ------------------ [<o>] or [L̪]	ek.seɤ, fɔɤ, te̍i.bɤ or ek.seɫ, fɔɫ, te̍i.bəɫ ------------------ eK.Se-<o>, F>AW<-<o>, TeᴱᴱB<o> or eK.SeL̪, F>AW<L̪, TeᴱᴱBuhL̪	

Key Words	Detailed American English Accent IPA ---------- Symbol	Shift to DR Congolese (Lingala) Accent of English IPA ---------- Symbol	Key Words Shifts IPA ---------- Symbol	Your Key Words
ju**dge**	dʒ ---------- J	[dʒ] or [ʒ] ---------- [J^CH] or [ZH]	dʒ₃dʒ or dʒ₃ʒ JUH^RJ^CH or JUH^RZH	
chur**ch** (*ch* at the end of a word)	tʃ ---------- CH	sometimes [ʃ] ---------- sometimes [SH]	t̪ʃəʃ CH>UH^R<SH	
see gue**ss**	[s̪] ---------- [S]	[s̪] ---------- [S] dentalized	s̪i, ges̪ SEE, GeS	
☛ boy**s** (final *s* in spelling when pronounced [z])	z ---------- Z	z̪ ---------- [Z^S] dentalized	boiz̪ Bo-EEZ^S	
lo**v**e (final *v* in spelling)	v ---------- V	v̥ ---------- V^F	lɑv̥ LAHV^F	
si**ng** (final *ng* in spelling)	ŋ ---------- NG	sometimes ŋ̊ ---------- sometimes NG^K	sĩŋ̊ SEENG^K	
readi**ng** (final *ing* in spelling)	ɪŋ ---------- ING	sometimes [iŋ^g] ---------- sometimes [EENG^G]	ɰi.d̃ĩŋ^g R^WEE.DEENG^G	
si**ng**ing (penultimate *ng* in spelling)	ŋ ---------- NG	sometimes ŋ.g ---------- sometimes NG.G	sĩŋ.gĩŋ SEENG.GEENG	

Vowel and Diphthong Sound Shift Notes!

Note!

On Vowels

The vowels of the Lingala language include:

IPA: [i], [e], [ɛ], [a], [u], [o], [ɔ]
SYMBOLS: [EE], [e], [EH], [Ah], [u], [o], [AW]

Knowing the vowels for the Lingala language will provide clues for the vowel shifts in the DR Congolese (Lingala) accent.

Note!

On Vowels and Diphthongs

When vowels or diphthongs precede or follow an [m]/[M], [n]/[N], or [ŋ]/[NG], they are nasalized.

Example: M̠im̠i, wro̠ng, a̠nswer

Notation for nasalized vowels → [ị̃]/[*EE*], [ɔ̃]/[*o*], [ą̃]/[*A̧H*]

Front Vowel Sound Shifts

Front Vowel Shifts				
The th*ie*f w*i*ll t*e*ll m*e* *a*fter w*e* tr*a*p h*i*m.				
IPA: ðə t̪if wɪɹ t̪eɫ mĩ ɑf.t̪ə wi t̪ɰap ĩm				
SYMBOLS: Duh TEEF WĒE-<o> TeL MEE A̧HF.Tu̲h WEE TRᵂAhP ĒEM				
Key Words	*Detailed American English Accent* *IPA* ------------------- *Symbol*	*Shift to DR Congolese (Lingala) Accent of English* *IPA* ------------------- *Symbol*	*Key Words Shifts* *IPA* ------------------- *Symbol*	*Your Key Words*
fl*ee*ce sn*ee*ze, pl*ea*d	i ------------------- EE	i̧ ------------------- EE	fliş ------------------- FLEES	
↦ k*i*t p*i*tch, d*i*m, l*i*p	ɪ ------------------- I	ɪ̧ ------------------- ĒE	kɪt̪, pɪt̪ʃ, d̪ĩm ------------------- KĒET, PĒECH, DĒEM	
countr*y* (*y* in final position of spelling)	ɪ̧ ------------------- ĒE	i ------------------- EE	kə̃n.t̪u̧i ------------------- KUHᴿN.TRᵂEE	
b*e*rated	[ɪ] in prefix ------------------- [ĒE] in prefix	i ------------------- EE	bi'ɹeⁱ.t̪ɪd ------------------- BEE.**Re̲**ᴱᴱ.TĒED	

Key Words	Detailed American English Accent	Shift to DR Congolese (Lingala) Accent of English	Key Words Shifts	Your Key Words
	IPA	*IPA*	*IPA*	
	Symbol	*Symbol*	*Symbol*	
dr<u>e</u>ss b<u>e</u>d, f<u>ea</u>ther, s<u>e</u>nd	ε	[e] or [ε]	dɹ̣e̩s, be̩d, fe.d̥ə or dɹ̣ε̩s, bε̣d, fε.d̥ə	
	EH	[e] or [EH]	DR^WeS, BeD, Fe.D<u>uh</u> or DR^WEHS, BEHD, FEH.D<u>uh</u>	
☛ tr<u>a</u>p m<u>a</u>d, r<u>a</u>t, c<u>a</u>ndle	æ	a	tɹ̣ap, mad̥, ɹ̣at̥	
	A	Ah	TR^WAhP, MAhD, R^WAhT	
☛ b<u>a</u>th *[a]/[Ah] <u>a</u>sk, <u>a</u>fter, d<u>a</u>nce, ex<u>a</u>mple, h<u>a</u>lf, m<u>a</u>sk, r<u>a</u>scal, tr<u>a</u>nsfer	æ	ɑ̟	bɑ̟θ, ɑ̟sk, ɑ̟f.t̥ə	
	A	AH	BAHth, AHSK, AHF.T<u>uh</u>	
In Chapter 1, there is a list of these words called the BATH or ASK list of words.				

Middle Vowel Sound Shifts

<table>
<tr><td colspan="5" align="center">Middle Vowel Shifts</td></tr>
<tr><td colspan="5">

In the summer, workers burned the underbrush.

With r-coloration: this is a DR Congolese (Lingala) accent that has a strong French influence:

IPA: ĩn də s̰ɜ.m̰ə̰ w̰ə̰.kə̰z b̰ə̰nd̰ də ɜn'd̰ɜ̰.bɥɜʃ

SYMBOLS: *EÉN* Duh S*UH*.M*er* W>U̲H̲R̲<.K*er*Z^S B>*U̲H̲R̲*<ND Duh U̲H̲^R̲N.**DUHR**.BR^WUH^RSH

Without r-coloration: this is a DR Congolese (Lingala) accent with a weak French influence:

IPA: ĩn də s̰ɑ.m̰ə̰ w̰ə.kə̰z b̰ə̰nd̰ də ɑ̰n.d̰ɜ.bɪ̰ɑ̰ʃ

SYMBOLS: *EÉN* Duh SA̰H.M*uh* W>U̲H̲^R<.K*uh*Z^S B>*U̲H̲R̲*<ND Duh A̰HN.**DU̲H̲^R̲**.BR̰A̰HSH

</td></tr>
<tr>
<td>Key Words</td>
<td>Detailed American English Accent

IPA

Symbol</td>
<td>Shift to DR Congolese (Lingala) Accent of English
IPA

Symbol</td>
<td>Key Words Shifts

IPA

Symbol</td>
<td>Your Key Words</td>
</tr>
<tr>
<td>⊷ b<u>ir</u>d
s<u>er</u>vice, l<u>ear</u>n
(ir, er, ear in spelling)</td>
<td>ɝ

ER</td>
<td>[ɜ] or [ɝ]

[UH^R] or [U̲H̲R̲]</td>
<td>bɜd, s̰ɜ.vɪ̰s, lɜn or bɝd, s̰ɜ̰.vɪ̰s, lɝn

BUH^RD, SUH^R.VE̲É̲S, LUH^RN or BU̲H̲RD, SU̲H̲R.VE̲É̲S, LU̲H̲RN</td>
<td></td>
</tr>
<tr>
<td>⊷ n<u>ur</u>se
w<u>or</u>k
(ur, or in spelling)</td>
<td>ɝ

ER</td>
<td>[ə] or [ɚ]

[>UH^R<] or [>U̲H̲R̲<]</td>
<td>nə̰s, wə̰k or nə̰.s, wə̰.k

N>UH^R<S, W>UH^R<K or N>U̲H̲R̲<S, W>U̲H̲R̲<K</td>
<td></td>
</tr>
</table>

Key Words	Detailed American English Accent	Shift to DR Congolese (Lingala) Accent of English	Key Words Shifts	Your Key Words
	IPA	IPA	IPA	
	Symbol	Symbol	Symbol	
sister traitor, hangar	ɚ	[ə] or [ɚ]	sɪs.tə, tɹeⁱ.tə, hãŋ.gə or sɪs.tɚ, tɹeⁱ.tɚ, haŋ.gɚ	
	er	[uh] or [er]	SEES.Tuh, TReᴱᴱ.Tuh, HАhNG.Guh SEES.Ter, TReᴱᴱ.Ter, HАhNG.Ger	
ɝ strut curry	ʌ̈	[ɜ] or [ɑ̟]	stɹɜt, kɜ.ɹi or stɹɑ̟t, kɑ̟.ɹi	
	U̟H	[UHᴿ] or [A̟H]	STRUHᴿT, KUHᴿ.REE or STRA̟HT, KA̟H.REE	
ɝ come, flood (in words spelled with *o* and sometimes *oo*)	ʌ̈	sometimes [ə]	kãm, fləd	
	U̟H	sometimes [>UHᴿ<]	K>UHᴿ<M, FL>UHᴿ<D	
about banana	ə	ə	ə.baut̪, bə.nã.nə	
	uh	uh	uh.BAh-OOT, Buh.NАh.Nuh	

Back Vowel Sound Shifts

	Back Vowel Shifts			
I thought my father would not stop being a bully but the truth is, I was wrong.				
IPA: ai θɔt mai fɑ.ðə̠ wu̠d nõt s̠top bĭŋ ə bu̠.li bɑ̠t ð̠ə tɹu̠θ ɪz ai wɑz ɯ̠ɔ̃ŋ̊				
SYMBOLS: Ah-EE th>AW<T MAh-EE FAH.THu̠h W>OO<D NᴏT SToP BEENG uh B>OO<.LEE BA̱HT THuh TR̠>OO<th E̱EZ^S Ah-EE WAHZ^S R^W>*AW*<NG^K				
Key Words	*Detailed American English Accent* IPA ------------------ *Symbol*	*Shift to DR Congolese (Lingala) Accent of English* IPA ------------------ *Symbol*	*Key Words Shifts* IPA ------------------ *Symbol*	*Your Key Words*
food grew, true, two	u ------------------ OO	u̠ ------------------ >OO<	fu̠d, gɯ̠ɯ̠, tu̠ɯ̠ ------------------ F>OO<D, GR^W>OO<, TR^W>OO<	
news	ɪɯ̠ (only when preceded by *n* in spelling) ------------------ I-O͞O (only when preceded by *n* in spelling)	ju̠ ------------------ Y>OO<	nju̠z̠ ------------------ NY>*OO*<Z^S	
foot put	ʊ ------------------ U	u̠ ------------------ >OO<	fu̠t, pu̠t ------------------ F>OO<T, P>OO<T	
thought tall, caulk, awful	ɔ ------------------ AW	ɔ̠ ------------------ >AW<	θɔ̠t, tɔ̠ɤ, kɔ̠k ------------------ th>AW<T, T>AW<-<o>, K>AW<K	

Key Words	Detailed American English Accent IPA	Shift to DR Congolese (Lingala) Accent of English IPA	Key Words Shifts IPA	Your Key Words
	Symbol	Symbol	Symbol	
cloth *[ɒ]/[O] dog, cough, wash, horrid	ɔ	ǫ	klǫt, dǫg, kǫf, wǫʃ	
	AW	>AW<	KL>AW<T, D>AW<G, K>AW<F, W>AW<SH	
father	ɑ	ɑ	ˈfɑ.də	
	AH	AH	FAH.Duh	
☞ lot *[ɒ]/[O] squad, wander	ɑ	[o] or [ɑ]	lot, skwod, wõn.də or lɑt, skwɑd, wãn.də	
	AH	[o] or [AH]	LoT, SKWod, WoN.Duh or LAHT, SKWAHd, WAHN.Duh	

Diphthong Sound Shifts

Diphthong Shifts				
_I_'d l_i_ke to _fly_ aw_ay_ somed_ay_ and g_o_ s_ou_th to the m_ou_ntains with the b_oys_.				
IPA: aid̪ laik t̪ṳ flai a.weⁱ s̰ə̰m.deⁱ ãn go s̰aṳθ t̪ṳ ð̰ə maṹⁿ.t̠ĩnẕ wᵻθ ð̰ə boiẕ				
SYMBOLS: Ah-EED LAh-EEK T>OO< FLAh-EE Ah.We^{EE} S*UH^R*M.De^{EE} *Ah*N Go SAh->OO<th T>OO< THuh MAh-*OO*^N.T*I*NZ^S WE̱̱Eth THuh Bo-EEZ^S				
Key Words	*Detailed American English Accent* *IPA* ------------ *Symbol*	*Shift to DR Congolese (Lingala) Accent of English* *IPA* ------------ *Symbol*	*Key Words Shifts* *IPA* ------------ *Symbol*	*Your Key Words*
↤ f**a**ce p**ai**n, d**ay**, w**ei**ght, st**ea**k	eɪ ---- AY	eⁱ ---- e^{EE}	feⁱs̰, pẽⁱn, deⁱ, weⁱt̠ ---- Fe^{EE}S, Pe^{EE}N, De^{EE}, We^{EE}T	
pr**i**ce **eye**s, d**ia**per, fl**y**, g**uy**, h**ei**ght	aɪ ---- EYE	ai ---- Ah-EE	p̠ɹais̰, aiẕ, dai.pə̰ ---- PRAh-EES, Ah-EEZ^S, DAh-EE.Pṳh	
ch**oi**ce b**oy**s	ɔɪ ---- OY	oi ---- o-EE	t̠ʃois̰, boiẕ ---- Cho-EES, Bo-EEZ^S	
g**oa**t s**ew**, g**o**, t**oe**	oʊ ---- OH	o ---- o	got̠, s̰o, go ---- GoT, So, Go	
m**ou**th t**ow**n	aʊ ---- OW	au ---- Ah-OO	maṵθ, t̠aṵn ---- MAh-OOth, TAh-*OO*N	

Diphthongs of R Sound Shifts

Note!

On r-coloration

The r-coloration in diphthongs of R in a Congolese (Lingala) accent can shift to ᴖ [ə]/[uh], [ɚ]/[er], [ɻ]/[R], [ɥ]/[Rʷ], [ɣ]/[R^GHH].

Because French is the official language, there are many variations of r-coloration. The more the accent is influenced by French, the stronger the r-coloration.

There is a [★] inserted where you can choose one or more of the r-coloration options above, in order to build the idiolect of your choice.

Diphthongs and Triphthongs of R Shifts				
Our friends st_ar_ted the _fire_ n_ear_ _your_ n_or_th _or_chard an _hour_ bef_ore_ we got th_ere_.				
IPA: a fɹɛ̃nz stɑə.tɹd ðə fa.jə niə jɔ noθ ɔ.t ʃɜd ãn aə bi.fɔ wi got ðeə				
SYMBOLS: Ah FRₑNZˢ STAH-uh.TĘ̄ED THuh FAh-Yuh NEE-uh YAW Noth AW.CHUHᴿD *Ah*N AH-uh BEE.FAW WEE GoT THe-uh				
Key Words	Detailed American English Accent IPA ------------------- Symbol	Shift to DR Congolese (Lingala) Accent of English IPA ---------------------- Symbol	Key Words Shifts IPA ---------------------- Symbol	Your Key Words
n<u>ear</u> b<u>eer</u>	ɪ˞ ------------------- EAR	[i] or [i★] ---------------------- [EE] or [EE-★]	nĩ, bi or nĩ★, bi★ ---------------------- N*EE*, BEE or N*EE*-★, BEE-★	
h<u>air</u> st<u>are</u>, p<u>ear</u>, squ<u>are</u>, th<u>ere</u>	ɛ˞ ------------------- AIR	[e] or [e★] ---------------------- [e] or [e-★]	he, ste, pe or he★, ste★, pe★ ---------------------- He, STe, Pe or He-★, STe-★, Pe-★	

Key Words	Detailed American English Accent IPA	Shift to DR Congolese (Lingala) Accent of English IPA	Key Words Shifts IPA	Your Key Words
	Symbol	Symbol	Symbol	
sure poor, your	ʊɚ	[ɔ] or [ɔ★]	ʃɔ, pɔ, jɔ, or ʃɔ★, pɔ★, jɔ★	
	UR	[AW] or [AW-★]	SHAW, PAW, YAW or SHAW-★, PAW-★, YAW-★	
north George, pour, warp, oar	ɔɚ	[o] or [o★] or [ɔ] or [ɔ★]	noθ̞, dʒodʒ̞, po or no★θ̞, dʒo★dʒ̞, po★ or nɔθ̞, dʒɔdʒ̞, pɔ or nɔ★θ̞ dʒɔ★dʒ̞, pɔ★	
	AWR	[o] or [o-★] or [AW] or [AW-★]	Noth, JoJ^(CH), Po or No-★th, Jo-★J^(CH), Po-★ or NAWth, JAWJ^(CH), PAW or NAW-★th, JAW-★J^(CH), PAW-★	
start heart	ɑɚ	[ɑ] or [ɑ★]	stɑt̞, hɑt̞ or stɑ★t̞, hɑ★t̞	
	AHR	[AH] or [AH-★]	STAHT, HAHT or STAH-★T, HAH-★T	
fire	aɪɚ	[a.j★]	fa.j★	
	EYER	[Ah-Y★]	FAh.Y-★	
hour	aʊɚ	[ɑ] or [ɑ★]	ɑ or ɑ★	
	OWR	[AH] or [AH-★]	AH or AH-★	

Key Sentences for Practice

Note!

• By practicing the sentences below, you can work through the sound shifts for a DR Congolese (Lingala) accent in the context of a simple thought. I suggest you think, imagine and speak actively from a point of view. As you begin to work with the operative words in the thoughts, the rhythm and melody of the accent will begin to emerge appropriately.

Consonants:

• **Example:** Mimi Story (Part 2) – 0:52

For lunch you have your fufu your rice your meats your

vegetable.

IPA: fɔʉ lə̃ʃ jʉ haʏ jɔ fʉfʉ jɔ‿ʉ̯aiṣ jɔ mi̯ts jɔ veʒ.tə.bə̩ɫ

SYMBOLS: FAWRᵂ L>UHᴿ<SH Y>OO<HAhVᶠ YAW F>OO<.F>OO<
YAW‿RᵂAh-EES YAW MEΕΤS YAW VeZH.Tuh.BuhL

And then around seven P.M. you will have your rice and beans

or you will have again milk and bread.

IPA: ēn ð̞ɛ̃ːn eⁱ.ɰaũnd̞ ˈse.ven pi̞ ēm ju̞ wɪ̞l hay jɔ‿ɰais̞ ãn bĩnz̞ ouɰ
          ju̞ hay e.gẽn mɪ̞ɾk ãn bɰe̞d̞

SYMBOLS: eN Thə̄N eᴱᴱ.RᵂAh-*OO*ND Se.VeN PEE *em* Y>OO< WĒ͇EL
          HAhVꟳ YAW‿RᵂAh-EES *Ah*N BEENZˢ oRᵂ Y>OO< HAhVꟳ
          e.GE*H*N MĒ͇E-<o>K *Ah*N BRᵂEHD

- ***I'll meet‿you at the ferry in an hour with the ten children.***

  IPA: aiɾ mĩt͡‿u̞ at ð̞ə fe.ɰi ĩn ãn ay wɪ̞θ ð̞ə tẽn ˈt͡ʃiɾ.d̞ie̞ⁿ

  SYMBOLS: Ah-EE-<o> MEETᶜᴴ‿>OO< AhT THuh Fe.RᵂEE *EE*N *Ah*N
            AHRᴳᴴᴴ WĒ͇Eth THuh Te*N* **CHĒ͇E-<o>**.DR*e*ᴺ

Front Vowels: Vowels made by arching or cupping the front of the tongue toward the front of the hard palate.

- ***The thief will tell me after we trap him.***

  IPA: d̞ə t̞if wɪ̞ɾ t̞eł mĩ ɑf.t̞ə wi tɰap ĩm

  SYMBOLS: Duh TEEF WĒ͇E-<o> TeḼ M*EE* A̞HF.T*uh* WEE TRᵂAhP Ē͇EM

Middle Vowels: Vowels made by arching or cupping the middle of the tongue toward the middle of the hard palate.

- ***In the summer, workers burned the underbrush.***

  <u>With r-coloration</u>: this is a DR Congolese (Lingala) accent that has a strong French influence:

  IPA: ĩn d̞ə s̃.mə̯̃ we̞.kə̯z bə̞̃nd̞ d̞ə ɜn'd̞ɜ̯.bɰɜʃ

  SYMBOLS: Ē͇EN Duh S*UH*.M*er* W>UHR<.K*er*Zˢ B>*UHR*<ND Duh
            *UH*ᴿN.D**UHR**.BRᵂUHᴿSH

  <u>Without r-coloration</u>: this is a DR Congolese (Lingala) accent with a weak French influence:

  IPA: ĩn d̞ə s̞ɑ.mə̯̃ we̞.kə̞z bẽnd̞ d̞ə ɑ̞n.d̞ɜ.bɹɑʃ

  SYMBOLS: Ē͇EN Duh SA̞H.M*uh* W>UHᴿ<.K*uh*Zˢ B>*UHR*<ND Duh
            A̞*H*N.D**UH**ᴿ.BR̞A̞HSH

Back Vowels: Vowels made by arching or cupping the back of the tongue toward the back of the hard palate.

- *I th**ou**ght my f**a**ther w**ou**ld n**o**t st**o**p being a b**u**lly but the tr**u**th is, I w**a**s wr**o**ng.*

  IPA: ai θɔt mai fɑ.ðə̠ wʊd nɔt stop bĩŋ ə bʊ.li bɑt ðə tɹ̪ʊθ ɪz̥ ai wɑz̥ ʮɔ̃̀ŋ̊

  SYMBOLS: Ah-EE th>AW<T MAh-EE FAH.TH**u̠h** W>OO<D NoT SToP B**EE**NG uh B>OO<.LEE BA̠HT THuh TR̠>OO<th **Ē̠E̠Z**ˢ Ah-EE WAHZˢ Rᵂ>*AW*<NGᴷ

Diphthongs: When two vowels are combined in one syllable.

- *I'd l**i**ke to fl**y** aw**ay** somed**ay** and g**o** s**ou**th to the m**ou**ntains with the b**oy**s.*

  IPA: aid̠ laik tʊ flai a.weⁱ s̠ə̃m.deⁱ ãn go s̠auθ tʊ ðə maũⁿ.tĩnz wɪ̠θ ðə boiz̠

  SYMBOLS: Ah-EED LAh-EEK T>OO< FLAh-EE Ah.We**ᴱᴱ** S*UH*ᴿM.De**ᴱᴱ** *Ah*N Go SAh->OO<th T>OO< THuh MAh-*OO*ᴺ.T*I*NZˢ W**E̠E̠**th THuh Bo-EEZˢ

Diphthongs of R: A diphthong in which the second vowel is rhotic (e.g., has r-coloration in the final sound).

Example: near → nɪɚ/NEAR

Triphthongs of R: A combination of three vowel sounds in which the third vowel is rhotic.

Example: fire → faɪɚ/FEYER

- *O**u**r friends st**a**rted the f**i**re n**ear** y**our** n**or**th **or**chard an h**ou**r bef**ore** we got th**ere**.*

  IPA: a fɹ̠ẽnz s̠tɑə̠.tɪd̠ ðə fa.jə niə̠ jɔ noθ ɔ.tʃɝd ãn aə̠ bi.fɔ wi got̠ ðeə̠

  SYMBOLS: Ah FR̠*e*NZˢ STAH-**u̠h**.T**E̠E̠**D THuh FAh-Yuh NEE-**u̠h** YAW Noth AW.CHUHᴿD *Ah*N AH-**u̠h** BEE.FAW WEE GoT THe-**u̠h**

Making Your Own Map of the Accent

Listen to the DR Congolese (Lingala) accent samples provided and investigate the resources suggested in the *Introduction and Resources* section. Compose (or steal) *Key Phrases* from your listening/viewing that challenge and/or ground you in the accent. Then get more specific and check your sounds against the sounds in the Workbook.

Your take on the sound shifts may be slightly different. That is okay. The breakdown is a tool, not a rule. Recheck what you hear and, if you still stand behind your discoveries, go with them. This will help you to develop **your own** idiolect of the accent.

> **Note!**
> **What is an Idiolect?**
> Each of us speaks differently even if we have the same general accent. The individualized way that each of us speaks is referred to as an idiolect. For the actor, idiolect is part of what creates character. It is the "how" of the accent, and influences the way we craft our thoughts through language.

KEY PHRASES WITH KEY SOUND SHIFTS

Speak your *Key Phrases*, shifting back and forth between your own home *idiolect of English* and the *DR Congolese (Lingala) accent* you are building. **Observe** the shifts <u>ONE by ONE</u> in your Articulators, Focus of Articulation, use of Melody/Pitch/Lilt, Rhythm/Stress/Pace, and Source & Path of Resonance as you shift back and forth between the two accents. Make note of the shifts in the table provided. Putting your understanding of the shifts into your <u>own words</u> will encourage you to develop a more clear and personal idiolect.

DR CONGOLESE (LINGALA) ACCENT *KEY POINTS OF FOCUS: VOCAL POSTURE AND CHARACTERISTICS*

JAW
LIPS
TONGUE
SOFT PALATE
PHARYNX

FOCUS OF ARTICULATION (TOWARDS TEETH, FRONT/MIDDLE/ BACK OF HARD PALATE, SOFT PALATE, ETC.)

MELODY/PITCH/LILT

RHYTHM/STRESS/PACE

SOURCE & PATH OF RESONANCE – Where does the resonance begin and what is the apparent path it travels through your body (chest, hard palate, sinuses, temples, crown, base of skull, etc.)? Refer to the Source & Path of Resonance and Resonators in the *DR Congolese (Lingala) Accent of English: Down & Dirty Warm-Up and Quick Look* on page 213.

OTHER CHARACTERISTICS (What are your observations?)

PERSONAL IMAGES (For many actors personal images can be the most powerful and effective triggers for their transformation into an accent)

Chapter 9

Senegalese (Wolof) Accent of English

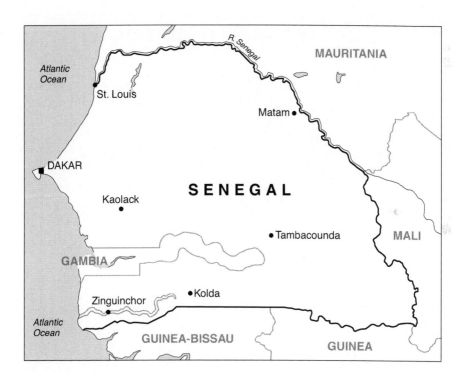

Introduction and Resources

The Wolof Language in Senegal

Although French is the official language of Senegal, the most widely spoken language is Wolof, a West Atlantic language of the Niger-Congo family group. Wolof is the preferred language of trade among Senegal's many ethnic and cultural groups. Other national languages include Jola, Manding, Pulaar, Sereer and Soninke. About 30% of the people of Senegal speak Wolof as their primary language and the other 70% can understand and speak it. The Wolof spoken in urban centers – like the capital city of Dakar – is influenced by French and Arabic.

The Berbers introduced Islam to Senegal in the 7th century. The Wolof moved into Senegal from northeast Africa in the 11th century. In the 17th century the French began building gum producing factories on the Senegal River as well as engaging in slave trade with many of the Wolof chiefs. Senegal was colonized by France in the 19th century and became independent in 1960. This intermingling of these converging languages has influenced how Wolof is spoken today.

Documentaries

Youssou N'Dour: I Bring What I Love, Senegal; *Africa: Through My Eyes*; *This Is Us: Video Stories from Senegalese Youth*; *Cry Sea*; *Touba* (in English, French and Wolof); *Yoole*

Films

Goodbye Solo; *Little Senegal*; *Badou Boy*; *Mossane*; films by the Senegalese filmmaker Ousmane Sembene in French and Wolof: *Faat Kine, L'heroime au quotidian, Guelwaar, Camp de Thiaroye, Ceddo, Xala, Taaw, Mandabi, Tableau Ferraille* (Wolof and French with English subtitles)

Television

Sunu TV – *Kor Dior*; *Buur Gueweul*; BBC's *Last Man Standing* (Season 1, Episode 7: "Senegalese Wrestling"); HBO's *Vice* (Season 1, Episode 8: "Senegalese Laamb Wrestling/The World is Sinking"); 2STV (most popular TV station)

Senegalese (Wolof) Plays

Belleville by Amy Herzog (two of the characters are from Senegal), *Battle of Black and Dogs* by Bernard-Marie Koltès

Music/Musicians

Mamadou Diop; Youssou N'Dour: *Nothing's in Vain*; Seckou Keita, Baba Maal: *Djam Leelii*; Ismael Lo (also a famous actor): *Tajabone*

Radio

Radio Seneweb, Radio Sud FM 98.5, WALF (most popular)

Personalities

Abdoulaye Wade (President of Senegal 2000–2012); Magatte Wade (entrepreneur); Akon (American-born, but spent much of his childhood in Senegal; his accent is American, but he is a very famous person of Wolof descent and culture); El Hadji Diouf (soccer player); Gorgui Dieng (NBA player); Balla Gaye (Laamb wrestler); Lamine Diack (President of the IAAF-International Association of Athletics Federation); Aminata Sow Fall (author); Kinee Diouf (model)

Down & Dirty Warm-up and Quick Look

Note!

On Symbols

● International Phonetic Alphabet Symbols will be listed first and Sound Symbols will be listed second. Example: [i]/[EE]

● Sound Symbol Users: bold-faced letters indicate the syllable is stressed.

1) **The Muscles:** Wake your mouth up so you can more easily discover the physical transformation in speaking the accent.

    a.   Scratch the front, middle and back of your tongue with your front top teeth.

    b.   Rub the front, middle and back of your hard palate with the tip of your tongue.

    c.   Imagine your mouth is numb from being at the dentist and you want to wake it up. Make tongue circles pressing against the back of your lips first clockwise, then counter clockwise (you are waking up your orbicularis muscle).

    d.   To get the breath flowing, blow through your lips, getting them to flap together. Travel up and down in pitch on a BBBB and PPP, feeling the vibration as you wiggle up and down your spine.

2) **Vocal Posture for a Senegalese (Wolof) Accent:** The Focus of Articulation is high towards the middle-back of the hard palate. The middle of the tongue rests fairly high in the mouth. The front of the tongue slopes down and rests behind the bottom front teeth. The middle of the tongue is slightly bunched up towards the middle of the hard palate while the back of the tongue slightly widens and lowers. The lips actively round for the rounded vowels and consonants. The jaw is fairly closed, but moves fluidly. For most speakers the soft palate is fairly lifted which results in hypo-nasality. The pharynx is slightly narrowed which creates oral twang.

3) **Resonators:** "occupy" the following spaces. This will prepare you to find the Source & Path of Resonance for a Senegalese (Wolof) accent. (By

"occupy", I mean just that; be in the space of it and find the pathway and flow of resonance, rather than "putting" the resonance there.)

a.   CHEST – Generously laugh at something – ha̲ ha̲ ha̲ / HA̲h HA̲h HA̲h
b.   HARD PALATE – As if you were discovering something – ho ho ho / Ho Ho Ho
c.   THE BONES AT THE BASE OF YOUR SKULL (THE OCCIPITAL BONE) – Use your hands to scoop the sound from the base of your skull with a Mississippi African-American dialect as if you're flirting with someone nearby – heː heː heː / Hē Hē Hē
d.   FLICK THE SOUND OUT OF YOUR CHEEKBONES with an Italian-American flourish, as if calling to someone across the street – heː heː heː / Hē Hē Hē
e.   WITH YOUR HANDS NEXT TO YOUR TEMPLES, SHAKE THE SOUND OUT WITH LOOSE FISTS – As if you were somewhat crazed – ji̲ ji̲ ji̲ / YEE YEE YEE
f.   IMAGINE A METAL DISK EXTENDING FROM YOUR HANDS THROUGH YOUR SKULL. Bring your hands to the sides of your head just above the temples, with your palms facing the floor, thumbs hooked behind your skull. *Lid* the vibration to create a muted brassy sound. Like a robot saying "Hi" – haːi haːi haːi / HA̅h-EE HA̅h-EE HA̅h-EE
g.   GIGGLE OUT OF THE TOP OF YOUR HEAD – As if you were tickled pink by something – hi̲ hi̲ hi̲ / HEE HEE HEE

4)   Source & Path of Resonance for a Senegalese (Wolof) Accent:
From a buoyant chest resonance, the sound travels through a pharynx that can be more or less narrowed, depending on the speaker. However, there will always be some narrowing to create the characteristic pharyngeal twang of the accent. The soft palate is fairly lifted, creating a hypo-nasality that travels into a very strong sinus resonance. Think of speaking into the backs of your cheekbones. By raising the middle of the tongue, resonance gets focused on the middle back of the hard palate. Most often the resonance gets lidded in the sinuses, but for some speakers it can travel up into the temples for a more brassy and bright sound.

5)   Get the sound changes into your body and imagination.
Say these phrases occupying the following places in your body, suggesting to yourself the following energetic associations:

●   pubic bone to tail bone – survival instinct

   zu̲ / Z>OO<
   I need it – ai ni̲d̲ it̲ / Ah-EE N*EE*D EET

●   pubic bone to navel & sacrum in back – sexuality, big feelings

   wo / Wo
   I desire it – ai di̲'z̲a.ju̲ɥ‿it̲ / Ah-EE DEE.**ZAh-EE**.YRᵂ‿EET

- rib cage to below heart – will

  ʒɔ / ZHAW
  I want it – ai wãn̪t̪ it̪ / Ah-EE W*Ah*NT EET

- heart – love

  ma̱ / M*Ah*
  I love it – ai l̠·ʌv it̪ / Ah-EE L̠UHV EET

- throat – communication (think of talking at a party)

  bʌ / BUH
  I have to say it – ai hav t̪u̱ s̪e it̪ / Ah-EE HAhV T>O͞O< Se EET

- forehead – intelligence/wisdom

  keː / Kē
  I know it – ai nõ it̪ / Ah-EE N*o* EET

- crown of head – spirituality

  r̪i̱ / RᴿEE
  I believe it – ai bi̱ˈl̠·iv it̪ / Ah-EE BĒE.**LEEV** EET

6) **Articulation** – using playful physical actions: punching, flicking, dabbing, slashing

  d̪u̱ d̪i ku̱ d̪u̱ d̪i ku̱ d̪u̱ d̪i ku̱ – d̪i
  d̪u̱ d̪i ku̱ d̪u̱ d̪i ku̱ d̪u̱ d̪i ku̱ – d̪eː
  d̪u̱ d̪i ku̱ d̪u̱ d̪i ku̱ d̪u̱ d̪i ku̱ – d̪aːi
  d̪u̱ d̪i ku̱ d̪u̱ d̪i ku̱ d̪u̱ d̪i ku̱ – d̪o
  d̪u̱ d̪i ku̱ d̪u̱ d̪i ku̱ d̪u̱ d̪i ku̱ – d̪u̱

  Repeat as needed, replacing [d̪] with [t̪], [p], [b], [k], [g], [f], [v]

D>O͞O< DEE K>O͞O< D>O͞O< DEE K>O͞O< D>O͞O< DEE K>O͞O< – DEE
D>O͞O< DEE K>O͞O< D>O͞O< DEE K>O͞O< D>O͞O< DEE K>O͞O< – Dē
D>O͞O< DEE K>O͞O< D>O͞O< DEE K>O͞O< D>O͞O< DEE K>O͞O< – DA͞h-EE
D>O͞O< DEE K>O͞O< D>O͞O< DEE K>O͞O< D>O͞O< DEE K>O͞O< – Do
D>O͞O< DEE K>O͞O< D>O͞O< DEE K>O͞O< D>O͞O< DEE K>O͞O< – D>OO<

  Repeat as needed, replacing [D] with [T], [P], [B], [K], [G], [F], [V]. [D] & [T] are both articulated with the blade of the tongue against the back of the top front teeth (dentalized).

Key Points of Focus

Characteristics and Vocal Posture

Senegalese (Wolof) Accent Characteristics

Note!

On Melody/Lilt/Pitch and Rhythm/Stress/Pace

Every accent contains shifts for some, but not necessarily all, of these elements of vocal variety.

Note!

On Use of Musical Notes

Follow the "musical notes" up and down to get a feel for the melody of the accent. The filled-in notes are shorter than the open notes. For those who are musically inclined, think of them as approximating quarter notes and half notes. This distinction will give you a feel for the rhythm of the accent.

Melody/Lilt/Pitch

Wolof is not a tonal language, unlike the Bantu languages in this workbook. The accent's melodic play is strongly influenced by French but Senegalese (Wolof) is much more melodically subdued. Both of these language characteristics manifest in the accent. The following characteristics tend to surface most often.

1. There are often internal glides up or down in pitch on or within operative words.
2. Multi-syllabic words often have an incremental rise or fall in pitch from syllable to syllable.
3. Words at the ends of thoughts tend to go up in pitch when the accent is more French-based, and down in pitch when it is more Wolof-based.
4. Pitch changes can often be on a characteristically French minor interval.

Example: Marietu Story (Part 1) – 0:00

I came to to join my husband, like ten years ago.

When you listen to Marietu, in contrast with the other speakers, you will hear that she has a relatively strong French accent. Also notice that when she speaks Wolof you can detect her French accent. In the sentence above she exhibits a typical French minor fall in pitch on the second syllable of *hus<u>band</u>* (#4, p. 248). She also glides in pitch in her operative words *join* and *years* (#1, p. 248). Notice that both of these words contain a diphthong. She maintains the Senegalese (Wolof) steady rhythm, which calls attention to her melodic shifts. Her fly-away lift in pitch on the final syllable of the final word of her thought: *a<u>go</u>* is also characteristic of a French influenced Senegalese (Wolof) accent (#3, p. 248)

Example: Aziz Story – 3:47

Well that's ha that's how I see things. I'm an African first

before being a Senegalese gentleman.

The melody in Aziz's thought above is an interesting mash-up of French, English and Senegalese (Wolof) melody. He travels a lot, so this is not surprising. He tends to lift in pitch at the end of his thoughts, but in the second sentence above, he ends his thought by dropping the pitch in *gentleman*, as would happen in Senegalese (Wolof) or English (#3, p. 248). You can hear the Senegalese (Wolof) accent characteristic of an internal glide within the words on: *well, how, things,* and *first* (#1, p. 248). The three, multisyllabic words *African, Senegalese* and *gentleman* all have an incremental rise and/or fall from syllable to syllable (#2, p. 248).

Rhythm/Stress/Pace

Words and syllables are most often consistent in length. This results in a very steady rhythm that can become rapid. Listen to the speakers Tyma, Gracya, Marietou and Mousa speak in the Senegalese (Wolof) language, and you will hear this very clearly. Also notice how the consistency in the rhythm calls attention to the shifts in pitch. Words do lengthen when the speakers use the characteristic pitch glide within a word.

Example: Papa Story – 0:00

I come to the states in the early nineties from uh Senegal.

Papa's syllables are consistent in length except for his lilt up on the first word *I*. It seems that he lengthens when he is thinking, on the words *early* and *uh*. The expression of his thought comes through in the melodic play much more than in rhythm, stress or pace. Notice how the consistency of the rhythm calls added attention to his shifts in pitch.

Example: Gracya Story (Part 1) – 0:18

She stayed there, like, seventeen years, but every summertime

she come back to Africa, we were there.

Gracya's only variation in length is in her glides. All of the glides are on words or syllables that would be diphthongs in D.A.E. Again, as with Papa, the expression of her thought comes through in the melodic play much more than in rhythm, stress or pace. Also, as with Papa, the consistency of the rhythm highlights her shifts in pitch.

Source & Path of Resonance

From a buoyant chest resonance, the sound travels through a pharynx that can be more or less narrowed, depending on the speaker. However, there will always be some narrowing to create the characteristic pharyngeal twang of the accent. The soft palate is fairly lifted; this creates a hypo-nasality that travels into a very strong sinus resonance. Think of speaking into the backs of your cheekbones. By raising the middle of the tongue, resonance gets focused on the middle-back of the hard palate. Most often the resonance gets lidded in the sinuses, but for some speakers it can travel up into the temples for a more brassy and bright sound.

Both Aziz and Gracya have a tendency to nasalize their sounds more than the other Senegalese (Wolof) speakers in the accent library. Tyma, Gracya and Aziz all lid their resonance in the temples, while the others tend to lid in their sinuses. Besides this variation, you will be able to hear the characteristic Path of Resonance for the accent as described above. It will make it easier for you to identify the Path of Resonance by listening to Tyma, Gracya, Marietou and Mousa speak in Wolof.

Senegalese (Wolof) Accent Vocal Posture

Note!

On Vocal Posture

These adjustments enable you to integrate the accent through physical transformation rather than solely relying on sound shifts.

- **Focus of Articulation:** High towards the middle-back of the hard palate.
- **Tongue:** The middle of the tongue rests fairly high in the mouth. The front of the tongue slopes down and rests behind the bottom front teeth. The middle of the tongue is slightly bunched up towards the middle of the hard palate while the back of the tongue slightly widens and lowers.
- **Lips:** The lips actively round for the rounded vowels and consonants.
- **Jaw:** The jaw is fairly closed, but moves fluidly.
- **Soft Palate:** For most speakers the soft palate is fairly lifted, which results in hypo-nasality.
- **Pharynx:** The pharynx is slightly narrowed which creates oral twang.

Distinct Sounds of the Language and/or Accent

> **Note!**
> **On Distinct Sounds**
> These are some of the sounds that the Senegalese use and American speakers do not. In speaking the sounds and/or the words that contain them, you can heighten your physical understanding of the Senegalese (Wolof) accent's *Vocal Posture* as compared to your own. This frame of reference will both inform and strengthen your own accent.

Consonants

1. *IPA:* [r] → alveolar trill.
   Symbol: [RR] → trilled [R].
   This sound is used in speaking the Senegalese (Wolof) language.
2. *IPA:* [ɾ] → alveolar tap.
   Symbol: [Rᴿ] → tapped [R].
   Used in place of [ɹ]/[R]: r̲ed, dr̲ess
   This sound is used in speaking both the language and accent of Senegalese (Wolof).
3. *IPA:* [x] → voiceless velar fricative.
   Symbol: [XX] → Rather like the sound of a cat with a furball.
   This sound is used in speaking the Senegalese (Wolof) language.
4. *IPA:* [ɰ] → velar approximant.
   Symbol: [Rᵂ] → [R] made on the soft palate.
   Used in place of [ɹ]/[R] in the middle of a word: me̲r̲ry, so̲r̲ry or in a diphthong of R: hear̲
   This sound is used in speaking a Senegalese (Wolof) accent of English.

Pre-nasalized Consonants

5.   *IPA:* [ᵐb], [ᵐp], [ⁿk], [ⁿd]
     Symbol: [ᴹB], [ᴹP], [ᴺK], [ᴺD]
     Although these consonants are used only in the Wolof language, there is a
     slight nasality that carries over into the accent.

Vowels

The vowels of the Senegalese (Wolof) language include:

   IPA: [i], [e], [ø], [a], [u], [o]
   Symbol: [EE], [e], [>e<], [Ah], [OO], [o]

Knowing the vowels for the Senegalese (Wolof) language will provide clues for
the vowel shifts in the accent.

6.   *IPA:* [e]
     Symbol: [e] → This is the first sound in the D.A.E. diphthong [AY] as in *face*.
     Used in place of [ɛ]/[EH]: *dress*, *bed*
     This sound is used in speaking both the language and accent of Senegalese
       (Wolof).
7.   *IPA:* [ø]
     Symbol: [>e<] → [e] made with rounded lips.
     This sound is used in speaking the Senegalese (Wolof) language.
8.   *IPA:* [a]
     Symbol: [Ah] → This is the first sound in the D.A.E. diphthong [EYE].
     Used in place of [æ]/[A]: *trap*, *bath*
     This sound is used in speaking both the language and accent of Senegalese
       (Wolof).
9.   *IPA:* [o]
     Symbol: [o] → This is the first sound in the D.A.E. diphthong [OH].
     Used in place of [oʊ]/[OH]: *goat*, *sew*
     This sound is used in speaking both the language and accent of Senegalese
       (Wolof).

Consonant Sound Shifts

- ⊶ indicates that this sound is a key sound shift
- You can begin to fold melody and rhythm with the sound changes by speaking the sample sentences that are before each section of sound changes.

Consonant Shifts

Example: Papa Story – 0:39

It's ju<u>st</u> gonna be f<u>ri</u>end<u>s</u> and <u>th</u>e way <u>the</u>

coun<u>tr</u>y i<u>s</u> <u>r</u>unning <u>sl</u>ower <u>th</u>an here.

IPA: is̬ dʒʌs̬ 'ga.nə̽ bi̬ f̬ɹ̪ẽn̬z̬ ãn ð̬ə: we: d̬ə 'kõn.t̪ɹi̬ iz̬ 'rʌ.niŋ 's̬lo.wə̬ d̬ẽn hi̬ə̬

SYMBOLS: EES JUHS GAh.N*uh* BEE F<u>R</u>eNZ^S *Ah*N THuh Wē Duh **KoN**.TRĒE
EĒZ^S **R^RUH**.NEENG **SL**o.W<u>uh</u> Den HEE-<u>uh</u>

I'<u>ll</u> mee<u>t</u> you a<u>t</u> <u>the</u> fe<u>rr</u>y in an hour wi<u>th</u> <u>the</u> <u>t</u>en <u>ch</u>il<u>dr</u>en.

IPA: ail̬ mit^s‿ju̬ ət̬ ðə 'fe.ri̬ ĩn ən 'a.wə wiθ̬ ðə t̬ẽn t͡ʃil.d̬r̃en

SYMBOLS: Ah-EE**L** MEET^{CH}‿Y>OO< uhT THuh Fe.R^RĒE *EE*N *uh*N **Ah**.Wuh
WEEth THuh TeN **CHEEL**.DR^ReN

Key Words	Detailed American English Accent	Shift to Senegalese (Wolof) Accent of English	Key Words Shifts	Your Key Words
	IPA	IPA	IPA	
	Symbol	Symbol	Symbol	
☞ team debt, did	[t]/[d]	t̪/d̪	t̪īm, det̪, did̪	
	[T]/[D]	[T]/[D] both dentalized	TEEM, DeT, DEED	
☞ these there, breathe	ð	[ð̪] or [d̪] or [z̪]	ð̪iz̪, ð̪eə, brið̪ or d̪iz̪, d̪eə, brid̪ or z̪iz̪, z̪eə, briz̪	
	TH	[TH] or [D] or [Z] all dentalized	THEEZ^S, THe-UH, BR^REETH or DEEZ^S, De-UH, BR^REED or ZEEZ^S, Ze-UH, BR^REEZ	
☞ thin thick, mouth	θ	[θ] or [t̪]	θin, θik, mau·θ or t̪in, t̪ik, mau·t̪	
	th	[th] or [T] both dentalized	thEEN, thEEK, MAh-ŌŌth	
stop population	p	sometimes [p˺]	stop˺, 'p˺op˺.ju.le·.ʃən	
	P	[P] sometimes there is no release of [H] after the [P]	SToP, PoP.Y>OO<. Lē.SHuhN	
☞ red dress, merry, sorry	ɹ	[ɹ̪] or [ɾ]	ɹed, dɹes, 'me.ɹi, 'sa.ɹi or red, dred, 'me.ri, 'sa.ri	
	R	[R] or [R^R]	ReD, DReS, Me.REE, SAh.REE or R^ReD, DR^ReS, Me.R^REE, SAh.R^REE	
☞ excel fall, table (final *l* in spelling)	l	l:	'ek.sel:, fɔl:, 'te:bəl:	
	L	L̲	EK.SēL̲, FAWL̲, Tē.BuhL̲	

Key Words	Detailed American English Accent	Shift to Senegalese (Wolof) Accent of English	Key Words Shifts	Your Key Words
	IPA	IPA	IPA	
	Symbol	Symbol	Symbol	
ju<u>dge</u>	dʒ	dʒ̥	dʒʌdʒ̥	
	J	J^{CH}	JUHJ^{CH}	
↤ bo<u>ys</u> (final *s* when pronounced [z])	z	z̪̥	bʌːiz̪̥	
	Z	Z^S	BU̅H-EEZ^S	
<u>s</u>ee <u>z</u>oo (*s* and *z* at the beginning of a word)	[s]/[z]	s̪/z̪	s̪i/z̪u	
		[S]/[Z] both dentalized	SEE/Z^S>OO<	
<u>h</u>istory (initial *h* in spelling)	h	often dropped in accents influenced by French	ˈis̪.t̪ə.ri̥	
	h	often dropped in accents influenced by French	**EES**.Tuh.R^REE	

Vowel and Diphthong Sound Shift Notes!

Note!
On Vowels and Diphthongs
When vowels or diphthongs precede or follow an [m]/[M], [n]/[N], or [ŋ]/[NG], they are nasalized.

Example: Mimi, wrong, answer

Notation for nasalized vowels → [ĩ]/[*EE*], [ɔ̃]/[*o*], [ã]/[*Ah*]

Note!
On Vowels
The vowels of the Senegalese (Wolof) language include:

IPA: [i], [e], [ø], [a], [u], [o]
Symbol: [EE], [e], [>e<], [Ah], [OO], [o]

Knowing the vowels for the Senegalese (Wolof) language will provide clues for the vowel shifts in the accent.

Front Vowel Sound Shifts

Front Vowel Shifts				
The thief will tell me after we trap him. *IPA:* ðə θif wil tel˞ mĩ ˈaf.tə wi trap˺‿ĩm *SYMBOLS:* THuh thEEF WEEL TeL̲ MEE **AhF**.Tuh WE TRᴿAhP‿*EEM*				
Key Words	*Detailed American English Accent* IPA ---- *Symbol*	*Shift to Senegalese (Wolof) Accent of English* IPA ---- *Symbol*	*Key Words Shifts* IPA ---- *Symbol*	*Your Key Words*
fl<u>ee</u>ce sn<u>ee</u>ze, pl<u>ea</u>d	i ---- EE	i̞ ---- EE	fl˙is, snĩ̞z, pl˙id ---- FL̲EES, SN*EEZ*ˢ, PL̲EED	
☞ k<u>i</u>t p<u>i</u>tch, d<u>i</u>m, l<u>i</u>p	ɪ ---- I	i ---- EE	ki̞t, p˺it̞ʃ, d̞ĩm ---- KEET, PEECH, D*EE*M	
countr<u>y</u> (*y* in final position of spelling)	I̞ ---- EE͞	i̞ ---- EE	ˈkõn.tr̞i̞ ---- K*o*N.TR̲EE	
b<u>e</u>rated	[ɪ] in prefix ---- [EE͞] in prefix	i̞ ---- EE͞	bi̞ˈɹeˑti̞d ---- BEE͞.R̲e͞.TID	
dr<u>e</u>ss b<u>e</u>d, f<u>ea</u>ther, s<u>e</u>nd	ɛ ---- EH	e ---- e	dr̞es, bed̞, ˈfe.d̞ə ---- DRᴿeS, BeD, **Fe**.D<u>uh</u>	

Key Words	Detailed American English Accent IPA	Shift to Senegalese (Wolof) Accent of English IPA	Key Words Shifts IPA	Your Key Words
	Symbol	Symbol	Symbol	
☛ tr<u>a</u>p m<u>a</u>d, r<u>a</u>t, c<u>a</u>ndle	æ	a	t̪ɹap˺, mãd̪, ɹat̪	
	A	Ah	TRAhP, M*Ah*D, RAhT	
☛ b<u>a</u>th *[a]/[Ah] <u>a</u>sk, <u>a</u>fter, d<u>a</u>nce, ex<u>a</u>mple, h<u>a</u>lf, m<u>a</u>sk, r<u>a</u>scal, tr<u>a</u>nsfer In Chapter 1, there is a list of these words called the BATH or ASK list of words.	æ	<u>a</u>	baθ, a̠sk, 'af.t̪ə	
	A	A<u>h</u>	BA<u>h</u>th, A<u>h</u>SK, **AhF**.Tu<u>h</u>	

Middle Vowel Sound Shifts

Middle Vowel Shifts				
In the summer, workers burned the underbrush.				
IPA: ĩn ð̥ə ˈsʌ.mə̰ ˈwɵ.kə̰z bə̃nd̥ ðə_ˈʌn.d̥ə.brʌʃ				
SYMBOLS: EEN THuh **SUH.**Muh **W>UH**R<.KuhZ**S** B>UHR<ND THuh_**UH**N.Duh.BRRUHSH				
Key Words	Detailed American English Accent IPA -------------- Symbol	Shift to Senegalese (Wolof) Accent of English IPA -------------- Symbol	Key Words Shifts IPA -------------- Symbol	Your Key Words
↤ bird learn, service, nurse, work (ir, er, ear, ur, or in spelling)	ɝ -------------- ER	[ə] or [ɚ] -------------- [>UHR<] or [UHR]	bəd, ˈl·ən, ˈsə.viṣ, nə̃ṣ, wək or bɝ·d̥, ˈl·ɝ·n, ˈsɝ·.viṣ, nɝ̃·ṣ, wɝ·k -------------- B>UHR<D, L̲>UHR<N, S>UHR<.VEES, N>UHR<S, W>UHR<K or BUHRD, L̲UHRN, SUHR.VEES, NUHRS, WUHRK	
sister traitor, hangar	ɚ -------------- er	[ə] or [ɚ] -------------- [uh] or [er]	ˈsiṣ.tə, t̯e·.tə, hã̃ŋ.ə or ˈsiṣ.tɚ, t̯e·.tɚ, hã̃ŋ.ɚ -------------- SEES.Tuh, TRē.Tuh, HAhNG.uh or SEES.Ter, TRē.Ter, HAhNG.er	

Key Words	Detailed American English Accent	Shift to Senegalese (Wolof) Accent of English	Key Words Shifts	Your Key Words
	IPA	IPA	IPA	
	Symbol	Symbol	Symbol	
str<u>u</u>t c<u>u</u>rry	Ä	ʌ	st̠ɹʌt̠, ˈkʌ.ɹ̠i̠	
	U̟H	UH	STR̠UHT, **KUH.R̠ĒE̠**	
← c<u>o</u>me fl<u>oo</u>d (in words spelled with *o* and sometimes *oo*)	Ä	sometimes o	kõm, fl̠od̠	
	U̟H	sometimes O	K*o*M, FL̠*o*D	
<u>a</u>bout b<u>anana</u>	ə	ə	əˈba̠·ut̠, bə.ˈna̠.nə	
	uh	uh	Uh.**BA̠H-OOT**, Buh.**NA̠h**.Nuh	

Back Vowel Sound Shifts

			Back Vowel Shifts		

I thought my father would not stop being a bully but the truth is, I was wrong.

IPA: aˑi θɔt maːi 'faˌðə wṳd nõt‿stop˺ biŋ ə 'bṳˌlːi̥ bʌt ðə t̬ru̬θ i̬z aˑi wɔ̬z r̃õŋ

SYMBOLS: Ah-EE thAWT MA͡h-EE **FAh**.THu͟h W>O͡O<D NoT‿SToP‿BEENG uh
B>O͡O<.L͟E͡E BUHT THuh TRᴿ>OO<th EEZˢ Ah-EE WAWZˢ Rᴿ₀NG

Key Words	Detailed American English Accent IPA / Symbol	Shift to Senegalese (Wolof) Accent of English IPA / Symbol	Key Words Shifts IPA / Symbol	Your Key Words
f<u>oo</u>d gr<u>ew</u>, tr<u>ue</u>, tw<u>o</u>	u -------- OO	u̬ -------- >OO<	fu̬d, gr̬u, t̬ru̬ --------------- F>OO<D, GR̬>OO<, TR̬>OO<	
⊷ f<u>oo</u>t p<u>u</u>t	ʊ -------- U	u̟ -------- >O͡O<	fu̟t, pu̟t ---------------- F>O͡O<T, P>O͡O<T	
th<u>ou</u>ght t<u>a</u>ll, c<u>au</u>lk, <u>aw</u>ful	ɔ -------- AW	ɔ -------- AW	θɔt, tɔlˑ, kɔk ---------------- thAWT, TAWL̲, KAWK	
⊷ cl<u>o</u>th *[ɒ]/[O] d<u>o</u>g, c<u>ou</u>gh, w<u>a</u>sh, h<u>o</u>rrid	ɔ -------- AW	[o] or [ɔ̬] ---------------- [o] or [AW]	kl̥ˑo̬θ, d̬og, kof, woʃ or kl̥ˑɔ̬θ, d̬ɔg, kɔf, wɔ̬ʃ ---------------- KL̲oth, DoG, KoF, WoSH or KL̲AWth, DAWG, KAWF, WAWSH	

Key Words	Detailed American English Accent	Shift to Senegalese (Wolof) Accent of English	Key Words Shifts	Your Key Words
	IPA	*IPA*	*IPA*	
	Symbol	*Symbol*	*Symbol*	
☛ f<u>a</u>ther	ɑ	<u>a</u>	'fa.ð<u>ə</u>	
	AH	A<u>h</u>	F<u>A</u><u>h</u>.TH<u>uh</u>	
☛ l<u>o</u>t *[ɒ]/[O] sq<u>ua</u>d, w<u>a</u>nder	ɑ	[o] or [<u>a</u>]	l'o̞t, s̞kwo̞d̞, 'wõn.d<u>ə</u> or l'<u>at</u>, s̞kw<u>a</u>d, 'w<u>ã</u>n.d<u>ə</u>	
	AH	[o] or [<u>Ah</u>]	L̲oT, SKWoD, W<i>o</i>N.D<u>uh</u> or L̲<u>Ah</u>T, SKW<u>Ah</u>D, W<u><i>Ah</i></u>N.Duh	

264

Diphthong Sound Shifts

	Diphthong Shifts			
I'd like to fly away someday and go south to the mountains with the boys.				
IPA: aˑiˑd̪ lˑaˑik tu̥ fl̪aːi əˈweː ˈs̪ʌm.d̪eˑ ɔ̃ go s̪auˑθ tu̥ ð̪ə ˈmãũːn.tẽⁿz̪ wiθ̪ ð̪ə bʌːiz̪				
SYMBOLS: Ah-EED L̪Āh-EEK T>O͞O< FL̪Āh-EE uh-**Wē SUHM**.De uh Go SAh-O͞Oth T>O͞O< THuh **M_Ah-OO_N**.TeⁿZˢ WEEth THuh BUH̄-EEZˢ				
Key Words	*Detailed American English Accent* IPA ------ *Symbol*	*Shift to Senegalese (Wolof) Accent of English* IPA ------ *Symbol*	*Key Words Shifts* IPA ------ *Symbol*	*Your Key Words*
☛ face pain, day, weight, steak	eɪ ------ AY	eː ------ ē	feːs̪, pẽːn, d̪eː ------ FēS, PēN, Dē	
price eyes, diaper, fly, guy, height	aɪ ------ EYE	aːi ------ Āh-EE	praːis̪, aːiz̪, ˈd̪aːi.pə ------ PRᴿĀh-EES, Āh-EEZˢ, D**Āh-EE**.P_uh_	
☛ choice boys	ɔɪ ------ OY	ʌːi ------ UH̄-EE	tʃʌːis̪, bʌːiz̪ ------ CHUH̄-EES, BUH̄-EEZˢ	
☛ goat sew, go, toe	oʊ ------ OH	oː ------ ō	goːt̪, s̪oː, goː ------ GōT, Sō, Gō	
mouth town	aʊ ------ OW	auː ------ Ah-O͞O	mauːθ, t̪aũːn ------ M_Ah_-OOth, T_Ah_-OON	

Diphthongs of R Sound Shifts

Note!

On r-coloration

The r-coloration in diphthongs of R in a Senegalese (Wolof) accent can shift to [ə]/[u̱h], [ɝ]/[U̱HR], [ɥ]/[R^W].

Because French is the official language, there are many variations of r-coloration. The stronger the accent is influenced by French, the stronger the r-coloration.

There is a [★] inserted where you can choose one of the options above for the idiolect you are building.

	Diphthongs and Triphthongs of R Shifts			
Our friends st_ar_ted the _fi_re n_ear_ _your_ n_or_th _or_chard an h_our_ bef_ore_ we got th_ere_.				
IPA: 'a.wə frɛ̃nẓ 'sta̱.tɹ̩d ð̱ə 'fa.jə nĩə̱ juə̱ nɔ̃ə̱θ 'o.t͡ʃəd ən 'a.wə bi'fɔ wi got ð̱eə̱				
SYMBOLS: **Ah**.Wuh FR^Re̱NZ^S **STA̱h**.TĒ̱ED THuh **FАh**.Yuh N*EE*-u̱h Y>O͞O<-u̱h N*A*W-u̱hth **o**.CH>UH^R<D *uh*N **Ah**.Wuh BEE.**FAW** WEE GoT THe-u̱h				
Key Words	*Detailed American English Accent* IPA --- *Symbol*	*Shift to Senegalese (Wolof) Accent of English* IPA --- *Symbol*	*Key Words Shifts* IPA --- *Symbol*	*Your Key Words*
n<u>ear</u> b<u>eer</u>	ɪɝ --- EAR	[i] or [i★] --- [EE] or [EE-★]	nĩ, bi or nĩ★ bi★ --- N*EE*, BEE or N*EE*-★, BEE-★	
h<u>air</u> st<u>are</u>, p<u>ear</u>, squ<u>are</u>, th<u>ere</u>	ɛɝ --- AIR	[eː] or [eː★] --- [ē] or [ē-★]	heː, steː, peː or heː★, steː★, peː★ --- Hē, STē, Pē or Hē-★, STē-★, Pē-★	

Key Words	Detailed American English Accent	Shift to Senegalese (Wolof) Accent of English	Key Words Shifts	Your Key Words
	IPA	*IPA*	*IPA*	
	Symbol	*Symbol*	*Symbol*	
<u>su</u>re <u>poor</u>, y<u>our</u>	ʊ˞	[u̯] or [u̯★] or [o] or [o★]	ʃu̯, pu̯, ju̯ or ʃu̯★, pu̯★, ju̯★ or ʃo, po, jo or ʃo-★, po-★, jo-★	
	UR	[>O͞O<] or [>O͞O<-★] or [o] or [o-★]	SH>O͞O<, P>O͞O<, Y>O͞O< or SH>O͞O<-★, P>O͞O<-★, Y>O͞O<-★ or SHo, Po, Yo or SHo-★, Po-★, Yo-★	
⊷ n<u>or</u>th Ge<u>or</u>ge, p<u>our</u>, w<u>ar</u>p, <u>oar</u>	ɔ˞	[o] or [o★] or [ɔ] or [ɔ★]	nðθ, dʒodʒ, po or nð★θ, dʒo★dʒ, po★ or nð̞θ, dʒɔdʒ, pɔ or nð̞★θ, dʒɔ★dʒ, pɔ★	
	AWR	[o] or [o-★] or [AW] or [AW-★]	No*th*, JoJ^CH, Po or No-★th, Jo-★J^CH, P-★o or NA*W*th, JAWJ^CH, PAW or NA*W*-★th, JAW-★J^CH, PAW-★	
⊷ st<u>ar</u>t h<u>ear</u>t	ɑ˞	[a̠] or [a̠★]	<u>sta</u>t̠, ha̠t̠ or <u>sta</u>★t̠, ha̠★t̠	
	AHR	[A<u>h</u>] or [A<u>h</u>-★]	STA<u>h</u>T, HA<u>h</u>T or STA<u>h</u>-★T, HA<u>h</u>-★T	
<u>fi</u>re	aɪ˞	[a.jə] or [a.j★]	ˈfa.jə or ˈfa.j★	
	EYER	[Ah-Yuh] or [Ah-Y-★]	**FAh**.Yuh or **FAh**-Y-★	
h<u>our</u>	aʊ˞	[a.wə] or [a.w★]	ˈa.wə or ˈa.w★	
	OWR	[Ah-Wuh] or [Ah-W-★]	Ah-Wuh or **Ah**.W-★	

Key Sentences for Practice

Note!

- By practicing the sentences below, you can work through the sound shifts for a Senegalese (Wolof) accent in the context of a simple thought. I suggest you think, imagine and speak actively from a point of view. As you begin to work with the operative words in the thoughts, the rhythm and melody of the accent will begin to emerge appropriately.

Consonants:

- **Example:** Papa Story – 0:39

> *IPA:* i̠s dʒʌs̠ 'ga.nə̄ bi̠ f̠ɹ̠ē̃nz̠ ãn ð̠ə: we: də 'kõn.tɹi̠ iz̠ 'ɾʌ.niŋ 's̠lo.wə̠ d̠ēn hi̠ə
>
> *SYMBOLS:* EES JUHS GAh.N*uh* BEE FR̠eNZˢ *Ah*N THu̅h̅ We̅ Duh **K**oN.TREE̅ EE̅Zˢ **Rᴿ**UH.NEENG **SLo**.W*u̠h* Den HEE-*u̠h*

- *I'll meet you at the ferry in an hour with the ten children.*

> *IPA:* ail̠ mit̠ˢ‿ju̠ ət̠ ð̠ə 'fe.ɾi̠ ĩn ən 'a.wə wi̠θ ð̠ə t̠ēn tʃil.dɹēn
>
> *SYMBOLS:* Ah-EEL̠ MEETᶜᴴ‿Y>OO< uhT THuh **Fe**.RᴿEE̅ *EE*N *uh*N **Ah**.Wuh WEEth THuh TeN **CHEEL̠**.DRᴿeN

Front Vowels: Vowels made by arching or cupping the front of the tongue toward the front of the hard palate.

- *The thief will tell me after we trap him.*

> *IPA:* ð̠ə θif wil̠ t̠el: mĩ 'af.t̠ə wi̠ trap˺‿ĩm
>
> *SYMBOLS:* THuh thEEF WEEL̠ TeL̠ *MEE* **Ah**F.T*uh* WE TRᴿAhP‿*EE*M

Middle Vowels: Vowels made by arching or cupping the middle of the tongue toward the middle of the hard palate.

- ***In the summer, workers burned the underbrush.***

    IPA: ĩn ðə 'sʌ.mə̰ 'we.kə̰z bɛ̃nd ̣ðə‿'ʌn.də.brʌʃ

    SYMBOLS: *EE*N THuh **SUH**.M*uh* **W**>**UH**ᴿ<.K*uh*Zˢ B>*UH*ᴿ<ND
    THuh‿*UH*N.Duh.BRᴿUHSH

Back Vowels: Vowels made by arching or cupping the back of the tongue toward the back of the hard palate.

- ***I thought my father would not stop being a bully but the truth is, I was wrong.***

    IPA: aˑi θɔt maːi 'fa.ðə̰ wʊd nõt‿stop̚ bĩŋ ə 'bʊ.l̰iˑi bʌt ðə trṵθ iz aˑi
    wɔ̰z ɾõŋ

    SYMBOLS: Ah-EE thAWT M**Ah**-EE **F**_**Ah**_.THu*h* W>O͞O<D N*o*T‿ST*o*P‿
    BEENG uh **B**>**O͞O**<.L̲E͞E BUHT THuh TRᴿ>OO<th EEZˢ
    Ah-EE WAWZˢ Rᴿ*o*NG

Diphthongs: When two vowels are combined in one syllable.

- ***I'd like to fly away someday and go south to the mountains with the boys.***

    IPA: aˑiˑd l̰ˑaˑik tu flaːi ə'weː 'sʌ̰m.deˑ ə̰ go saṵˑθ tu ðə̰ 'mãũːn.tẽⁿz̰
    wiθ ðə bʌːiz̰

    SYMBOLS: Ah-EED L̲**Ah**-EEK T>O͞O< F**L**_**Ah**_-EE uh-W**ẽ** **SUHM**.De *uh*
    Go SAh-O͞Oth T>O͞O< THuh **M**_**Ah**_-**OON**.TeᴺZˢ WEEth THuh
    BU͞H-EEZˢ

Diphthongs of R: A diphthong in which the second vowel is rhotic (e.g., has r-coloration in the final sound).

Example: near → nɪɝ-/NEAR

Triphthongs of R: A combination of three vowel sounds, in which the third vowel is rhotic.

Example: fire → faɪɚ-/FEYER

- ***Our friends started the fire near your north orchard an hour before we got there.***

    IPA: 'a.wə frẽnz 'sta.tɾd̰ ðə 'fa.jə nĩə̰ juə̰ nõə̰θ 'o.tʃəd̰ ə̃n 'a.wə bi'fɔ
    wi goṭ ðḛə

    SYMBOLS: **Ah**.Wuh FRᴿ*e*NZˢ **ST**_**Ah**_.TEED THuh **F**_**Ah**_.Yuh N*EE*-*uh*
    Y>O͞O<-*uh* N*A*W-*uh*th **o**.CH>UHᴿ<D *uh*N **Ah**.Wuh BEE.**FAW**
    WEE G*o*T THe-*uh*

Making Your Own Map of the Accent

Listen to the Senegalese (Wolof) accent samples provided and investigate the resources suggested in the *Introduction and Resources* section. Compose (or steal) *Key Phrases* from your listening/viewing that challenge and/or ground you in the accent. Then get more specific and check your sounds against the sounds in the Workbook.

Your take on the sound shifts may be slightly different. That is okay. The breakdown is a tool, not a rule. Recheck what you hear and, if you still stand behind your discoveries, go with them. This will help you to develop **your own** idiolect of the accent.

> *Note!*
> **What is an Idiolect?**
> Each of us speaks differently even if we have the same general accent. The individualized way that each of us speaks is referred to as an idiolect. For the actor, idiolect is part of what creates character. It is the "how" of the accent, and influences the way we craft our thoughts through language.

KEY PHRASES

Speak your *Key Phrases*, shifting back and forth between your own home *idiolect of English* and the *Senegalese (Wolof) accent* you are building. **Observe** the shifts <u>ONE by ONE</u> in your Articulators, Focus of Articulation, use of Melody/Pitch/Lilt, Rhythm/Stress/Pace, and Source & Path of Resonance as you shift back and forth between the two accents. Make note of the shifts in the table provided. Putting your understanding of the shifts into your <u>own words</u> will encourage you to develop a more clear and personal idiolect.

SENEGALESE (WOLOF) ACCENT *KEY POINTS OF FOCUS: VOCAL POSTURE AND CHARACTERISTICS*

JAW
LIPS
TONGUE
SOFT PALATE
PHARYNX

FOCUS OF ARTICULATION (TOWARDS TEETH, FRONT/MIDDLE/ BACK OF HARD PALATE, SOFT PALATE, ETC.)

MELODY/PITCH/LILT

RHYTHM/STRESS/PACE

SOURCE & PATH OF RESONANCE – Where does the resonance begin and what is the apparent path it travels through your body (chest, hard palate, sinuses, temples, crown, base of skull, etc.)? Refer to the Source & Path of Resonance and Resonators in the *Senegalese Accent of English: Down & Dirty Warm-Up and Quick Look* on page 245.

OTHER CHARACTERISTICS (What are your observations?)

PERSONAL IMAGES (For many actors personal images can be the most powerful and effective triggers for their transformation into an accent)

Chapter 10

Nigerian (Igbo) Accent of English

Introduction and Resources

The Igbo Language in Nigeria

Igbo is a Bantu language of the Niger-Congo family group and is spoken by over twenty million people, mainly in southern Nigeria. There are many dialects of Igbo, but the Onitscha-Owerri dialect is the basis for standard Igbo. The British colonized Nigeria at the end of the 19th century and did not leave until the middle of the 20th century. A number of different cultural groups speak Igbo. It was during colonization that these groups united as a distinct group unified by ethnicity and language. Since there were many different cultural groups speaking Igbo in the country, there were many different dialects. It was not until the 20th century that the current standard Igbo was developed. Over 250 languages are spoken in Nigeria; English is the official language. Two thirds of the country speaks either Hausa, Igbo, Yoruba or Fulani.

Documentaries

Re-emerging: The Jews of Nigeria, On the Nigeria-Biafra War

Films

Bursting Out, Living in Bondage, Umu Escochi Egbu, Umu Agbara Na-Eti Eti, Ndi Apama

Television

Ka Anyi Siebi, Igbo Amaka TV, House of Wahala, Africa Independent Television (AIT), Ay's Crib (pidgin languages; Igbo mixed with Yoruba)

Nigerian (Igbo) Plays

In English: *Wedlock of the Gods, Queen Omu-Ako of Oligbo, Old Wines Are Tasty, Memories in the Moonlight, The Wizard of Law*, all by Zulu Sofola

In Igbo: *Umu Ejima* by S.O. Mezu, *Aku Fechaa* and *Udo ka Mma* by A.B. Chukwuezi, *Nwa Ngwii Puo Eze* by B.I.N. Osuagwu, *Obidiya* by Enyinna Akoma,

Ojadili by Odunke; *Obi Nwanne* by Kalu Okpi; *Oguamalam* by Chika Gbuje; *Ugomma* by Godson Echebima; *Nka Di Na Nti* by B.C. Okoro; *Erimma* by T. Nzeako, Nwata Rie Awo; *Abu Na Egwuregwe Odinala Igbo* by N. Ugonna; *Uwa Ntoo, Oku Ghere Item, Eriri Mara Ngwugwu by Goddy Onyekaonwu; Nwadike Okwe Agbaala, Onye Kpa Nku Ahuhu, Nwata Bulie Nna, Ya Elu* by Innocent Nwadike

Music

Chiomam, Osondi Owendi, Darlington Nwangwu, King Prof. Obewe

Radio

RadioPalmwine Igbo, Igbo Radio

Personalities

Genevieve Nnaji (actress), Chimamanda Ngozi Adichie (author), Ngozi Okonjo-Iweola (Minister of Finance), Pat Utomi (professor & politician), Chinua Achebe (writer), Philip Emeagwali (computer scientist), Mike Ezuronye (actor), Nnamdi Azikiwe (first President of Nigeria), John Obi Mikel (football player), Oliver De Coque (singer/guitarist)

Down & Dirty Warm-up and Quick Look

Note!

On Symbols

- International Phonetic Alphabet Symbols will be listed first and Sound Symbols will be listed second. Example: [i]/[EE]
- Sound Symbol Users: bold-faced letters indicate the syllable is stressed.

1) **The Muscles:** Wake your mouth up so you can more easily discover the physical transformation in speaking the accent.

   a. Scratch the front, middle and back of your tongue with your front top teeth.

   b. Rub the front, middle and back of your hard palate with the tip of your tongue.

   c. Imagine your mouth is numb from being at the dentist and you want to wake it up. Make tongue circles pressing against the back of your lips first clockwise, then counter clockwise (you are waking up your orbicularis muscle).

   d. To get the breath flowing, blow through your lips, getting them to flap together. Travel up and down in pitch on a BBBB and PPP, feeling the vibration as you wiggle up and down your spine.

2) **Vocal Posture for a Nigerian (Igbo) Accent:** The tongue rests slightly forward behind the lower teeth, in the front of the mouth. The middle of the tongue is low. It sometimes helps to think of a nickel resting on the middle of the tongue. The back of the tongue is slightly raised. The body of the tongue is fairly wide and easy. The blade and middle-back of the tongue are both active in articulation. The lips are very active for rounded sounds. The jaw is active, but does not open wide. The soft palate is wide and easy. The pharynx is slightly narrowed, creating a very warm-sounding pharyngeal twang. The focus of articulation is split between the back of the hard palate with the back of the tongue articulating, and the front of the hard palate with the blade of the tongue articulating.

3) **Resonators:** "occupy" the following spaces. This will prepare you to find the Source & Path of Resonance for a Nigerian (Igbo) accent. (By "occupy", I mean just that; be in the space of it and find the pathway and flow of resonance, rather than "putting" the resonance there.)

a. CHEST – Generously laugh at something – hɑ hɑ hɑ / HAH HAH HAH

b. HARD PALATE – As if you were discovering something – hoː hoː hoː / Hō Hō Hō

c. THE BONES AT THE BASE OF YOUR SKULL (THE OCCIPITAL BONE) – Use your hands to scoop the sound from the base of your skull with a Mississippi African-American dialect as if you're flirting with someone nearby – heː heː heː / Hē Hē Hē

d. FLICK THE SOUND OUT OF YOUR CHEEKBONES with an Italian-American flourish, as if calling to someone across the street – heː heː heː / Hē Hē Hē

e. WITH YOUR HANDS NEXT TO YOUR TEMPLES, SHAKE THE SOUND OUT WITH LOOSE FISTS – As if you were somewhat crazed – ji̩ ji̩ ji̩ / YEE YEE YEE

f. IMAGINE A METAL DISK EXTENDING FROM YOUR HANDS THROUGH YOUR SKULL. Bring your hands to the sides of your head just above the temples, with your palms facing the floor, thumbs hooked behind your skull. *Lid* the vibration to create a muted brassy sound. Like a robot say "Hi" – haɨ haɨ haɨ / HAh-E̱E̱ HAh-E̱E̱ HAh-E̱E̱

g. GIGGLE OUT OF THE TOP OF YOUR HEAD – As if you were tickled pink by something – hi̩ hi̩ hi̩ / HEE HEE HEE

4) **Source & Path of Resonance for a Nigerian (Igbo) Accent:**
The image that comes to mind for the vibration's texture is one of warm velvet steel wool in the middle of the skull. The entire resonance is robust. Chest resonance is strong, and moves up through a slightly narrowed pharynx. It then feels as if it moves into the back of the neck and from there, onto what feels like a widened hard palate. Think of a nickel on the middle of the tongue, and imagine sending the resonance to the middle-back of the hard palate. The resonance then feels as if it goes into the side bones of the skull, and is pitched forward by a slightly raised back of the tongue, into the sinuses. Finally, it is lidded at the "metal disk" area of the skull (see #3b and #3f above). **Get the sound changes into your body and imagination.**

Say these phrases occupying the following places in your body, suggesting to yourself the following energetic associations:

● pubic bone to tail bone – survival instinct

zu̩ː / Z>O̅O̅<
I need it – aɨ ni̩d ɪ̩t / Ah-E̱E̱ NEED E̅ĒT

● pubic bone to navel & sacrum in back – sexuality, big feelings

woː / Wō
I desire it – aɨ 'di̩.'zaᵃ‿ɪ̩t / Ah-E̱E̱ **DE.ZAh**ᴬᴴ‿RᴿE̅ĒT

- rib cage to below heart – will

  ʒoː / ZHō
  I want it – aɪ wont ɪt̬ / Ah-EE WoNT EET

- heart – love

  mɑː / MAH
  I love it – aɪ lɔv ɪt̬ / Ah-EE LAWV EET

- throat – communication (think of talking at a party)

  bɵ / Bǫ
  I have to say it – aɪ hav tǫ seː ɪt̬ / Ah-EE HAhV TOO Sē EET

- forehead – intelligence/wisdom

  keː / Kē
  I know it – aɪ noː ɪt̬ / Ah-EE Nō EET

- crown of head – spirituality

  rɪ̞ː / RᴿEE
  I believe it – aɪ ˈbɪˈlɪv ɪt̬ / Ah-EE **BEE.LEEV** EET

6) **Articulation** – using playful physical actions: punching, flicking, dabbing, slashing

dǫ dɪ kǫ dǫ dɪ kǫ dǫ dɪ kǫ – dɪ
dǫ dɪ kǫ dǫ dɪ kǫ dǫ dɪ kǫ – deː
dǫ dɪ kǫ dǫ dɪ kǫ dǫ dɪ kǫ – daɪ
dǫ dɪ kǫ dǫ dɪ kǫ dǫ dɪ kǫ – doː
dǫ dɪ kǫ dǫ dɪ kǫ dǫ dɪ kǫ – dǫ

Repeat as needed, replacing [d̪] with [t̪], [p], [b], [k], [g], [f], [v]

DOO DEE KOO DOO DEE KOO DU DEE KOO – DEE
DOO DEE KOO DOO DEE KOO DU DEE KOO – Dē
DOO DEE KOO DOO DEE KOO DU DEE KOO – DAh-EE
DOO DEE KOO DOO DEE KOO DU DEE KOO – Dō
DOO DEE KOO DOO DEE KOO DU DEE KOO – D>OO<

Repeat as needed, replacing [D] with [T], [P], [B], [K], [G], [F], [V]. [D] & [T] are both articulated with the blade of the tongue against the back of the top front teeth (dentalized).

Key Points of Focus
Characteristics and Vocal Posture

Nigerian (Igbo) Accent Characteristics

> *Note!*
> **On Melody/Lilt/Pitch and Rhythm/Stress/Pace**
> Every accent contains shifts for some, but not necessarily all, of these
> elements of vocal variety.

> *Note!*
> **On Use of Musical Notes**
> Follow the "musical notes" up and down to get a feel for the melody of
> the accent. The filled-in notes are shorter than the open notes. For those
> who are musically inclined, think of them as approximating quarter notes
> and half notes. This distinction will give you a feel for the rhythm of the
> accent.

Melody/Lilt/Pitch

The melody for a Nigerian (Igbo) accent is quite different from that of a General
American accent of English. Below are some of the characteristics that mark the
difference.

1. Over the course of a thought, the melody for a Nigerian (Igbo) accent goes
   up and down like a bumpy road, whereas General American English is more
   like driving up and down an easy grade hill.
2. In the Igbo language, mid-level tones can only follow high tones – not low
   tones. This characteristic sometimes manifests in a Nigerian (Igbo) accent
   of English as an unexpected dramatic lift in pitch from syllable to syllable
   or word to word.

3. Often, there is <u>not</u> a full drop in pitch at the conclusion of a thought or sentence, as there is in General American English. The pitch can stay the same or rise.
4. In a Nigerian (Igbo) accent, vowels in operative words have more length than lengthened vowels in General American English. This length is often accompanied by a lifting or lowering in pitch.
5. Prefixes and suffixes are sometimes stressed through pitch change and/or lengthening.
6. In words with multiple syllables, Nigerian (Igbo) speakers often stress the middle syllable(s) through pitch change, and/or lengthening.
7. In compound words – unlike in General American English – the pitch remains steady in both syllables.
8. Weak forms of vowels are rarely used, which results in the syllables that are unstressed in General American English becoming stressed, through pitch change, and/or lengthening.

Example: Linda Story – 0:08

I went for a holiday precisely

In this thought, Linda speaks with a *bumpy road* melodic pattern (#1, p. 280). She stresses the final syllable in the compound word *holiday* by matching the pitch in the first syllable and by lengthening the vowel in the last syllable (#2, p. 280 and #7 above). The operative word *went* lifts in pitch and *holiday* and *precisely* both contain syllables that lift in pitch (#4 above). Linda does not conclude her short thought with a drop in pitch, but keeps the last two syllables floating on a middle tone (#3 above).

Example: Chinedu Story – 1:02

Because their activities are causing a lot of havoc on the road.

Even in all our express road.

Chinedu's impassioned protest about traffic and road conditions in Lagos is ironically expressed through *bumpy road* clusters of melody, with a progressive rise in pitch toward the words *activities, havoc* and *express* (#1, p. 280). His lifts in pitch are extreme in the words *activities* and *even* (#2, p. 280). Operative words *activities, lot, causing, havoc, express* all contain vowels that are lengthened, emphasizing the importance of these words in his thought.

This is accompanied by a lift in pitch in *activities* and *causing* (#4, p. 281). The prefix in *express*, which would be unstressed in General American English, is given equal length and pitch as the second syllable (#5, p. 281). To an American ear, this makes the prefix sound stressed. Vowels that would be pronounced in their weak forms in D.A.E. are pronounced in their strong forms and emphasized through pitch and length in *activities*, *causing*, *express* (#8, p. 281).

Rhythm/Stress/Pace

The expressive quality of this accent is largely driven by the variation in rhythm. There is a back and forth in the lengthening and shortening of the syllables and words, which creates a playful and syncopated dynamic. Be aware of the specific characteristics below.

1. Prefixes and suffixes are sometimes stressed through lengthening and/or pitch change.
2. In multiple-syllable words, the middle syllable(s) is/are often stressed through lengthening and pitch change.
3. The vowels in operative words have more length than the lengthened vowels in General American English. This length is often accompanied by a lifting or lowering of pitch.
4. Weak forms of vowels are rarely used, which results in the syllables that are normally unstressed in General American English becoming stressed, through lengthening and/or pitch change.
5. In compound words, the normally unstressed part of the word often gets stressed through lengthening.

   Example: Emmanuel Story (Part 1) – 2:19

They never knew we are sleeping in one of the classrooms in

the barracks.

There are a number of characteristics contributing to the expression of Emmanuel's wonderfully syncopated thought above. Note that he uses strong forms of vowels, which, in General American English, would be pronounced in weak forms: *sleeping* and *barracks*. This, along with the lengthening of these vowels, allows these otherwise weak syllables to match the stress in the stressed first syllables (#4 above). As mentioned above, the suffix in *sleeping* is stressed (#1 above). He lengthens the vowels in all of his operative words: *knew*, *sleeping*, *classrooms*, *barracks* (#3 above). In the compound word *classrooms*, he stresses the syllables equally by lengthening the vowels in both (#5 above). Notice how the pitch remains fairly steady.

Example: Nonyelum Story (Part 1) – 1:15

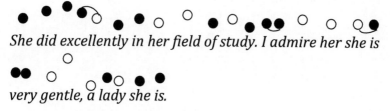

She did excellently in her field of study. I admire her she is

very gentle, a lady she is.

Nonyelum's accent beautifully illustrates with rhythm and stress, the *bumpy road* characteristic. In the four-syllable word *excellently*, she lengthens one of the middle syllables, *lent*, giving it stress; in a General American accent, it would be relatively unstressed (#2, p. 282). The vowels in operative words *excellently, field, study, admire, her, gentle, lady* are lengthened considerably (#3, p. 282). Strong forms of vowels, rather than weak forms, are used in *a lady*. These vowels are also lengthened, resulting in a speech dynamic that is rhythmically opposite to that of a General American accent, where the first syllable of *lady* would be stressed (#4, p. 282).

Source & Path of Resonance

The image that comes to mind for the resonance's texture is one of warm velvet steel wool in the middle of the skull. The entire resonance is robust. Chest resonance is strong, and moves up though a slightly narrowed pharynx. It then feels as if it moves into the back of the neck and from there, onto what feels like a widened hard palate. Think of a nickel on the middle of the tongue, and imagine sending the resonance to the middle-back of the hard palate. The resonance then feels as if it goes into the side bones of the skull, and is pitched forward by a slightly raised back of the tongue, into the sinuses. Finally, it is lidded at the "metal disk" area of the skull (see #3b and #3f on page 278).

The Source & Path of Resonance is present in all of the Nigerian (Igbo) accents in the audio library. It is most clear in the stronger accents of Ijeoma, Linda, Nonyelum, Emmanuel, Chibuzo and Chineda.

Nigerian (Igbo) Accent Vocal Posture

Note!
On Vocal Posture
These adjustments enable you to integrate the accent through physical transformation rather than solely relying on sound shifts.

- **Focus of Articulation:** The focus of articulation is split between the back of the hard palate and the front of the hard palate, with the blade of the tongue actively articulating in both places.
- **Tongue:** The tongue rests slightly forward in the front of the mouth. The middle of the tongue is low. The back of the tongue is slightly raised. The body of the tongue is fairly wide and easy. The blade and middle-back of the tongue are both very active in articulation. It sometimes helps to think of a nickel on the middle of the tongue.
- **Lips:** The lips are very active on rounded sounds.
- **Jaw:** The jaw is active, but stays fairly closed.
- **Soft Palate:** The soft palate is wide and easy.
- **Pharynx:** The pharynx is slightly narrowed, creating a very warm pharyngeal twang.

Distinct Sounds of the Language and/or Accent

Note!
On Distinct Sounds
These are some of the sounds that Nigerian (Igbo) speakers use and American speakers do not. In speaking the sounds and/or the words that contain them, you can heighten your physical understanding of the Nigerian (Igbo) accent's *Vocal Posture* as compared to your own. This frame of reference will both inform and strengthen your accent.

Consonants

1. *IPA:* [c] → palatal plosive.
    Symbol: [K̟ʸ] → [K] made more forward in the mouth with a little [ʸ] following.
    This sound is used in speaking the Nigerian (Igbo) language.
2. *IPA:* [kp]: voiceless labial velar implosive.
    Symbol: [KP]: made by sucking the air in rather than exploding the air out.
    This sound is used in speaking the Nigerian (Igbo) language.
3. *IPA:* [gb]: voiced labial velar implosive.
    Symbol: [GB]: made by sucking the air in rather than exploding the air out.
    This sound is used in speaking the Nigerian (Igbo) language.
4. *IPA:* [r] → alveolar trill.
    Symbol: [RR] → trilled [R].
    Used in place of [ɹ]/[R]: *red, dress*
    This sound is used in speaking the Nigerian (Igbo) language.
5. *IPA:* [ɾ] → alveolar tap.
    Symbol: [Rᴿ] → tapped [R], made by lightly tapping the top of the tip of the tongue on the alveolar ridge.
    Used in place of [ɹ]/[R]: *ran, ferry*
    This sound is used in speaking a Nigerian (Igbo) accent of English.

6. *IPA:* [ɣ]: voiced velar fricative.
    Symbol: [R^{GHH}]: made by vibrating the back of the tongue against the soft
    palate.
    This sound is used in speaking the Nigerian (Igbo) language.

Vowels

The vowels of the Nigerian (Igbo) language include:

IPA: [i], [ɪ], [ɛ], [a], [ɵ], [u], [o]
Symbol: [EE], [I], [EH], [Ah], [ọ], [OO], [o]

Knowing the vowels for the Nigerian (Igbo) language will provide clues for the
vowel shifts in the accent.

7. *IPA:* [e]
    Symbol: [e] → This is the first sound in the D.A.E. diphthong [AY] as in *face*.
    Used in place of [ɛ]/[Eh]: *dress*, *bed*
    This sound is used in speaking both the language and accent of Nigerian
    (Igbo).
8. *IPA:* [ɵ] → centralized [o].
    Symbol: [ọ] → [o] made in the middle of the mouth.
    This sound is used in speaking both the language and accent of Nigerian
    (Igbo).
9. *IPA:* [a]
    Symbol: [Ah] → This is the first sound in the D.A.E. diphthong [EYE].
    Used in place of [æ]/[A]: *trap*, *bath*
    This sound is used in speaking both the language and accent of Nigerian
    (Igbo).

Consonant Sound Shifts

- ☞ indicates that this sound is a key sound shift
- You can begin to fold melody and rhythm with the sound changes by speaking the sample sentences that are before each section of sound changes.

Note!

On End of Word Consonant Clusters *nt* and *nd*

Sometimes in words ending in [NT] or [ND], the consonants [T] and [D] are dropped.

Example: pla<u>nt</u> → pla<u>n</u>, sta<u>nd</u> → sta<u>n</u>

Consonant Shifts
Chinedu Story – 1:14

<u>The pot hol<u>es</u>, AH, even <u>the</u> pl<u>aces</u> <u>where</u> they a<u>re</u></u>

appea<u>ring</u>...

IPA: ḏi poṭˢ hoːʁẓ ʔa iː.vẽn ḏi 'pɫeː.sɪẓ weↃ ḏe ɑː‿ɾ‿'ɑ̣.'pïə.ɾen

SYMBOLS: DEE PoTˢ Hō<o>Zˢ ʔAh E̅E̅.VǫN DEE PL̲e̅.SIZˢ De A̅H‿Rᴿ‿A̱H.PI̲uh. RᴿeN

I'<u>ll</u> mee<u>t</u> you a<u>t</u> <u>the</u> fe<u>rr</u>y in an hour wi<u>th</u> <u>the</u> <u>t</u>en chil<u>dr</u>en.

IPA: aɪ̈ɾ mĩ̱ṭˢ‿jụ aṭ ḏa 'fe'ri ĩn an ãn wɪ̣ṭ ḏa ṭˢẽn 'tʃɪ̈ɾ'ḏɾen

SYMBOLS: Ah-E̲E̅-<o> MEETᶜᴴ‿Y>OO< AhT DAH Fe.RᴿEE E̅E̅N AhN ʔAhↃ WE̅E̅T DAh Tˢen CHE̅E̅-<oo>.DRᴿeN

288 Nigerian (Igbo) Accent of English

Key Words	Detailed American English Accent *IPA* *Symbol*	Shift to Nigerian (Igbo) Accent of English *IPA* *Symbol*	Key Words Shifts *IPA* *Symbol*	Your Key Words
<u>t</u>eam <u>taught</u>	t	[t̪] or [t̪ˢ]	t̪ĩm, t̪ot̪ or t̪ˢĩm, t̪ˢot̪	
	T	[T] or [Tˢ] both dentalized	TEEM, ToT or TˢEEM, TˢoT	
<u>d</u>eb<u>t</u> <u>d</u>i<u>d</u>	d	[d̪] or [d̪ᶻ]	d̪et̪, d̪ɪd̪ or d̪ᶻet̪, d̪ᶻɪd̪	
	D	[D] or [Dᶻ] both dentalized	DeT, DEED or DᶻeT, DᶻEED	
⊷ <u>th</u>ese <u>th</u>ere, brea<u>the</u>	ð	[ð̪] or [d̪]	ð̪iz, ð̪eːↃ, bríð̪ or d̪iz, d̪eːↃ, bríd̪	
	TH	[TH] or [D] both dentalized	THEEZS, Thē↘, BRᴿEETH or DEEZˢ, Dē↘, BRᴿEED	
⊷ <u>th</u>in <u>th</u>ick, mou<u>th</u>	θ	[θ] or [t̪]	θin, θɪk, mɑːθ or t̪in, t̪ɪk, mɑːt̪	
	th	[th] or [T] dentalized	thEEN, thEEK, MĀHth or TEEN, TEEK, MĀHT	
⊷ <u>r</u>ed d<u>r</u>ess, me<u>rr</u>y, so<u>rr</u>y	ɹ	sometimes [r]	red̪, d̪res, 'mē'ri	
	R	sometimes [Rᴿ]	RᴿeD, DRᴿeS, **Me.RᴿEE**	
⊷ exce<u>l</u> fa<u>ll</u>, tab<u>le</u> (final *l* in spelling)	l	[ɫ] or [ɤ]	'ek.seɫ, foɫ, 'teː'bɫ or 'ek.seɤ, foɤ, 'teː'bɤ	
	L	[L] or [<o>]	**eK.Se-L, Fo-L, Tĕ.BL** or **eK.Se-<o>, Fo-<o>, Tĕ.B<o>**	
ju<u>dge</u>	dʒ	d̪ʒ	d̪ʒəd̪ʒ	
	J	Jᶜᴴ	JᶜᴴₒJᶜᴴ	

Key Words	Detailed American English Accent IPA	Shift to Nigerian (Igbo) Accent of English IPA	Key Words Shifts IPA	Your Key Words
	Symbol	Symbol	Symbol	
<u>ch</u>ur<u>ch</u>	tʃ ---- CH	sometimes [ʃ] ---- sometimes [SH]	ʃəʃ ---- SHǫSH	
boy<u>s</u> (final *s* when pronounced [z])	z ---- Z	z̥ ---- Zˢ	bʌiz̥ ---- BUH-EEZˢ	
si<u>ng</u>	ŋ ---- NG	sometimes [ŋ̊] ---- sometimes [NGᴷ]	sĩŋ̊ ---- SEĔNGᴷ	
rea<u>ding</u> (final *ing* in spelling)	ɪŋ ---- ING	sometimes [in] ---- sometimes [EEN]	'ɾi̥'dĩn ---- Rᴿ**EE.DEEN**	
si<u>ng</u>ing (penultimate *ng* in spelling)	ŋ ---- NG	sometimes [ŋ.g] ---- sometimes [NG.G]	'sĩŋ'gĩn ---- SEĔNG.GEEN	
↦ a<u>sk</u>	sk ---- SK	sometimes [ks] ---- sometimes [KS]	aks ---- AhKS	

Front Vowel Sound Shifts

Note!

On Vowels

The vowels of the Nigerian (Igbo) language include:

IPA: [i], [ɪ], [ɛ], [a], [ө], [u], [o]
SYMBOL: [EE], [I], [EH], [Ah], [ǫ], [OO], [o]

Knowing the vowels of the Igbo language will provide clues for the vowel shifts in the accent.

Note!

On Vowels

Vowels are often nasalized when they precede or follow [n]/[N], [m]/[M], [ŋ]/[NG]

Example: meet → mĩt/M*EE*T
           nice → nãĩs/N*Ah-EE*S
           home → hõːm/H*ō*M
           fun → fẽn/F*ǫ*N
           ring → rĩŋ/R^R*EE*NG

		Front Vowel Shifts		

The *thief* wi**ll *tell* m**e** *after* w**e** *trap* h**i**m.**

IPA: ḍɑ ṭif wɪ̈ɤ ṭeɤ mi̧ 'af.tä̈ wi̧ ṭˢrap hi̧m

SYMBOLS: DAH TEEF WEĔ-<o> Te<o> MEE **AhF**.TUḨ WEE TˢRᴿAhP HEĔM

Key Words	Detailed American English Accent IPA ----- Symbol	Shift to Nigerian (Igbo) Accent of English IPA ----- Symbol	Key Words Shifts IPA ----- Symbol	Your Key Words
fl<u>ee</u>ce sn<u>ee</u>ze, pl<u>ea</u>d	i ----- EE	i̧ ----- EE	fli̧s, pli̧ḍ ----- FLEES, PLEED	
☞ k<u>i</u>t p<u>i</u>tch, d<u>i</u>m, l<u>i</u>p	ɪ ----- I	ɪ̧ ----- EĔ	kɪ̧ṭ, pɪ̧ṭʃ, ḍi̧m ----- KEĔT, PEĔCH, DEĔM	
countr<u>y</u> (*y* in final position of spelling)	ɪ̧ ----- EĔ	i ----- EE	'kɘn'ṭˢɹii ----- KO̧N.TˢREE	
☞ b<u>e</u>rated (this includes prefixes like *be, re,* and *de,* as in the words b<u>e</u>rated, r<u>e</u>pair, d<u>e</u>light)	[ɪ̧] in prefix ----- [EĔ] in prefix	[i] the prefix is <u>not</u> unstressed ----- [EE] the prefix is <u>not</u> unstressed	'bi'reː.ṭiḍ ----- **BEE.Rᴿɛ̧.TEED**	
dr<u>e</u>ss b<u>e</u>d, f<u>ea</u>ther, s<u>e</u>nd	ɛ ----- EH	e ----- e	ḍres, beḍ, 'fe.ḍä ----- DRᴿeS, Bed, Fe.DUḨ	
☞ tr<u>a</u>p m<u>a</u>d, r<u>a</u>t, c<u>a</u>ndle	æ ----- A	a ----- Ah	ṭˢɹap, maḍ, 'kän'ḍɤ ----- TˢRAhP, MAhD, K*Ah*N.D<o>	
☞ b<u>a</u>th *[a]/[Ah] <u>a</u>sk, <u>a</u>fter, d<u>a</u>nce, ex<u>a</u>mple, h<u>a</u>lf, m<u>a</u>sk, r<u>a</u>scal, tr<u>a</u>nsfer In Chapter 1, there is a list of these words called the BATH or ASK list of words.	æ ----- A	a ----- Ah	baθ, aks, 'af'ṭä ----- BAhth, Ahks, **AhF.TUḨ**	

Middle Vowel Sound Shifts

	Middle Vowel Shifts			
In the summer, workers burned the underbrush.				
IPA: ɪn ḍɑ 'sɔ'mã 'wə'kä̱z bēnḍ ọ̈i 'ən'ḍä.brʌʃ				
SYMBOLS: ĒEN DAH **SAW.M*AH* Wọ.KU̲HZ**^S BọND THEE ọN.DU̲H.BR^RUHSH				
Key Words	*Detailed American English Accent* IPA ------------------- Symbol	*Shift to Nigerian (Igbo) Accent of English* IPA ------------------- Symbol	*Key Words Shifts* IPA ------------------- Symbol	*Your Key Words*
☛ bi̲rd service, lea̲rn (*ir, er, ear* in spelling)	ɝ ------------------- ER	[ɛ] or [ə] ------------------- [E̱H] or [ọ]	bɛḍ, 'sɛ'vis, lɛ̱n or bọḍ, 'sə'vis, lə̱n ------------------- BE̱HD, **SE̱H.VEES**, LE̱HN or BọD, **Sọ.VEES**, Lọ̱N	
☛ nu̲rse wo̲rk (*ur, or* in spelling)	ɝ ------------------- ER	ɵ ------------------- ọ	nẽs, wək ------------------- NọS, WọK	
☛ siste̲r traito̲r, hanga̲r	ɚ ------------------- er	ʌ̈ ------------------- UH̱	'sɪs'ṯä, 't^Sreː'ṯä ------------------- SE̱ES.TUH̱, T^SR^Rē.TUH̱	
☛ stru̲t cu̲rry	ʌ̈ ------------------- UH̱	[ɵ] or [ɔ] or [ʌ] ------------------- [ọ] or [AW] or [UH]	st^Srɵṯ, 'kə.ɾi or st^Srɔṯ, 'kɔ.ɾi or st^Srʌṯ, 'kʌ.ɾi ------------------- ST^SRọT, **Kọ.R^REE** or ST^SRAWT, **KAW.R^REE** or ST^SRUHT, **KUH.R^REE**	

Key Words	*Detailed American English Accent* *IPA* ---------- *Symbol*	*Shift to Nigerian (Igbo) Accent of English* *IPA* ---------- *Symbol*	*Key Words Shifts* *IPA* ---------- *Symbol*	*Your Key Words*
⊶ c<u>o</u>me fl<u>oo</u>d (in words spelled with *o* and sometimes *oo*)	ʌ̈ ---------- UH̟	ɔ ---------- AW	kɔ̃m, flɔd̪ ---------- K*AW*M, FLAWD	
⊶ <u>a</u>bout b<u>a</u>nan<u>a</u>	ə ---------- uh	ɑ̟ ---------- AH̟	'ɑ̟.baːt̪, 'bɑ̟'nã.nɑ̟̃ ---------- **AH**.BĀHT, **BAH̟.N*Ah***.N*AH̟*	
⊶ <u>con</u>sider <u>com</u>pare	[ə] in *con* and *com* prefixes ---------- [uh] in *con* and *com* prefixes	o ---------- o	'kõn'sɪ̞.d̪ʌ̈, 'kõm.peː↘ ---------- **K*o*N.SĒ̆E**.DUH̟, **K*o*M**.Pē↘	

Back Vowel Sound Shifts

	Back Vowel Shifts			
I thought my father would not stop being a bully but the truth is, I was wrong.				
IPA:	ai θɔt mai 'fɑ.ðʌ̈ wʊd nɔt stɒp bĩŋ ɑ 'bʊ.li bʌt ðə truθ ɪz ai wɑz ɾɒŋ̊			
SYMBOLS:	Ah-EE thoT MAh-EE **FAH**.THUH WOOD NoT SToP B*EE*NG^K AH **BOO**.LEE BUHT THAH TR^R>OO<th EEZ^S Ah-EE WAHZ^S R^RoNG^K			
Key Words	*Detailed American English Accent* IPA ------------------- Symbol	*Shift to Nigerian (Igbo) Accent of English* IPA ------------------- Symbol	*Key Words Shifts* IPA ------------------- Symbol	*Your Key Words*
f<u>oo</u>d gr<u>ew</u>, tr<u>ue</u>, tw<u>o</u>	u ------------------- OO	ṵ ------------------- >OO<	fṵd, gɾṵ, t^sɾṵ, t^sṵ ------------------- F>OO<D, GR^R>OO<, T^sR^R>OO<, T^s>OO<	
d<u>u</u>ty t<u>u</u>ne, n<u>ew</u>s	[ɪʊ] when preceded by *t, d, n* in spelling ------------------- [I-OO] when preceded by *t, d, n* in spelling	ṵ ------------------- >OO<	dṵ.t^si, t^sṵn, nṵz ------------------- D>OO<.T^sEE, T^s>OO<N, N>OO<Z^s	
f<u>oo</u>t p<u>u</u>t	ʊ ------------------- U	ṵ ------------------- OO	fṵt, pṵt ------------------- FOOT, POOT	
⊢ th<u>ou</u>ght t<u>a</u>ll, c<u>au</u>lk, <u>aw</u>ful	ɔ ------------------- AW	[o] or [ɔ] ------------------- [o] or [AW]	t^sot, t^soʏ, kok or t^sɔt, t^sɔʏ, kɔk ------------------- T^soT, T^so-<o>, KoK or T^sAWT, T^sAW-<o>, KAWK	

Key Words	Detailed American English Accent IPA ------------------ Symbol	Shift to Nigerian (Igbo) Accent of English IPA ------------------ Symbol	Key Words Shifts IPA ------------------------ Symbol	Your Key Words
☞ cl<u>o</u>th *[ɒ]/[O] d<u>o</u>g, c<u>ou</u>gh, w<u>a</u>sh, h<u>o</u>rrid	ɔ ------------------ AW	ɔ̧ ------------------ o	klɔ̧θ, dɔ̧g, kɔf, wɔʃ, hɔ̧.rɪ̧d ------------------------ KLoth, DoG, KoF, WoSH, Ho.Rᴿ E̅E̅D	
f<u>a</u>ther	ɑ ------------------ AH	ɑ ------------------ AH	ˈfɑ.ð̧ä ------------------------ **FAH**.THŲH	
☞ l<u>o</u>t *[ɒ]/[O] sq<u>ua</u>d, w<u>a</u>nder	ɑ ------------------ AH	[o] or [ɑ] ------------------ [o] or [AH]	lo̧t, skwo̧d, ˈwõn.ḑä or la̧t, skwa̧d, ˈwãn.ḑä ------------------------ LoT, SKWoD, **Wo**N.DUH or LAHT, SKWAHD, **WAH**N.DUH	

Diphthong Sound Shifts

		Diphthong Shifts		

I'd like to fly away someday and go south to the mountains with the boys.

IPA: aiḍ laik t̪ˢu̜ flai 'ạ'weː 'sẽm'deˑ ạ̈n goː sɑːθ t̪ˢu̜ ọ̈ị 'mɑ̃ːn.tạ̈nz wị̈θ ð̪ạ̈ bʌiz̪

SYMBOLS: Ah-EED LAh-EEK TˢŌŌ FLAh-EE **AH-Wē SọM.Dē** ẠHN Gō SĀHth TˢŌŌ THẠH **MĀHN.TẠHNZ**ˢ WĒETH THẠH BUH-EEZˢ

Key Words	Detailed American English Accent	Shift to Nigerian (Igbo) Accent of English	Key Words Shifts	Your Key Words
	IPA ------------------- Symbol	IPA ------------------- Symbol	IPA ------------------- Symbol	
☛ face pain, day, weight, steak	eɪ ------------------- AY	eː ------------------- ē	feːs, pẽːn, ḍeː weːt̪ ------------------- Fēs, Pēn, Dē, WēT	
price eyes, diaper, fly, guy, height	aɪ ------------------- EYE	aɨ ------------------- Ah-EE	pɾais, aiz̪, dai.pʌ̈ ------------------- PRᴿAh-EES, Ah-EEZˢ, DAh-EE.PUḦ	
☛ choice boys	ɔɪ ------------------- OY	ʌɨ ------------------- UH-EE	t̪ʃʌis, bʌiz̪ ------------------- CHUH-EES, BUH-EEZˢ	
☛ goat sew, go, toe	oʊ̆ ------------------- OH	oː ------------------- ō	goːt̪ˢ, soː, goː ------------------- GōTˢ, Sō, Gō	
☛ mouth town	aʊ̆ ------------------- OW	ɑː ------------------- ĀH	mɑ̃ːt̪, t̪ɑ̃ːn ------------------- MĀHT, TĀHN	

Diphthongs of R Sound Shifts

Note!
On r-coloration
A Nigerian (Igbo) accent has no r-coloration in diphthongs or triphthongs of R.

Note!
On Falling Tone in Diphthongs of R Turned Monophthong
When the diphthong becomes a monothong, there is often a falling tone: ↘

Example: h<u>air</u> ↘   heː↘ / Hē
         h<u>our</u>↘   aː↘ / A͞H

Diphthongs and Triphthongs of R Shifts				

<u>Our</u> friends st<u>ar</u>ted the f<u>ire</u> n<u>ear</u> <u>your</u> n<u>or</u>th <u>or</u>chard an h<u>our</u> bef<u>ore</u> we got th<u>ere</u>.

IPA: aʽ↘ frɛ̃nẓ stɑ˞.tṛd dǫ faᵃ nï j↘ǫ noˑṭ ꞌoːꞌtʃǫd ą̈n ꞌa.wa ꞌbi.fǫ wị goṭ deː↘

SYMBOLS: Ah↘ FRᴿeNZˢ STA͞H.TE͞ED DAḤ FAhᴬᴴ NI̦ Yo↘ NōT ō̦.CHǫD A̦HN
Ah.WAH **BEE**.Fo WEE GoT Dē↘

Key Words	Detailed American English Accent IPA	Shift to Nigerian (Igbo) Accent of English IPA	Key Words Shifts IPA	Your Key Words
	Symbol	Symbol	Symbol	
↤ n<u>ear</u> b<u>eer</u>	ɪ˞	[iˑə] or [ï͐↘]	niˑə, biˑə or nï↘, bï↘	
	EAR	[E͞E-uh] or [I̦]	NE͞E-uh, BE͞E-uh or NI̦↘, BI̦↘	
↤ h<u>air</u> st<u>are</u>, p<u>ear</u>, squ<u>are</u>, th<u>ere</u>	ɛ˞	eː↘	heː↘, steː↘, peː↘	
	AIR	ē↘	Hē↘, STē↘, Pē↘	

Key Words	Detailed American English Accent IPA ---------- Symbol	Shift to Nigerian (Igbo) Accent of English IPA ---------- Symbol	Key Words Shifts IPA ---------- Symbol	Your Key Words
☛ s<u>ure</u> p<u>oor</u>, y<u>our</u>	ʊɝ˞ ---------- UR	ɔ↘ ---------- AW↘	ʃɔ↘, pɔ↘, jɔ↘, ---------- SHAW↘, PAW↘, YAW↘	
☛ n<u>orth</u> Ge<u>or</u>ge, p<u>our</u>, w<u>ar</u>p, <u>oar</u>	ɔɝ˞ ---------- AWR	oː↘ ---------- ō↘	nõːθ↘, d̥ʒoːd̥ʒ↘, poː↘ ---------- Nōth↘, J^{CH}ōJ^{CH}↘, Pō↘	
☛ st<u>art</u> h<u>eart</u>	ɑɝ˞ ---------- AHR	ɑˑ↘ ---------- ĀH↘	st̥ɑˑt̥↘, hɑˑt↘ ---------- STĀHT↘, HĀHT↘	
f<u>ire</u>	aɪɝ˞ ---------- EYER	aᵃ ---------- Ah^{AH}	faᵃ ---------- FAh^{AH}	
h<u>our</u>	aʊɝ˞ ---------- OWR	[a↘] or [ˈa.wɑ] ---------- [Ah↘] or [**Ah-WAH**]	a↘ or ˈa.wɑ ---------- Ah↘ or **Ah**.WAH	

Key Sentences for Practice

> **Note!**
> - By practicing the sentences below, you can work through the sound shifts for a Nigerian (Igbo) accent in the context of a simple thought. I suggest you think, imagine and speak actively from a point of view. As you begin to work with the operative words in the thoughts, the rhythm and melody of the accent will begin to emerge appropriately.

Consonants:

- **Example:** Chinedu Story – 1:14

The pot holes, AH, even the places where they

are appearing...

IPA:　　ɖi potˢ hoːɤẓ ʔa iː.vẽn ɖi ˈpɬeː.sɪẓ weˎ ɖe ɑːˏɾˏˈɑ.ˈpïə.ɾen

SYMBOLS:　DEE PoTˢ Hō<o>Zˢ ʔAh ĒE.VǫN DEE PḺē.SIZˢ De ĀH̲ˏRᴿˏ A̲H.PĪuh.RᴿeN

- ***I'll meet you at the ferry in an hour with the ten children.***

IPA:　　aɪɤ mĩtˢˏju at ɖa ˈfeˈɾi ĩn an ãn wɪt ɖa t̪ˢẽn ˈt̪ʃɪɤˈɖɾen

SYMBOLS:　Ah-ĒE-<o> MEETᶜᴴˏY>OO< AhT DAH **Fe.Rᴿ̲EE** *ĒĒN Ah*N ʔAhˎ WĒET DAh Tˢen **CHĒĒ-<oo>.DRᴿeN**

Front Vowels: Vowels made by arching or cupping the front of the tongue toward the front of the hard palate.

- ***The thief will tell me after we trap him.***

IPA:　　ɖa t̪if wɪɤ t̪eɤ mi̲ ˈaf.tä wi̲ t̪ˢɾap him

SYMBOLS:　DAH TEEF WĒE-<o> Te<o> MEE AhF.TU̲H WEE TˢRᴿAhP HĒ̆EM

Middle Vowels: Vowels made by arching or cupping the middle of the tongue toward the middle of the hard palate.

- *In the summer, workers burned the underbrush.*

  IPA: ɪn dạ 'sɔ'mã 'wə'kặz̧ bẽnḍ ọi 'ẽn'ḍặ.brʌʃ

  SYMBOLS: ẼEN DAH **SAW.M*A*H W*ọ*.KU*Ḥ*Z*^{S} Bọ̧ND THEE
  ọN.DU̧H.BR^{R}UHSH

Back Vowels: Vowels made by arching or cupping the back of the tongue toward the back of the hard palate.

- *I thought my father would not stop being a bully but the truth is, I was wrong.*

  IPA: aɨ θoṭ maɨ 'fɑ.ọ̈ẍ wụd nǫ̇ṭ sṭop bĩŋ ɑ 'bụ.li bʌṭ ọ̧ạ tṛụθ ɪz̧ aɨ wạ̧z̧
  ɾoŋ̇

  SYMBOLS: Ah-E̱E thoT MAh-E̱E **FAH**.THU̧H WO͞OD NoT SToP BE̱E̱NG^K
  A̧H **BO͞O**.LEE BU̧HT THA̧H TR^R>OO<th E̱E̱Z^S Ah-E̱E WA̧̧HZ^S
  R^{R}oNG^K

Diphthongs: When two vowels are combined in one syllable.

- *I'd like to fly away someday and go south to the mountains with the boys.*

  IPA: aɨḍ laɨk ṭˢụ flaɨ 'ạ'weː 'sẽm'deˑ ạ̧n goː sɑːθ ṭˢụ ọ̧ɪ 'mãːn.ṭạ̧nz̧
  wɪθ ọ̧ạ bʌɨz̧

  SYMBOLS: Ah-E̱E̱D LAh-E̱EK TˢO͞O FLAh-EE **A̧H-Wē** Sọ̧M.Dē *A̧H*N
  Gō SA͞Hth TˢO͞O THA̧H **M*A͞H*N.T*A̧H*NZ**^{S} WE͞ETH THA̧H
  BUH-E̱EZ^S

Diphthongs of R: A diphthong in which the second vowel is rhotic (e.g., has r-coloration in the final sound).

Example: near → nɪɚ̃/NEAR

Triphthongs of R: A combination of three vowel sounds, in which the third vowel is rhotic.

Example: fire → faɪɚ̃/FEYER

- *Our friends started the fire near your north orchard an hour before we got there.*

  IPA: a↘ frẽnz̧ sṭɑˑṭɪḍ dạ faᵃ nɨ jↄ̧↘ noˑt 'oːtʃəd ạ̧n 'a.wɑ 'bi.fↄ̧ wɪ
  goṭ ḍeː↘

  SYMBOLS: Ah↘ FR^R*e*NZ^S STA͞H.TE̱ED DA̧H FAh^{AH} NI̧ Yo↘ NōT **ō.CHọ̧D**
  *A̧H*N **Ah**.WAH **BEE**.Fo WEE GoT Dē↘

Making Your Own Map of the Accent

Listen to the Nigerian (Igbo) accent samples provided and investigate the resources suggested in the *Introduction and Resources* section. Compose (or steal) *Key Phrases* from your listening/viewing that challenge and/or ground you in the accent. Then get more specific and check your sounds against the sounds in the Workbook.

Your take on the sound shifts may be slightly different. That is okay. The breakdown is a tool, not a rule. Recheck what you hear and, if you still stand behind your discoveries, go with them. This will help you to develop **your own** idiolect of the accent.

Note!

What is an Idiolect?

Each of us speaks differently even if we have the same general accent. The individualized way that each of us speaks is referred to as an idiolect. For the actor, idiolect is part of what creates character. It is the "how" of the accent, and influences the way we craft our thoughts through language.

KEY PHRASES WITH KEY SOUND SHIFTS

Speak your *Key Phrases*, shifting back and forth between your own home *idiolect of English* and the *Nigerian (Igbo) accent* you are building. **Observe** the shifts <u>ONE by ONE</u> in your Articulators, Focus of Articulation, use of Melody/ Pitch/Lilt, Rhythm/Stress/Pace, and Source & Path of Resonance as you shift back and forth between the two accents. Make note of the shifts in the table provided. Putting your understanding of the shifts into your <u>own words</u> will encourage you to develop a more clear and personal idiolect.

NIGERIAN (IGBO) ACCENT *KEY POINTS OF FOCUS: VOCAL POSTURE AND CHARACTERISTICS*

JAW
LIPS
TONGUE
SOFT PALATE
PHARYNX

FOCUS OF ARTICULATION (TOWARDS TEETH, FRONT/MIDDLE/
BACK OF HARD PALATE, SOFT PALATE, ETC.)

MELODY/PITCH/LILT

RHYTHM/STRESS/PACE

SOURCE & PATH OF RESONANCE – Where does the resonance begin and
what is the apparent path it travels through your body (chest, hard palate,
sinuses, temples, crown, base of skull, etc.)? Refer to the Source & Path of
Resonance and Resonators in the *Nigerian (Igbo) Accent of English: Down
& Dirty Warm-Up and Quick Look* on page 277.

OTHER CHARACTERISTICS (What are your observations?)

PERSONAL IMAGES (For many actors personal images can be the most
powerful and effective triggers for their transformation into an accent)

Chapter 11

Ghanaian (Akan: Twi and Fante) Accent of English

Introduction and Resources

The Akan Language in Ghana

Ghanaians have been exposed to the English language for over five hundred years. British traders first came to Ghana in the late 15th century. By the middle of the 16th century, they had established a strong trade in gold, ivory, spices and slaves. The first British missionaries arrived in the middle of the 18th century and with missionaries came a more formal push towards teaching Ghanaians English. It was not until the late 1950s that Ghanaians were finally free of British rule.

Today, English is the official language of Ghana, but nine other languages are popularly spoken. The most widely spoken languages include Akan, Ga, Dagomba and Ewe. Akan is the largest ethnic group in Ghana and about 80% of the population speaks Akan as a first or second language. Twi, Fante, Asante Twi and Kwapim are all dialects of Akan and are mutually understandable. Akan belongs to the Kwa group of the Niger-Congo language family.

Documentaries

Sakawa Boys Internet Scamming in Ghana, Out of Informality: Ghana's way to decent work, The Witches of Gambaga, Living the Hiplife

Films

Sankofa (Kofi Ganoba is Akan), *Through a Film, Darkly, Boys Abre, Ware Me, Oseifuo, Emmaa Pe Aware, Aboa Sika, What A Shock, Obaatan Mmo Dua, Kae Dabi*

Television

Tracey Towers, Concert Party, Showcase in Akan, Osofo Dadzie, Adehye Drama Group, Daakye Drama Group, Obra, Ntease Drama Group, Adassa Drama Group

Ghanaian Akan (Twi & Fante) Plays

The Dilemma of a Ghost and *Anowa* by Ama Ata Aidoo, *Foriwa*, *Edufa*, and *The Marriage of Anansewa* by Efua Sutherland, *The Blinkards* by Kobina Seyi (written in English and interspersed with Fanti), *Abibigoro* and *The Witch of Mopti* by Mohammed Ben Abdallah (written in English and interspersed with Akan; the narrator speaks only in Akan.)

Music/Musicians

Ebo Taylor: *Ohemaa Mercy* (There are a couple of wonderful interviews with Mr. Taylor on the web), Daddy Lumba, Reggie Rockstone, Sarkodie, Osei Kwame. Azonto is a popular music and dance.

Radio

Adom FM

Personalities

Kofi Annan (Former Secretary-General of U.N.), James Kwesi Appiah (coach of Ghanaian football team), Abedi Pele (footballer), Michael Essien (footballer), Sulley Muntari (footballer), Mawuli Okudjeto (fashion designer), Azumah Nelson (boxer), Joshua Clotted (boxer), Apostle Kwadwo Safo (Steve Jobs of Ghana), Agya Koo (actor), Van Vicker (actor), Majid Michael (actor), S.K. Oppong (actor)

Down & Dirty Warm-up and Quick Look

> *Note!*
> **On Symbols**
> - International Phonetic Alphabet Symbols will be listed first and Sound Symbols will be listed second. Example: [i]/[EE]
> - Sound Symbol Users: bold-faced letters indicate the syllable is stressed.

1) **The Muscles:** Wake your mouth up so you can more easily discover the physical transformation in speaking the accent.

   a. Scratch the front, middle and back of your tongue with your front top teeth.
   b. Rub the front, middle and back of your hard palate with the tip of your tongue.
   c. Imagine your mouth is numb from being at the dentist and you want to wake it up. Make tongue circles pressing against the back of your lips first clockwise, then counter clockwise (you are waking up your orbicularis muscle).
   d. To get the breath flowing, blow through your lips, getting them to flap together. Travel up and down in pitch on a BBBB and PPP, feeling the vibration as you wiggle up and down your spine.

2) **Vocal Posture for a Ghanaian Akan (Twi & Fante) Accent:** These adjustments enable you to integrate the accent through physical transformation rather than solely relying on sound shifts.

   The blade of the tongue rests behind the lower bottom teeth, while the middle of the tongue is slightly raised, and the soft palate is low; this keeps the articulation focused toward the middle and front of the mouth. The lip corners are slightly pulled back, but the lips actively round for rounded vowels: [ʉˑ]/[O͡O], [ʊ]/[O͡O], [ɔ]/[>A̹W<]. The pharynx narrows actively to create a slight nasal twang.

3) **Resonators:** "occupy" the following spaces. This will prepare you to find the Source & Path of Resonance for a Ghanaian Akan (Twi & Fante) accent.

(By "occupy", I mean just that; be in the space of it and find the pathway and flow of resonance, rather than "putting" the resonance there.)

a. CHEST – Generously laugh at something – ha ha ha / HAh HAh HAh
b. HARD PALATE – As if you were discovering something – hǝː hǝː hǝː / Hǭ Hǭ Hǭ
c. THE BONES AT THE BASE OF YOUR SKULL (THE OCCIPITAL BONE) – Use your hands to scoop the sound from the base of your skull with a Mississippi African-American dialect as if you're flirting with someone nearby – heˑ heˑ heˑ / Hē Hē Hē
d. FLICK THE SOUND OUT OF YOUR CHEEKBONES with an Italian-American flourish, as if calling to someone across the street – heˑ heˑ heˑ / Hē Hē Hē
e. WITH YOUR HANDS NEXT TO YOUR TEMPLES, SHAKE THE SOUND OUT WITH LOOSE FISTS – As if you were somewhat crazed – jį jį jį / YEE YEE YEE
f. IMAGINE A METAL DISK EXTENDING FROM YOUR HANDS THROUGH YOUR SKULL. Bring your hands to the sides of your head just above the temples, with your palms facing the floor, thumbs hooked behind your skull. *Lid* the vibration to create a muted brassy sound. Like a robot say "Hi" – häː häː häː / H̲Ah H̲Ah H̲Ah
g. GIGGLE OUT OF THE TOP OF YOUR HEAD – As if you were tickled pink by something – hį hį hį / HEE HEE HEE

4) **Source & Path of Resonance for a Ghanaian Akan (Twi & Fante) Accent:** The resonance is grounded robustly in the chest. It moves through a slightly narrowed pharynx, creating a light nasal twang. Because the focus of articulation is in the middle and front of the mouth, the resonance travels onto the middle of the hard palate. Resonance passes through the sinuses and becomes slightly nasalized. The sound becomes lidded at the *metal disk* area, just above the temples (refer to #3f above).

5) **Get the sound changes into your body and imagination.**
    Say these phrases occupying the following places in your body, suggesting to yourself the following energetic associations:

- pubic bone to tail bone – survival instinct

    zu̱ˑ / ZO͞O
    I need it – ä nị̱d ị̈t / A̲h NEED E̲͞ET

- pubic bone to navel & sacrum in back – sexuality, big feelings

    wǝː / W>U͞H^R<
    I desire it – ä dị̱'za.jă̱ɾ‿į̱'ṱ / A̲h DE̲͞E.**ZAh**.Yã̱h.R^R‿E̲͞ET

- rib cage to below heart – will

    ɔ̱ɔ / ZH>A̱W<
    I want it – ä wonṱ ị̈t / A̲h WoNT E̲͞ET

- heart – love

    ma / MAH

    I love it – ä ləv ɪ̈t̪ / Aḫ LʉV E̋ET

- throat – communication (think of talking at a party)

    bə / Be̲

    I have to say it – ä haẙ tʉ se· ɪ̈t̪ / Aḫ HAhVᶠ TU Se̅ E̋ET

- forehead – intelligence/wisdom

    ke· / Ke̅

    I know it – ä nə: ɪ̈t̪ / Aḫ N>UHᴿ< E̋ET

- crown of head – spirituality

    ri̪ / RᴿEE

    I believe it – ä bɪ̈'lɪ̈v ɪ̈t̪ / Aḫ BE̋E.**LE̲E̲V** E̋ET

6) **Articulation** – using playful physical actions: punching, flicking, dabbing, slashing

    d̪ʉ dï kʉ d̪ʉ dï kʉ d̪ʉ dï kʉ – d̪i̪
    d̪ʉ dï kʉ d̪ʉ dï kʉ d̪ʉ dï kʉ – d̪e·
    d̪ʉ dï kʉ d̪ʉ dï kʉ d̪ʉ dï kʉ – d̪ä:ï
    d̪ʉ dï kʉ d̪ʉ dï kʉ d̪ʉ dï kʉ – d̪ə:
    d̪ʉ dï kʉ d̪ʉ dï kʉ d̪ʉ dï kʉ – d̪ʉ·

Repeat as needed, replacing [d̪] with [t̪], [p], [b], [k], [g], [f], [v].

    DO͝O DEE KO͝O DO͝O DEE KO͝O DO͝O DEE KO͝O – DE̲E̲
    DO͝O DEE KO͝O DO͝O DEE KO͝O DO͝O DEE KO͝O – De̅
    DO͝O DEE KO͝O DO͝O DEE KO͝O DO͝O DEE KO͝O – DA̲H-Ĭ
    DO͝O DEE KO͝O DO͝O DEE KO͝O DO͝O DEE KO͝O – DU̲
    DO͝O DEE KO͝O DO͝O DEE KO͝O DO͝O DEE KO͝O – DO̲͝O

Repeat as needed, replacing [D] with [T], [P], [B], [K], [G], [F], [V]. [D] & [T] are both articulated with the blade of the tongue against the back of the top front teeth (dentalized).

Key Points of Focus
Characteristics and Vocal Posture

Ghanaian Akan (Twi & Fante) Accent Characteristics

Note!
On Melody/Lilt/Pitch and Rhythm/Stress/Pace
Every accent contains shifts for some, but not necessarily all, of these elements of vocal variety.

Note!
On Use of Musical Notes
Follow the "musical notes" up and down to get a feel for the melody of the accent. The filled-in notes are shorter than the open notes. For those who are musically inclined, think of them as approximating quarter notes and half notes. This distinction will give you a feel for the rhythm of the accent.

Melody/Lilt/Pitch

1. The melody travels like little hills: up and down.
2. The lengthened vowels and diphthongs in the stressed syllables do not lilt, but they do go up or down in pitch. Pitch shifts occur mainly in syllables containing a diphthong.

   Example: Kwesi Story – 0:57

She went to the riverside and was just about to throw herself

in the water

Note the words *riverside* and *about* have a downward pitch thrust in their second syllables, which contain diphthongs (#2, p. 312). The whole thought contains many little melodic hills going up and down (#1, p. 312).

Example: Mary Story – 0:42

I was the only girl among them

This small phrase illustrates the gentle hills that occur when pitch changes. There are no lilts in this accent's pitch variation.

Rhythm/Stress/Pace

The stress is most often created by simultaneously lengthening and changing the pitch of the vowels and diphthongs in the stressed syllables of operative words. This is clearly heard in Mary's story on *after*, *very*, *runner* and in Kwesi's story on *beautiful* and *girl*.

Example: Mary Story – 2:05

The one after me was a very good runner

Example: Kwesi Story – 0:29

She grew up to be a beautiful girl

Source & Path of Resonance

The resonance is grounded robustly in the chest. It moves through a slightly narrowed pharynx, creating a light nasal twang. Because the focus of articulation is in the middle and front of the mouth, the resonance travels strongly up onto the middle of the hard palate. Resonance passes through the sinuses and becomes slightly nasalized. The sound becomes lidded at the *metal disk* area, just above the temples (refer to #3f on page 310).

This is clearly heard in the stronger accents of Gertrude, Mary, Ama, Paul and Kwesi, as well as in Nana's accent, when he speaks Fante in Part 2 of his story. Dorothy speaks at a higher pitch, so her chest resonance is not as pronounced as the others'. These resonance characteristics can be heard even in the lighter accents of Francis and Nana when they are speaking English.

Ghanaian Akan (Twi & Fante) Accent Vocal Posture

> *Note!*
> **On Vocal Posture**
> These adjustments enable you to integrate the accent through physical transformation rather than solely relying on sound shifts.

- **Focus of Articulation:** The focus of articulation is toward the middle and front of the mouth.
- **Tongue:** The blade of the tongue rests behind the lower bottom teeth. The middle of the tongue is slightly raised, which keeps the articulation forward.
- **Lips:** The lip corners are slightly pulled back, but the lips actively round for rounded vowels: [u̟˔]/[O̟͡O], [ʊ̞]/[O͝O], [ɔ̹̟]/[>A̟W<] as well as for the rounded consonants.
- **Jaw:** The jaw is moderately active.
- **Soft Palate:** The soft palate is low.
- **Pharynx:** The pharynx is active, creating a slight nasal twang.

Distinct Sounds of the Language and/or Accent

> *Note!*
>
> **On Distinct Sounds**
>
> These are some of the sounds that Ghanaian (Akan: Twi and Fante) speakers use and American speakers do not. In speaking the sounds and/or the words that contain them, you can heighten your physical understanding of the Ghanaian (Akan: Twi and Fante) accent's *Vocal Posture* as compared to your own. This frame of reference will both inform and strengthen your accent.

Consonants

1. *IPA:* [r] → alveolar trill.
   Symbol: [RR] → Trilled [R].
   This sound is used in speaking the Ghanaian Akan language.
2. *IPA:* [ɾ] → alveolar tap.
   Symbol: [R^R] → Tapped [R].
   Sometimes used in place of [ɹ]/[R]: *red*, *ferry*
   This sound is used in speaking both the language and accent of Ghanaian Akan.
3. *IPA:* [ɲ] → Palatal nasal.
   Symbol: [NG^Y] → [NG]. Made on the hard palate with a little [^{Y}] following.
   Used in place of [ŋ]/[NG]: *sing*
   This sound is used in speaking both the language and accent of Ghanaian Akan.
4. *IPA:* [ç] → Voiceless palatal fricative.
   Symbol: [SH^Y] → Articulated in the middle of the mouth with a little [^{Y}] following.
   This sound is used in speaking the Ghanaian Akan language.
5. *IPA:* [h] → Voiceless glottal fricative.
   Symbol: [H^{XXX}] → This sound is made by blowing air through a slightly closed throat.
   This sound is used in speaking the Ghanaian Akan language.

6. *IPA:* [pʷ], [bʷ], [tʷ], [dʷ], [kʷ], [gʷ], [çʷ], [hʷ], [nʷ], [ɲʷ] → The [ʷ] indicates that this set of consonants is made while rounding the lips for a [ʷ].

   Symbol: [P ʷ], [B ʷ], [T ʷ], [D ʷ], [K ʷ], [G ʷ], [SH ʷ], [H ʷ], [N ʷ], [NG ʷ] → The [ʷ] indicates that this set of consonants is made while rounding the lips for a [ʷ].

   These sounds are used in speaking the Ghanaian Akan language.

   * ***These sounds indicate how active the lips are in rounding for a Ghanaian Akan accent of English and are key to the Vocal Posture.***

Vowels

The Vowels of the Ghanaian Akan language include:

IPA: [i], [y], [ɪ], [e], [ɛ], [a], [u], [ʊ], [ɔ]

Symbol: [EE], [>EE<] (with rounded lips), [I], [e], [EH], [Ah], [OO], [U], [AW]

Knowing the vowels of the Ghanaian Akan language will provide clues for the vowel shifts in the accent.

7. *IPA:* [e]

   Symbol: [e] → This is the first sound in the D.A.E. diphthong [AY] as in f*a*ce.

   Used in place of [ɛ]/[EH] and sometimes [ʌ]/[UH] and made more in the middle of the mouth [e̞]/[e̞]: dr*e*ss, b*e*d and str*u*t, c*u*rry

   This sound is used in speaking both the language and accent of Ghanaian Akan.

8. *IPA:* [a]

   Symbol: [Ah] → This is the first sound in the D.A.E. diphthong [EYE].

   Used in place of [æ]/[A]: tr*a*p, b*a*th

   This sound is used in speaking both the language and accent of Ghanaian Akan.

9. *IPA:* [ə] → centralized [e].

   Symbol: [e̞] → [e] made in the middle of the mouth.

   Used in place of [ʌ]/[UH]: str*u*t, c*u*rry

   This sound is used in speaking a Ghanaian Akan accent of English.

10. *IPA:* [ɵ] → centralized [o].

    Symbol: [o̞] → [o] made in the middle of the mouth.

    Used in place of [ʌ]/[UH] for *o* in spelling: c*o*me, fl*oo*d

    This sound is used in speaking a Ghanaian Akan accent of English.

Consonant Sound Shifts

- ↤ indicates that this sound is a key sound shift
- You can begin to fold melody and rhythm with the sound changes by speaking the sample sentences that are before each section of sound changes.

Consonant Shifts
Example: Paul Story (Part 1) – 0:00

One dream I remember having which felt so real was I was

running in the woods .

IPA: wən d͡sɹɪmː ä͡ɪ ɹ̩ˈmɛm.bə̥ ˈha.vɪ̈n wɪ̈t͡ʃː fɛx̣t sə ɹ̣ɹ̈ woẓ ä͡ɪ woẓ ˈɹən.nɪ̈n ɪ̈n ð̥ə wʊ̥dẓ

SYMBOLS: WǫN >Dˢ<REEM Ah-EE REE.MeM.BUH HAh.VEEN WEECH Fe-<o>T S>UHᴿ< >R<EE->o< WoZˢ Ah-EE WoZˢ Re.NEEN EEN THUH WOODZˢ

I'll meet you at the ferry in an hour with the ten children.

IPA: ä͡ɹ mɪ̣t jṳ ä̤t ð̥ə ˈfɛ.rɪ ɪ̈n än ˈa.wä wɪ̈θ ð̥ə tɛn ˈt͡ʃɪ̈ɹ.drɛn

SYMBOLS: Ah-<o> MEET YOO AhT THUH Fe.RᴿEE EEN AhN Ah.WAh WEEth THUH TeN CHEE-<o>.DRᴿeN

Key Words	Detailed American English Accent	Shift to Ghanaian Accent of English	Key Words Shifts	Your Key Words
	IPA	*IPA*	*IPA*	
	Symbol	*Symbol*	*Symbol*	
team deb<u>t</u>, <u>d</u>i<u>d</u>	[t]/[d] ------------------ [T], [D]	[t̪]/[d̪] ------------------ [T]/[D] both dentalized	t̪im, d̪et̪, d̪ïd̪ ------------------ TEEM, DeT, DEED	
↦ <u>th</u>ese <u>th</u>ere, brea<u>th</u>e	ð ------------------ TH	ð̪ ------------------ [TH] dentalized	ð̪iz, ð̪e:, brïð̪ ------------------ THEEZ^S, THē, BR^REETH	
↦ <u>th</u>in <u>th</u>ick, mou<u>th</u>	θ ------------------ th	θ̪ ------------------ [th] dentalized	θ̪ïn, θ̪ïk, mä·ŭθ ------------------ thEEN, thEEK, MAh-Ŭth	
↦ <u>r</u>ed d<u>r</u>ess, me<u>rr</u>y, so<u>rr</u>y	ɹ ------------------ R	sometimes [ɾ̪] or [ɾ] ------------------ sometimes [R] or [R^R]	ɹed, dɹes, 'me·ɾ̪i, 'so·ɾ̪i or red, dres, 'me·ɾi, 'so·ɾi ------------------ Red, DReS, Mē.REE, Sō.REE or R^Red, DR^ReS, Mē.R^REE, Sō.R^REE	
↦ exce<u>l</u> fa<u>ll</u>, tab<u>le</u> (final *l* in spelling)	l ------------------ L	[l] often dropped or [ɤ] ------------------ [L] often dropped or [<o>] ([o] made with no lip rounding)	'ek.seɤ, fɔɤ, 'te·bɤ ------------------ eK.Se<o>, F>AW<-<o>, Te.B<o>	
boy<u>s</u> (final *s* when pronounced [z])	z ------------------ Z	z̪ ------------------ Z^S	boiz̪ ------------------ bo-EEZ^S	
si<u>ng</u> (final *ng* in spelling)	ŋ ------------------ NG	ɲ ------------------ NG⁺^Y	sïɲ ------------------ SEENG⁺^Y	

Key Words	Detailed American English Accent	Shift to Ghanaian Accent of English	Key Words Shifts	Your Key Words
	IPA ------------------ *Symbol*	*IPA* ---------------------- *Symbol*	*IPA* --------------------------- *Symbol*	
singing (medial *ng* in spelling)	ŋ ------------------ NG	ŋg̊ ---------------------- NGᴷ	ˈsɪ̈ ŋg̊.ɪ̈n ------------------------- **SE̱ENG**ᴷ**.E̱EN**	
reading (final *ing* in spelling)	ɪŋ ------------------ ING	ɪ̈n ---------------------- E̱EN	ˈrɪ̠.dɪ̈n ------------------------- **RᴿEE̱.DEE̱N**	
explain, export (*ex* in prefix)	ɛks ------------------ EKS	[k] is sometimes dropped in this prefix ---------------------- [K] is sometimes dropped in this prefix	esˈpleˑn ------------------------- e̱S.**PL**e̱**N**	

Front Vowel Sound Shifts

Note!

On Vowels

The Vowels of the Ghanaian Akan language include:

IPA: [i], [y], [ɪ], [e], [ɛ], [a], [u], [ʊ], [ɔ]

Symbols: [EE], [EE] (with rounded lips), [I], [e], [EH], [Ah], [OO], [U], [AW]

Knowing the vowels of the Ghanaian Akan language will provide clues for the vowel shifts in the accent.

Front Vowel Shifts				

The thief will tell me after we trap him.

IPA: ð̟ə θi̠f wɪ̈ɤ te̠ɤ mi̠ ˈaf.t̠ə̃ wi̠ t̠ɾap hi̠m

SYMBOLS: THUH thE̠EF WE̠E<o> Te̠<o> ME̠E **AhF**.TUH WE̠E TR^RAhP HE̠EM

Key Words	Detailed American English Accent IPA ------------------ Symbol	Shift to Ghanaian Accent of English IPA ------------------ Symbol	Key Words Shifts IPA ---------------------- Symbol	Your Key Words
↤ fleece sneeze, plead	i ------------------ EE	i̠ ------------------ [E̠E] [EE] articulated more in the middle of the mouth	fli̠s, sni̠z, pli̠d ---------------------- FLE̠ES, SNEE̠Z^S, PLEE̠D	
↤ kit pitch, dim, lip	ɪ ------------------ I	ï̠ ------------------ [Ë̠E] [I] made almost like [EE]	ki̠t, pi̠tʃ, di̠m ---------------------- KE̠ET, PEE̠CH, DE̠EM	

Key Words	Detailed American English Accent IPA / Symbol	Shift to Ghanaian Accent of English IPA / Symbol	Key Words Shifts IPA / Symbol	Your Key Words
country (*y* in final position of spelling)	ɪ̠ / EE̠	i / [EE]	ˈkən.t̠r̠i / Ke̠·N.TREE̠	
be̠rated	[ɪ̠] in prefix / [EE̠] in prefix	ï̠ / [EE̠]	ˌbï ˈr̠e·.t̠ïd / BEE̠.Rᴿe̠.TEED	
☛ dre̠ss be̠d, fe̠ather, se̠nd	ɛ / EH	e̠ / [e] ([e] articulated more in the middle of the mouth)	dr̠e̠s, be̠d, ˈfe·.ð̠ə̠ / DRᴿe̠s, Be̠D, Fe̠.THUH	
☛ tra̠p ma̠d, ra̠t, ca̠ndle	æ / A	a / Ah	t̠ra̠p, ma̠d̠, ˈkan.d̠r̠ / TRᴿAhP, MAhD, KAhN.D<o>	
☛ ba̠th *[a]/[Ah] a̠sk, a̠fter, da̠nce, exa̠mple, ha̠lf, ma̠sk, ra̠scal, tra̠nsfer In Chapter 1, there is a list of these words called the BATH or ASK list of words.	æ / A	a̠ / [Ah] ([Ah] articulated more in the middle of the mouth)	ba̠θ, a̠ks / BAhth, AhKS	

Middle Vowel Sound Shifts

Middle Vowel Shifts				
In the summer, workers burned the underbrush.				
IPA: ĭn ð̣ə̣ 'sɔ.mə̰̃ 'wɛ.kə̰z bənḍ ð̣ị̣ 'ən.dę̃,brəʃ				
SYMBOLS: ĚEN THUH **Se̱**.MŬH **Wę**.KUHZ^S B>UH^R<ND THEE **ę**N.DŬH.BR^ReSH				
Key Words	*Detailed American English Accent* IPA ---------------------- *Symbol*	*Shift to Ghanaian Accent of English* IPA ---------------------- *Symbol*	*Key Words Shifts* IPA ---------------------- *Symbol*	*Your Key Words*
↤ nurse work (*ur, or* in spelling)	ɝ ---------------------- ER	[e] or [ə] ---------------------- [e] ([e] made more in the middle of the mouth) or [>UH^R<] ([UH^R] made with rounded lips)	[nes], [wek] or [nəs], [wək] ---------------------- NeS, WeK or N>UH^R<S, W>UH^R<K	
↤ bird service, learn (*ir, er, ear* in spelling)	ɝ ---------------------- ER	[e˙] or [eɚ] ---------------------- [ē] or [e-uȟ^R]	be˙ḍ, 'se˙.vïs, le˙n or beə̄ḍ, 'seɚ.vïs, leɚn ---------------------- BēD, **Sę**.VĒES, LēN or Be-uȟ^RD, **Se-uȟ^R**.VĒES, Le-uȟ^RN	
sister traitor, hangar	ɚ ---------------------- er	ə̰̃ ---------------------- UȞ	'sïs.tə̰̃, 'tre˙.tə̰̃, 'haŋ.ĝə̰̃ ---------------------- S**EĒ**S.TUȞ, TRhē̆.TUȞ, HAhNG.^KUȞ	

Key Words	Detailed American English Accent IPA / Symbol		Shift to Ghanaian Accent of English IPA / Symbol		Key Words Shifts IPA / Symbol		Your Key Words

Key Words	Detailed American English Accent — IPA / Symbol	Shift to Ghanaian Accent of English — IPA / Symbol	Key Words Shifts — IPA / Symbol	Your Key Words
☛ str<u>u</u>t c<u>u</u>rry	Ʌ / UH	ə / [e] ([e] made more in the middle of the mouth)	st̺r̺ət, ˈkə.r<u>i</u> / STRᴿ<u>e</u>T, **K<u>e</u>**.Rᴿ<u>EE</u>	
☛ c<u>o</u>me fl<u>oo</u>d (in words spelled with *o* and sometimes *oo*)	Ʌ / [UH]	ɵ / [o̧] ([o] made more in the middle of the mouth)	kəm, flo̧d / Ko̧M, FLo̧D	
<u>a</u>bout b<u>a</u>n<u>a</u>n<u>a</u>	ə / uh	ə̧ / UH	ə̧ˈbä·ŭt̺, ˌbaˈna·.nə̧ / UH.**BA͞h**-ŬT, BAh.**NA͞h**.NUH	
☛ c<u>o</u>n**sider** c<u>o</u>m**pare**	[ə] in *con* and *com* prefixes / [uh] in *con* and *com* prefixes	[kon]/[kom] / [KoN]/[KoM]	konˈsï.də̧, komˈpeə̧ / KoN.**S͞E͞E**.DŬH, KoM.**P<u>e</u>**-UH	

324

Back Vowel Sound Shifts

Back Vowel Shifts				
I thought my father would not stop being a bully but the truth is, I was wrong.				
IPA: ä θǫt maˑ 'fa.ðə̌ wǔd not stǫp 'bɪn ạ 'bǔ.lị bǝt ðǝ trụˑθ ĭz ä woẓ ṛᴿǫ̌ŋ				
SYMBOLS: A̱h thoT MAh **FAh**.THUH WOOD NoT SToP BEEN UH **BOŎ**.LE̱E̱ BUHT THUH TRᴿO̱Oth E̱E̱Zˢ A̱h WoZˢ RᴿAWNGᴷ				
Key Words	*Detailed American English Accent* *IPA* --- *Symbol*	*Shift to Ghanaian Accent of English* *IPA* --- *Symbol*	*Key Words Shifts* *IPA* --- *Symbol*	*Your Key Words*
f<u>oo</u>d gr<u>ew</u>, tr<u>ue</u>, tw<u>o</u>	u --- OO	ʉˑ --- O̱O̱	fʉˑd, grʉˑ, trʉˑ --- FOŎD, GRᴿO̱O̱, TRᴿO̱O̱	
⊶ f<u>oo</u>t p<u>u</u>t	ʊ --- U	ʊ̣ --- [O̱O̱] ([U] made almost like [OO])	fʊ̣t, pʊ̣t --- FOŎT, POŎT	
⊶ d<u>u</u>ty t<u>u</u>ne, n<u>ew</u>s	[ɪʊ̣] when preceded by *t, d, n* in spelling --- [I-O̱O̱] when preceded by *t, d, n* in spelling	ɪʲu --- IʸOO	'drʲu.tị --- **DI**ʸ**OO**.TE̱E̱	

Key Words	Detailed American English Accent	Shift to Ghanaian Accent of English	Key Words Shifts	Your Key Words
	IPA	*IPA*	*IPA*	
	Symbol	*Symbol*	*Symbol*	
thought t<u>a</u>ll, c<u>au</u>lk, <u>aw</u>ful	ɔ ――――――― AW	ɔ̞ ――――――― [>A̟W<] ([AW] made with lips more rounded and made more in the middle of the mouth)	θɔ̞t, tɔ̞ɹ, kɔ̞k, 'ɔ̞.fɹ ――――――― th>A̟W<t, T>A̟W<-<o>, K>A̟W<K >A̟W<.F<o>	
cl<u>o</u>th *[ɒ]/[O] d<u>o</u>g, c<u>ou</u>gh, w<u>a</u>sh, h<u>o</u>rrid	ɔ ――――――― AW	ɔ̞ ――――――― [AW] articulated with the back of the tongue lowered toward an [AH]	klɔ̞θ, dɔ̞g, kɔ̞f ――――――― KLAWTh, DAWG, KAWF	
f<u>a</u>ther	ɑ ――――――― AH	a ――――――― Ah	'fa.ð̞ə̞ ――――――― **FAh.THŬH**	
☛ l<u>o</u>t *[ɒ]/[O] sq<u>ua</u>d, w<u>a</u>nder	ɑ ――――――― AH	o ――――――― o	lot, skwod, 'won.d̞ə̞ ――――――― LoT, SKWoD, **WoN.Dŭh**	

Diphthong Sound Shifts

> ***Note!***
> **On Diphthongs**
> In a Ghanaian Akan (Twi and Fante) accent of English, when the diphthong becomes a monophthong, as is often the case with [eɪ]/[AY] and [oʊ]/[OH], there is a falling melodic tone: ↘
>
> Example: price ↘   präː↘s / PR^RA̱ẖ↘S

Diphthong Shifts				
I̱'d lı̱ke to flỵ awạy somedạy and gǫ sọuth to the mǫuntains with the bǫỵs.				
IPA: ä̱d läˈɪ̱k tṳ fläːɪ̱ aˈweˑ↘ ˈsəm.de an gəː säˑʊθ tṳ ð̥ə̱ ˈmäʊn.tə̱nẕ wɪ̱θ̥ ð̥ə̱ boɪẕ				
SYMBOLS: A̱hD LA̱ẖ-Ĭ̱K TŌŌ FLA̱ẖ-Ĭ̱ Ah.**We̅↘** Sə̱m.De AhN G>U̅H^R< SA̱ẖ-Ŭth TU THUH **MA̱ẖ-ŬN**.TUHNZ^S WI̱th THUH Bo-EEZ^S				
Key Words	*Detailed American English Accent* IPA ---------------------- *Symbol*	*Shift to Ghanaian Accent of English* IPA ---------------------- *Symbol*	*Key Words Shifts* IPA ---------------------- *Symbol*	*Your Key Words*
↤ fa̱ce pa̱in, dạy, we̱ight, stea̱k	eɪ ---------------------- AY	eˑ ---------------------- e̅	feˑs, peˑn, d̥eˑ ---------------------- FēS, PēN, Dē	
prı̱ce eỵes, dı̱aper, flỵ, guỵ, he̱ight	aɪ ---------------------- EYE	[äːɪ̱] or [äː] ---------------------- [A̱ẖ-Ĭ̱] or [A̱ẖ]	präːɪ̱s, äːɪ̱ẕ, ˈd̥äːɪ̱.pə̥̌ or präːs, äːẕ, ˈd̥äː.pə̥̌ ---------------------- PR^RA̱ẖ-Ĭ̱S, A̱ẖ-Ĭ̱Z^S, **DA̱ẖ-Ĭ̱**.Pu̱h or PR^RA̱ẖS, A̱ẖZ^S, **DA̱ẖ**.Pu̱h	

Key Words	Detailed American English Accent *IPA* ---- *Symbol*	Shift to Ghanaian Accent of English *IPA* ---- *Symbol*	Key Words Shifts *IPA* ---- *Symbol*	Your Key Words
ch<u>oi</u>ce b<u>oy</u>s	ɔɪ ---- OY	oi ---- o-EE	t͡ʃois, boiz̦ ---- Cho-EES, Bo-EEZ[S]	
⌐ g<u>oa</u>t s<u>ew</u>, g<u>o</u>, t<u>oe</u>	oʊ ---- OH	ɘː ---- [>ŪH[R]<] ([UH[R]] made with rounded lips)	gɘːt, sɘː, gɘː ---- G>ŪH[R]<T, S>ŪH[R]<, G>ŪH[R]<	
m<u>ou</u>th t<u>ow</u>n	aʊ ---- OW	ä·ʊ ---- Ā̱h-Ŭ	mä·ʊ̞θ, tä·ʊn ---- MĀ̱h-ŬTh, TĀ̱-ŬN	

Diphthongs of R Sound Shifts

> *Note!*
> **On r-coloration**
> A Ghanaian Akan (Twi & Fante) accent has no r-coloration in diphthongs
> and triphthongs of R.

Diphthongs and Triphthongs of R Shifts

__Our__ friends st__a__rted the __fi__re n__ear__ __your__ n__or__th __or__chard an h__our__ bef__ore__ we got th__ere__.

IPA: ˈa.wă frɛnz̥ ˈsta.tɪ̈d ɒ̯ə̯ ˈfa.jă nɪ̈ə̯ jʊ̯ nɔ̯θ ˈɔ.tʃəd an ˈa.wă ˈbɪ̈.fɔ wɪ̯ gɒt ðɛːə̯

SYMBOLS: **Ah**.WĀh FRᴿₑNZˢ **STAh**.TĒ̠ED THUH **FAh**.YĀh NĒ̠E-UH YAW
N>AW<th >AW<.CH>UHᴿ<D AhN **Ah**.WĀh **BĒ̠E**.F>AW< WE̠E GoT
Th̠ē-ŪH

Key Words	Detailed American English Accent	Shift to Ghanaian Accent of English	Key Words Shifts	Your Key Words
	IPA	IPA	IPA	
	-------------------	-------------------	-------------------	
	Symbol	Symbol	Symbol	
n__ear__ b__eer__	ɪɚ̯	ɪ̈ə̯	nɪ̈ə̯, bɪ̈ə̯	
	-----------------	-----------------	-----------------	
	EAR	I̠-ŪH	NI̠-ŪH, BI̠-ŪH	
↦ __hair__ st__are__, p__ear__, squ__are__, th__ere__	ɛɚ̯	[e̠ː] or [e̠ə̯]	he̠ː, ste̠ː, pe̠ː or he̠ə̯, ste̠ə̯, pe̠ə̯	
	-----------------	-----------------	-----------------	
	AIR	[ē̠] or [e̠-ŪH]	HĒ̠, STĒ̠, PĒ̠ or He̠-ŪH, STe̠-ŪH, Pe̠-ŪH	
s__ure__ p__oor__, y__our__	ʊɚ̯	[ʊ̯] or [ʊ̯ə̯]	ʃʊ̯, pʊ̯, jʊ̯ or ʃʊ̯ə̯, pʊ̯ə̯, jʊ̯ə̯	
	-----------------	-----------------	-----------------	
	UR	[U] or [U-UH]	SHU, PU, YU or SHU-UH, PU-UH, YU-UH	

Key Words	Detailed American English Accent *IPA*	Shift to Ghanaian Accent of English *IPA*	Key Words Shifts *IPA*	Your Key Words
	Symbol	*Symbol*	*Symbol*	
⊢ n<u>or</u>th G<u>eor</u>ge, p<u>our</u>, w<u>ar</u>p, <u>oar</u>	ɔɚ	ɔ̞̈	nɔ̞̈·θ, d̠ʒ̊ɔ̞̈·d̠ʒ̊, pɔ̞̈·	
	AWR	[>A̅W<] ([AW] made with lips more rounded)	N>A̅W<th, J^SH>A̅W<J^SH, P>A̅W<	
st<u>ar</u>t h<u>ear</u>t	ɑɚ	[a·] or [a˞]	sta·t, ha·t or sta·t, ha·t	
	AHR	[A̅h] or [Ah^R]	STA̅hT, HA̅hT or STAh^RT, HAh^RT	
f<u>ire</u>	aɪɚ	ˈa.jã	ˈfa.jã	
	EYER	Ah-Yah	**FAh-YAh**	
h<u>our</u>	aʊɚ	ˈa.wã	ˈa.wã	
	OWR	Ah-WA̅h	**Ah-WA̅h**	

Key Sentences for Practice

> **Note!**
> • By practicing the sentences below, you can work through the sound
>   shifts for a Ghanaian Akan (Twi & Fante) accent in the context of a
>   simple thought. I suggest you think, imagine and speak actively from
>   a point of view. As you begin to work with the operative words in the
>   thoughts, the rhythm and melody of the accent will begin to emerge
>   appropriately.

Consonants:

• **Example:** Paul Story (Part 1) – 0:00

One dream I remember having which felt so real was I

was running in the woods .

  IPA: wən d̠ˢɹiːmː ä̈ɪ ɹ̈ɪˈmem.bə̤ ˈha.vɪ̈n wɪ̈tʃː feɤt sɐ ɹ̈ɪɤ woz ä̈ɪ woz
      ˈɹən.nɪ̈n ɪ̈n ð̠ə̤ wʊ̆dz̥

  SYMBOLS: WǫN >Dˢ<REEM Ah-EĒ REĒ.**M̧eM**.BUH **HAh**.VEĒN WEĒCH
      Fe.<o>T S>UHᴿ< >R<EĒ->o< WoZˢ Ah-EĒ WoZˢ Re̞.NEĒN
      EĒN THUH WŎODZˢ

• ***I'll meet you at the ferry in an hour with the ten children.***

  IPA: äːɤ mit ju̱ ăt ð̠ə̤ ˈfe.ɾi ɪ̈n ăn ˈa.wă wɪ̈θ ð̠ə̤ ten ˈtʃɪ̈ɤ.dɹen

  SYMBOLS: Ãh-<o> MEĒT YO̱O ÃhT THUH **Fe̞**.RᴿEE EĒN ÃhN **Ah**.WÃh
      WEĒth THUH Te̞N **CHEĒ**-<o>.DRᴿe̞N

Front Vowels: Vowels made by arching or cupping the front of the tongue toward the front of the hard palate.

- **The th*ie*f w*i*ll t*e*ll m*e* *a*fter w*e* tr*a*p h*i*m.

    IPA: ð̮ə θ̮if wɪ̽ʏ t̮eʏ mi̮ 'af.t̮ə̽ wi̮ t̮rap hɪ̮m

    SYMBOLS: THUH thEE͞F WE͞E<o> Te<o> ME͟E **A͟hF**.TU͞H WEE TRᴿAhP HE͞EM

Middle Vowels: Vowels made by arching or cupping the middle of the tongue toward the middle of the hard palate.

- **In th*e* s*u*mm*er*, w*or*kers b*ur*ned the *u*nderbr*u*sh.**

    IPA: ɪ̮n ð̮ə̮ 'sə.mə̽ 'we.k̮əz̮ bənd̮ ð̮i̮ 'ən.d̮ə̽ˌbrəʃ

    SYMBOLS: E͞EN THUH **S*e***.MU͞H **W*e***.KUHZˢ B>UHᴿ<ND THE͟E **e͟N**.DU͞H.BRᴿ*e*SH

Back Vowels: Vowels made by arching or cupping the back of the tongue toward the back of the hard palate.

- **I th*ou*ght my f*a*ther w*ou*ld n*o*t st*o*p being a b*u*lly but the tr*u*th is, I w*a*s wr*o*ng.**

    IPA: ä θ̮ɔt ma· 'fa.ð̮ə̽ wʊ̮d nŏt̮ st̮op 'bɪ̮n a̮ 'bʊ̮.li̮ bət̮ ð̮ə t̮rṳ·θ ɪ̮z ä woz̮ rɔ̮ŋ⁺

    SYMBOLS: A͟h thoT MAh **FAh**.THUH WOOD NoT SToP **BEEN UH BO͞O.LE͟E** BUHT THUH TRᴿOOth E͞Eᴢˢ A͟h WoZˢ Rᴿ͟AWNGᴷ

Diphthongs: When two vowels are combined in one syllable.

- **I*'d* l*i*ke to fl*y* aw*ay* somed*ay* and g*o* s*ou*th to the m*ou*ntains with the b*oy*s.**

    IPA: äd̮ lä·ɪ̆k t̮ṳ flä:ɪ̆ a'we·↘ 'səm.d̮e an gɔɪ sä·ʊθ t̮ṳ ð̮ə 'mäʊn.t̮ənz̮ wɪ̮θ ð̮ə boiz̮

    SYMBOLS: A͟hD LA͟I̯H-Ĭ̮K TO͞O FLA͟I̯H-Ĭ̮ Ah.**We͞**↘ **S*e*m**.De AhN G>U͞Hᴿ< SA͟I̯H-Ŭth TU THUH **MA͟h-Ŭ̮N**.TUHNZˢ WIth THUH Bo-EEZˢ

Diphthongs of R: A diphthong in which the second vowel is rhotic (e.g., has r-coloration in the final sound).

Example: near → nɪɚ̃/NEAR

Triphthongs of R: A combination of three vowel sounds, in which the third vowel is rhotic.

Example: fire → faɪɚ̃/FEYER

- ***Our friends started the fire near your north orchard an hour before we got there.***

  IPA: ˈa.wă frɛn̥z̥ ˈsta.tɪ̥d ðə̥ ˈfa.jă nɪ̃ɚ̃ jʊ̥ nɔ̥θ ˈɔ.tʃəd an ˈa.wă ˈbɪ̈.fɔ̥ wɪ̥ got̥ ðe̥ːɚ̥

  SYMBOLS: **Ah**.WÃh FRᴿ<u>e</u>NZˢ **STAh**.T<u>EE</u>D THUH **FAh**.YÃh N<u>EE</u>-UH
  YAW N>AW<th >**AW**<.CH>UHᴿ<D AhN **Ah**.WÃh
  B<u>EE</u>.F>AW< W<u>EE</u> GoT Th<u>e</u>-ŬH

Making Your Own Map of the Accent

Listen to the Ghanaian Akan (Twi & Fante) accent samples provided and investigate the resources suggested in the *Introduction and Resources* section. Compose (or steal) *Key Phrases* from your listening/viewing that challenge and/or ground you in the accent. Then get more specific and check your sounds against the sounds in the Workbook.

Your take on the sound shifts may be slightly different. That is okay. The breakdown is a tool, not a rule. Recheck what you hear and, if you still stand behind your discoveries, go with them. This will help you to develop **your own** idiolect of the accent.

> *Note!*
> **What is an Idiolect?**
> Each of us speaks differently even if we have the same general accent. The individualized way that each of us speaks is referred to as an idiolect. For the actor, idiolect is part of what creates character. It is the "how" of the accent, and influences the way we craft our thoughts through language.

KEY PHRASES WITH KEY SOUND SHIFTS

Speak your *Key Phrases*, shifting back and forth between your own home *idiolect of English* and the *Ghanaian Akan (Twi & Fante) accent* you are building. **Observe** the shifts <u>ONE by ONE</u> in your Articulators, Focus of Articulation, use of Melody/Pitch/Lilt, Rhythm/Stress/Pace, and Source & Path of Resonance as you shift back and forth between the two accents. Make note of the shifts in the table provided. Putting your understanding of the shifts into your <u>own words</u> will encourage you to develop a more clear and personal idiolect.

GHANAIAN AKAN (TWI & FANTE) ACCENT *KEY POINTS OF FOCUS: VOCAL POSTURE AND CHARACTERISTICS*

JAW
LIPS
TONGUE
SOFT PALATE
PHARYNX

FOCUS OF ARTICULATION (TOWARDS TEETH, FRONT/MIDDLE/ BACK OF HARD PALATE, SOFT PALATE, ETC.)

MELODY/PITCH/LILT

RHYTHM/STRESS/PACE

SOURCE & PATH OF RESONANCE – Where does the resonance begin and what is the apparent path it travels through your body (chest, hard palate, sinuses, temples, crown, base of skull, etc.)? Refer to the Source & Path of Resonance and Resonators in the *Ghanaian Akan (Twi & Fante) Accent of English: Down & Dirty Warm-Up and Quick Look* on page 309.

OTHER CHARACTERISTICS (What are your observations?)

PERSONAL IMAGES (For many actors personal images can be the most powerful and effective triggers for their transformation into an accent)

Chapter 12

Liberian Accent of English

Introduction and Resources

The History of Liberian English

Liberia, "land of the free," was founded by the American Colonization Society (ACS) in 1821. The ACS was a society that supported the return of freed African-American slaves to Africa. In the 15th century, the Portuguese engaged in trade along the *Grain Coast*, the coast nicknamed for the large amount of melegueta peppers – or *grains of paradise* – traded in that area. The British and Dutch had trading posts on the Grain Coast in the 16th century, but did not stay long. Linguistically, this is significant because the Portuguese, English and Dutch languages all shaped the African Pidgins in Liberia before the freed American slaves arrived.

English is the official language of Liberia; however, Kru Pidgin English and Liberian Pidgin English are both widely spoken. Since Liberia was founded by freed African-American slaves, it is the only African country whose English accent is deeply rooted in American English. The original English, spoken by the freed American slaves, developed into a creole called Americo-Liberian (Merico). Currently, Liberian English uses many of the same vowel and diphthong distinctions as American Southern English.

In addition to English, there are over thirty African languages spoken in Liberia. Kru and Kpelle, both of the Niger-Congo family, are the most widely spoken.

Note!

On Pidgin

A pidgin is a language of necessity created when people speaking different languages are forced to communicate over an extended period of time. It is a down and dirty way of communicating. Historically it has been a makeshift language for traders. It does not have a distinct grammar or a developed vocabulary.

Documentaries

Liberia: America's Stepchild, Bill Moyers Journal: Pray the Devil Back to Hell, Liberia: an Uncivil War, Iron Ladies of Liberia, No More Selections! We Want Elections!

Films

Imported Bride, My African Queen

Television

Monseo TV – on the web

Screenplays

Terminal Island (1995 Scenario Magazine-WGA-E Student Finalist/Sundance Writer's Lab), *In Quest of Liberty* by Womi E. Neal

Plays with Liberian Characters

Eclipsed by Danai Gurira, *SIA* by Matthew MacKenzie, *Agnes Under the Big Top: a tall tale* by Aditi Brennan Kapil (the character of Agnes)

Books

Slaves no More: Letters from Liberia 1833–1869 by Bell I. Wiley, *Selected Letters of Edward Wilmot Blyden* (both of these books would translate into excellent staged readings)

Music

Coupe Decale, Liberian a Capella Singers, Sundaygar Dearboy, Morris Dorley, Kakpindi Band

Radio

Radio LIB

Personalities

Elwood Dunn (author), Robtel N. Pailey (author), Ellen Johnson Serlief (President at time of publication), Charles Taylor (former President), Samuel Doe (former President), Cheryl Dunye (director), Izetta Sombo Wesley (head of the Liberia Football Association), Angie Elizabeth Brooks (Liberian diplomat and former President of the U.N. General Assembly), George Weah (footballer), Leymah Gbowee (peace activist and Noble Peace Prize recipient)

Down & Dirty Warm-up and Quick Look

Note!
- International Phonetic Alphabet Symbols will be listed first and Sound Symbols will be listed second.
- Sound Symbol Users: bold-faced letters indicate the syllable is stressed.

1) **The Muscles:** Wake your mouth up so you can more easily discover the physical transformation in speaking the accent.

    a. Scratch the front, middle and back of your tongue with your front top teeth.

    b. Rub the front, middle and back of your hard palate with the tip of your tongue.

    c. Imagine your mouth is numb from being at the dentist and you want to wake it up. Make tongue circles pressing against the back of your lips first clockwise, then counter clockwise (you are waking up your orbicularis muscle).

    d. To get the breath flowing, blow through your lips, getting them to flap together. Travel up and down in pitch on a BBBB and PPP, feeling the vibration as you wiggle up and down your spine.

2) **Vocal Posture for a Liberian Accent:** The tongue is wide and flat, and articulates with an easy effort. It may help to imagine it as somewhat swollen. The back of the tongue raises and retracts. The lips actively round on the rounded vowels in words like: nurse, strut, curry, love, bird, food, foot, thought, cloth, lot. In other articulation the lips are relaxed and easy. The jaw is half open and relaxed. The articulation of the tongue and shape of the mouth cavity are focused toward the middle of the hard palate. The soft palate has a domed, wide feel to it. The pharynx actively narrows in varying degrees, depending on the speaker. There can be a bit of creakiness in the vocal quality, which is a result of stiffening the vocal folds.

3) **Resonators:** "occupy" the following spaces. This will prepare you to find the Source & Path of Resonance for the Liberian accent. (By "occupy", I

mean just that; be in the space of it and find the pathway and flow of resonance, rather than "putting" the resonance there.)

a. CHEST – Generously laugh at something – ha ha ha / HAh HAh HAh
b. HARD PALATE – As if you were discovering something – ho ho ho / Ho Ho Ho
c. THE BONES AT THE BASE OF YOUR SKULL (THE OCCIPITAL BONE) – Use your hands to scoop the sound from the base of your skull with a Mississippi African-American dialect as if you're flirting with someone nearby – heː heː heː / Hē Hē Hē
d. FLICK THE SOUND OUT OF YOUR CHEEKBONES with an Italian-American flourish, as if calling to someone across the street – heː heː heː / Hē Hē Hē
e. WITH YOUR HANDS NEXT TO YOUR TEMPLES, SHAKE THE SOUND OUT WITH LOOSE FISTS – As if you were somewhat crazed – ji̧ ji̧ ji̧ / YĒE YĒE YĒE
f. IMAGINE A METAL DISK EXTENDING FROM YOUR HANDS THROUGH YOUR SKULL. Bring your hands to the sides of your head just above the temples, with your palms facing the floor, thumbs hooked behind your skull. *Lid* the vibration to create a muted brassy sound. Like a robot say "Hi" – ha·ĭ ha·ĭ ha·ĭ / HAh-Ĭ HAh-Ĭ HA-Ĭ
g. GIGGLE OUT OF THE TOP OF YOUR HEAD – As if you were tickled pink by something – hi̧ hi̧ hi̧ / HĒE HĒE HĒE

4) Source & Path of Resonance for a Liberian Accent:

The vibration in this accent begins robustly in the chest, travels up through the hard palate of the mouth into the facial mask right behind the eyes. Although the resonance is predominantly hypo-nasal (no nasality), nasal consonants color the vowels around them. Sometimes, these nasal consonants are dropped altogether and replaced by a lilting nasalized vowel or diphthong. The effect can sound like a muted trumpet.

Note!

For Symbol Users

When vowels are italicized, it means they are nasalized. Example: no → N*o*

5) Get the sound changes into your body and imagination.

Say these phrases occupying the following places in your body, suggesting to yourself the following energetic associations:

- pubic bone to tail bone – survival instinct

  zu̧ / Z>OO<
  I need it – aĭ ni̧d ɪt / Ah-Ĭ N*EE*D *EE*T

- pubic bone to navel & sacrum in back – sexuality, big feelings

  wo / Wo
  I desire it – aĭ dɪˈzaɪ.jəɹ‿ɪt̪ / Ah-Ĭ DĔE.**ZEYE**.YuhR‿ĔET

- rib cage to below heart – will

  ɜǫ / ZHAW
  I want it – aĭ wǫ̃n ɪt̪ / Ah-Ĭ W*A*WN ĔET

- heart – love

  ma / MAh
  I love it – aĭ ləv ɪt̪ / Ah-Ĭ L>UHᴿ<V ĔET

- throat – communication (think of talking at a party)

  bə / B>UHᴿ<
  I have to say it – aĭ hay̆ t̪ŭ seː ɪt̪ / Ah-Ĭ HAhVᶠ TŎO Sē ĔET

- forehead – intelligence/wisdom

  keː / Kē
  I know it – aĭ nõ ɪt̪ / Ah-Ĭ N*o* ĔET

- crown of head – spirituality

  ɹi̧ / RĔE
  I believe it – aĭ bɪˈli̧v ɪt̪ / Ah-Ĭ BI.**LĔEV** ĔET

6) **Articulation** – using playful physical actions: punching, flicking, dabbing, slashing

d̪ʊ̧ d̪i̧ kʊ̧ d̪ʊ̧ d̪i̧ kʊ̧ d̪ʊ̧ d̪i̧ kʊ̧ – d̪i̧
d̪ʊ̧ d̪i̧ kʊ̧ d̪ʊ̧ d̪i̧ kʊ̧ d̪ʊ̧ d̪i̧ kʊ̧ – d̪eː
d̪ʊ̧ d̪i̧ kʊ̧ d̪ʊ̧ d̪i̧ kʊ̧ d̪ʊ̧ d̪i̧ kʊ̧ – d̪aĭ
d̪ʊ̧ d̪i̧ kʊ̧ d̪ʊ̧ d̪i̧ kʊ̧ d̪ʊ̧ d̪i̧ kʊ̧ – d̪o
d̪ʊ̧ d̪i̧ kʊ̧ d̪ʊ̧ d̪i̧ kʊ̧ d̪ʊ̧ d̪i̧ kʊ̧ – d̪u

Repeat as needed, replacing [d̪] with [t̪], [p], [b], [k], [g], [f], [v]

DŎO DĔE KŎO DŎO DĔE KŎO DŎO DĔE KŎO – DĔE
DŎO DĔE KŎO DŎO DĔE KŎO DŎO DĔE KŎO – Dē
DŎO DĔE KŎO DŎO DĔE KŎO DŎO DĔE KŎO – DAh-Ĭ
DŎO DĔE KŎO DŎO DĔE KŎO DŎO DĔE KŎO – Do
DŎO DĔE KŎO DŎO DĔE KŎO DŎO DĔE KŎO – D>OO<

Repeat as needed, replacing [D] with [T], [P], [B], [K], [G], [F], [V]. [D] & [T] are both articulated with the blade of the tongue against the back of the top front teeth (dentalized).

Key Points of Focus
Characteristics and Vocal Posture

Liberian Accent Characteristics

> *Note!*
> **On Melody/Lilt/Pitch and Rhythm/Stress/Pace**
> Every accent contains shifts for some, but not necessarily all, of these elements of vocal variety.

> *Note!*
> **On use of Musical Notes**
> Follow the "musical notes" up and down to get a feel for the melody of the accent. The filled-in notes are shorter than the open notes. For those who are musically inclined, think of them as approximating quarter notes and half notes. This distinction will give you a feel for the rhythm of the accent.

Melody/Lilt/Pitch

There is a gentle yet unexpected and lively rhythmic rise and fall in the melody of this accent, largely due to the following:

1. Vowels or diphthongs in stressed syllables of either operative words or final words of a thought, are often elongated on the same note, or on a minor glide up or down in pitch. This can be heard in all of the audio samples.
2. For nouns that are grouped together like "diaper pail" or "reference librarian", i.e. one noun becomes possessive of the other: the second syllable of the first "noun" tends to go up in pitch rather than down, as it would in General American English.
3. There are often unexpected, and/or minor, lifts or falls in pitch in the syllables of operative words.

4. Operative words are normally contrasted by a pitch change.
5. Nasalized consonants [m]/[M], [n]/[N], [ŋ]/[NG] are often dropped and replaced with a nasalized minor lilt on their preceding vowel.

Example: Alice Story (Part 1) – 0:55

All the Krahn people ran to the soldier barracks.

In this sentence Alice elongates syllables in her operative words: *people*, *soldiers*, *barracks* (#1, p. 344). She also drops the nasal consonant [n]/[N] and replaces it with a nazalized minor lilt on the one syllable operative word *Krahn* (#4 above). Finally, she demonstrates the interesting "pitching down rather than up" in the word *soldier* in the noun set *soldier barracks* (#2, p. 344).

Example: Jesse Story – 1:03

We thought that things were going to stay forever but

unfortunately war came.

Jesse's sentence above has a very steady rhythm with a gentle up and down movement in pitch on his operative words *thought, going, forever, war, came* (#4 above). He nasalizes and lilts on the vowels preceding the nasal conso-nants in *things, going* and *came*, and in doing so, softens these consonants (#5 above). The unexpected lifts in pitch occur on the middle syllable in *forever* and the first part of the lilt in *came*. These unexpected lifts are a salient characteristic of the Liberian accent (#3, p. 344). In both of these places, most General American English speakers would expect some sort of downward pitch resolve (#3, p. 344)

Rhythm/Stress/Pace

Most of the rhythmic characteristics of this accent overlap with the melodic characteristics. A distinct stress characteristic is the stressing of prefixes. Pace is rapid and is made to seem faster because of consonant-dropping, coupled with the consistent syncopation of syllables.

Example: Julia Story (Part 2) – 2:01

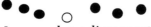

I never show disrespect.

Notice how Julia stresses the prefix in *disrespect*, which would not normally be stressed in General American English: she uses a little volume, but mainly distinguishes it with a minor lift in pitch.

Example: Emery Story – 1:13

Me and my brother we are twins. I have a twin brother.

And we dream the same thing.

Emery has been living in America for much of his adult life so his accent is not as strong as the others in the accent library. You can hear this in how he doesn't quite drop his final nasal consonants in *twin*, *dream* and *thing*. That said he still keeps a steady rapid fire rhythm going, which is so characteristic of this accent. His syllables are nearly all equal in length. He lengthens on the most operative word in the thought, *twins*, which also happens to end with a nasal consonant, lending itself to nasalizing and lengthening of the vowel. The final word of his thought, *thing*, also gets nasalized and lengthened through lilt.

Source & Path of Resonance

The vibration in this accent begins robustly in the chest, travels up through the hard palate of the mouth into the facial mask right behind the eyes. Although the resonance is predominantly hypo-nasal (no nasality), nasal consonants color the vowels around them. Sometimes, these nasal consonants are dropped altogether and replaced by a lilting nasalized vowel or diphthong. The effect can sound like a muted trumpet.

With some variation, you can hear the *Path of Resonance* characteristics in all of the speakers in the accent library. A marked variation is that Alice, Marcia, Emery and Kona all speak with more creakiness in their voices.

Liberian Accent Vocal Posture

> *Note!*
> **On Vocal Posture**
> These adjustments enable you to integrate the accent through physical transformation rather than solely relying on sound shifts.

- **Focus of Articulation:** The articulation of the tongue and shape of the mouth cavity are focused toward the middle of the hard palate.
- **Tongue:** The tongue is wide and flat, and articulates with an easy effort. It may help to imagine it as somewhat swollen. The back of the tongue raises and retracts.
- **Lips:** The lips actively round on the rounded vowels in words like n<u>ur</u>se, str<u>u</u>t, c<u>u</u>rry, l<u>o</u>ve: [ɵ]/[>UH^R<]; b<u>ir</u>d: [ɵɪ]/[>UH^R< – I]; f<u>oo</u>d: [u]/[OO]; f<u>oo</u>t: [ʊ̈]/[OO]; th<u>ou</u>ght: [o̞]/[AW]; cl<u>o</u>th: [o̞]/[o]; l<u>o</u>t: [ɔ]/[AW]. In other articulation, the lips are relaxed and easy.
- **Jaw:** The jaw is half-open and relaxed.
- **Soft Palate:** The soft palate has a domed, wide feel to it.
- **Pharynx:** The pharynx actively narrows in varying degrees, depending on the speaker. There can be a bit of creakiness in the vocal quality, which is a result of stiffening in the vocal folds.

Distinct Sounds of the Language and/or Accent

> *Note!*
> **On Distinct Sounds**
> These are some of the sounds that Liberians use and American speakers do not. In speaking the sounds and/or the words that contain them, you can heighten your physical understanding of the Liberian accent's *Vocal Posture* as compared to your own. This frame of reference will both inform and strengthen your accent.

Consonants

1. *IPA:* [ɾ] → alveolar tap.
    Symbol: [R^R] → This is a tapped [R] and is made by lightly tapping the tip of the tongue on the alveolar ridge.
    Often used in place of "ter": w*ater*, be*tter*
    This sound is used in speaking a Liberian accent of English.

Vowels

2. *IPA:* [e] → This is the first sound in the D.A.E. diphthong [AY] as in *face*.
    Symbol: [e] → This is the first sound in the D.A.E. diphthong [AY].
    Used in place of [eɪ]/[AY]: *face*, w*ei*ght
    This sound is used in speaking a Liberian accent of English.
3. *IPA:* [a]
    Symbol: [Ah] → This is the first sound in the diphthong [EYE].
    Used in place of [æ]/[A]: tr*a*p, b*a*th
    This sound is used in speaking a Liberian accent of English.
4. *IPA:* [ɜ]
    Symbol: [>UH^R<] → [UHR] with no r-coloration and made with rounded lips.
    Used in place of [ɝ]/[UHR]: *nu*rse, w*o*rk, s*e*rvice
    This sound is used in speaking a Liberian accent of English.

5. *IPA:* [ɤ]

   Symbol: [<o>] → Pronounce [o] with slightly pulled back lip corners.

   This sound is used in place of final [l]/[L]: *exce<u>l</u>, fa<u>ll</u>*

   This sound is used in speaking a Liberian accent of English.

6. *IPA:* [o]

   Symbol: [o]. This is the first sound in the D.A.E. diphthong [OH].

   Used in place of [oŏ]/[OH]: *g<u>oa</u>t, s<u>ew</u>*

   This sound is used in speaking a Liberian accent of English.

Consonant Sound Shifts

- ↦ indicates that this sound is a key sound shift
- You can begin to fold melody and rhythm with the sound changes by speaking the sample sentences that are before each section of sound changes.

> **Note!**
> Some Liberian speakers drop consonants liberally. This can make it challenging to an audience unfamiliar with the accent. It is useful to start off with the consonant dropping as you learn the accent, since it greatly affects the pace and rhythm. As you begin to gear up towards performance, you can add consonants to help with intelligibility. Remember that you are an actor, not a linguist. Your purpose is to illuminate character and text and to tell a story, not to fool the indigenous speakers of the accent.

> **Note!**
> Consonants are key to this accent, so the consonant sentences have been customized into condensed examples that do not occur in the sound samples in the audio library.

	Consonant Shifts	

The melody breakdowns below are hypothetical:

The stuff there on table came from the first love.

IPA: ðə stə dɪʌ ɔ̃ 'teː.bɣ kẽː fɹẽ ðə fës ʟəɣ

SYMBOLS: Duh ST>UH^R< DI-UH *AW̄* TE.B<o> K*ē* FR>*UH^R*< Duh F*e*S L>UH<V^F

Compare that judge to other and he bad.

IPA: 'kõ.pɛ ɖa ʒɜʒ tə 'ə.ɖə̰ ã hḭ ba

SYMBOLS: **Ko**.PEH DAh ZHUHZH Tuh >**UH^R**<.DUH *Ah* HE̋E BAh

I'll meet you at the ferry in an hour with the ten children.

IPA: aɪ̆ɣ mḭ̃t̪‿ʃʊ̰ ɛ ðə 'fɛ̰.ɹe ḭ̃n ã 'a.wə̰ wɪ̰t̪ ðə tɛ̰̃ ʃɪɣ.ɖɹẽn

SYMBOLS: Ah-Ĭ -<o> M*EET*_CHOO EH Duh **FEH**.Re *ĔĔN Ah* **Ah**.WUH WĔ̈ET
Duh T*EH* SHĔ̈E-<o>.DR*EH*N

Key Words	Detailed American English Accent IPA	Shift to Liberian Accent of English IPA	Key Words Shifts IPA	Your Key Words
	Symbol	*Symbol*	*Symbol*	
☛ team debt, did	[t]/[d]	[t̪]/[d̪]	tĩm, d̪ɛ̰t	
	[T]/[D]	[T]/[D] both dentalized	TE̋EM, DEHT	
☛ water fighter	*t* in middle of a word followed by *er* in spelling	ɾ	wɔɾ, faĭɾ	
	T	R^R	WAW R^R, FAh-ĬR^R	
☛ got	final *t* in spelling when word is not followed by another word	t̪	gɔ̰t	
	T	[T] (dentalized)	GAWT	

Key Words	Detailed American English Accent IPA	Shift to Liberian Accent of English IPA	Key Words Shifts IPA	Your Key Words
	Symbol	*Symbol*	*Symbol*	
☛ go<u>t</u> away	final *t* in spelling when next word begins with a vowel	ḓ̥	gɔḓ̥	
	T	[D] (dentalized)	GAWD	
☛ go<u>t</u> now	final *t* in spelling when next word begins with a consonant	dropped	gɔ năŭ̃	
	T	dropped	GAW N>*AH*<-*OŎ*	
☛ sto<u>p</u> (final *p* in spelling)	p	p˺	stop˺	
	P	[P] with no audible release of air after the [P]	SToP	
☛ <u>th</u>ese <u>th</u>ere (initial *th* in spelling)	ð	ḓ̥	ḓ̥iz̥	
	TH	[D] (dentalized)	DEEZ͞ˢ	
☛ brea<u>the</u> (final *th* in spelling)	ð	often [v]	bŭiv	
	TH	often [V]	BŎO-EĔV	
☛ <u>th</u>in <u>th</u>ick (initial *th* in spelling)	θ	t̪	t̪ĩn	
	th	[T] (dentalized)	T*I*N	
☛ mou<u>th</u> (final *th* in spelling)	θ	often [f]	măŭf	
	th	often [F]	M>*OW*<F	
☛ lo<u>ve</u> (final *v* in spelling)	v	v̥	lɜv̥	
	V	Vᶠ	L>*UH*ᴿ<Vᶠ	
☛ boy<u>s</u> (final *s* when pronounced [z])	z	z̥	boiz̥	
	Z	Zˢ	Bo-EĔZˢ	

Key Words	Detailed American English Accent IPA Symbol	Shift to Liberian Accent of English IPA Symbol	Key Words Shifts IPA Symbol	Your Key Words
☛ exce<u>l</u> fa<u>ll</u> (final *l* in spelling)	l <hr> L	ɤ <hr> [<o>] ([L] made like an [o] without rounding your lips)	ɛk'sɛɤ, fɔɤ <hr> EHK.**SE**<o>, FAW<o>	
☛ ta<u>bl</u>e peo<u>pl</u>e, ho<u>ld</u>	l in consonant clusters of *bl, pl, ld* at end of words <hr> L	ɤ <hr> <o>	'tei̯.bɤ, 'pi.pɤ <hr> T**ĕ**.B<o>, **PEE**.P<o>	
ju<u>dg</u>e	dʒ <hr> J	ʒ <hr> ZH	ʒʌʒ <hr> ZHAWZH	
☛ <u>ch</u>ur<u>ch</u>	tʃ <hr> CH	ʃ <hr> SH	ʃəʃ <hr> SH>UHᴿ<SH	
read<u>ing</u> (final *ing* in spelling)	ŋ <hr> ING	ɪn <hr> IN	'ɹi̯.dĩn <hr> R**Ĭ**.D*I*N	
stu<u>ff</u> lo<u>v</u>e, fa<u>t</u>, ba<u>d</u>, ki<u>ss</u>, bu<u>zz</u>, bu<u>sh</u>, bei<u>ge</u> (*f, v, t, d, s, z, sh, ge* in spelling at end of word)	f, v, t, d, s, z, ʃ, ʒ <hr> F, V, T, D, S, Z, SH, ZH	sometimes dropped <hr> sometimes dropped	st̪ə <hr> ST>UHᴿ<	
sta<u>nd</u> fir<u>st</u>, twe<u>nty</u>, exa<u>ctl</u>y, hol<u>d</u>ing, tra<u>des</u> consonant clusters in final positions of a word root		one or the other of the consonants are almost always dropped. If the consonant cluster begins with an *n*, the *n* gets dropped, and the preceding vowel gets nasalized.	st̪ã <hr> ST*A*	
co<u>me</u> ra<u>n</u>, si<u>ng</u> (final *m, n, ng* in spelling)	[m], [n], [ŋ] <hr> [M], [N], [NG]	often dropped and preceding vowel is nasalized <hr> often dropped and preceding vowel is nasalized	kã, ɹaã̃, sĩ <hr> K>*UH*ᴿ<, R*Ah-uh*, S*EE*	

Front Vowel Sound Shifts

Note!
Although the resonance is predominantly hypo-nasal (no nasality), nasal consonants color the vowels around them.

Note!
For Symbol Users
When vowels are italicized, it means they are nasalized. Example: no → N*o*

		Front Vowel Shifts		
The thief will tell me after we trap him.				
IPA: də t̪if wɪɣ tɛɣ mĩ ˈaf.tə̪ wḭ ʈɹap˥ hĩm				
SYMBOLS: Duh TEĒF WEĒ<o> TEH<o> M*EĒ* **AhF.TUH** WEĒ TRAhP H*EĒ*M				
Key Words	*Detailed American English Accent* *IPA* ------------------ *Symbol*	*Shift to Liberian Accent of English* *IPA* ------------------ *Symbol*	*Key Words Shifts* *IPA* ------------------ *Symbol*	*Your Key Words*
fl<u>ee</u>ce sn<u>ee</u>ze, pl<u>ea</u>d	i ---------------- EE	i̧ ---------------- E*Ē*	flḭs, snḭẓ ---------------- FLE*Ē*S, SN*EĒ*Z^S
↤ k<u>i</u>t p<u>i</u>tch, d<u>i</u>m, l<u>i</u>p	ɪ ---------------- I	ḭ ---------------- [I] moves toward [EE] as in fl<u>ee</u>ce	kɪ̪t ---------------- KE*Ē*T
↤ countr<u>y</u> (*y* in final position of spelling)	i̧ ---------------- EE	e ---------------- e	ˈkẽn.t̪ʲɹe ---------------- **K>*UH*^R<N**.T^SHRe

Key Words	Detailed American English Accent	Shift to Liberian Accent of English	Key Words Shifts	Your Key Words
	IPA ---- Symbol	IPA ---- Symbol	IPA ---- Symbol	
berated	[ɪ] in prefix ---- [I] in prefix or suffix	i̧ ---- [EE] articulated further back in the mouth	bi̧'ɹeː.ti̧d ---- BEE.**Rē**.TEED^T	
dress bed, feather, send	ε ---- EH	ε̧ ---- EH (made with a lowered front of tongue)	dɹε̧s ---- DREHS	
⊶ trap mad, rat, candle	æ ---- A	[a] or [ε] ---- [Ah] or [EH]	tɹap̚, mãd̪, ɹat̪ or tɹεp̚, mε̃d̪, ɹεt̪ ---- TRAhP, MAhD, RAhT or TREHP, MEHD, REHT	
⊶ can't rank, man, chance (*an* in spelling)	æ ---- A	ã͡ə ---- [Ah-uh] nasalized	kã͡ə, ɹã͡ə, mã͡ə, ʃã͡əs ---- KAh-uh, RAh-uh, MAh-uh, SHAh-uhS	
⊶ bath *[a]/[Ah] after, dance, example, half, mask, rascal, transfer In Chapter 1, there is a list of these words called the BATH or ASK list of words.	æ ---- A	a ---- Ah	baf, 'af.t̪ə, dã͡əs ---- BAhf, **AhF**.TUH, DAh-uhS	

Middle Vowel Sound Shifts

	Middle Vowel Shifts			
In the summer, workers burned the underbrush.				
IPA: ĭn də 'sə.mə̃ də 'wə.kə̱z bə̃nd dɪ̯ 'ə̃n.də̹,bɹəʃ				
SYMBOLS: IN Duh **S>UH**ᴿ**<**.M*UH* Duh W>UHᴿ<.KUHZˢ B>*UH*ᴿ<ND DĒĒ >*UH*ᴿ**<**N.DUH.BR>UHᴿ<SH				
Key Words	*Detailed American English Accent* IPA -------------------- *Symbol*	*Shift to Liberian Accent of English* IPA --------------------- *Symbol*	*Key Words Shifts* IPA --------------------- *Symbol*	*Your Key Words*
☛ nurse work, service, learn (*ur, or, er, ear* in spelling)	ɝ -------------------- ER	[ə] or sometimes [ɜ] --------------------- >UHᴿ< ([UHᴿ] with rounded lips)	nəs, wək, 'sə.vɪs or nɜs, wɜk, 'sɜ.vɪs --------------------- N>*UH*ᴿ<S, W>UHᴿ<K, **S>UH**ᴿ**<**.VĒĒS	
☛ bird (*ir* in spelling)	ɝ -------------------- ER	ë --------------------- e̩	bëḏ --------------------- B_eD	
☛ sister traitor, hangar	ɚ -------------------- er	ə̹ --------------------- UH	'sis.tə̹, 'tɹeːtə̹, 'hãŋ.ə̹ --------------------- **SEES**.TUH, TRē.TUH, **H***h***NG**.UH	
☛ strut curry	ʌ̈ -------------------- U̞H	[ə] and sometimes [ɜ] --------------------- [>UHᴿ<] and sometimes [UHᴿ]	stɹə̩t, stɹɜt --------------------- STR>UHᴿ<T, STRUHᴿT	

Key Words	Detailed American English Accent IPA Symbol	Shift to Liberian Accent of English IPA Symbol	Key Words Shifts IPA Symbol	Your Key Words
☞ come flood (in words spelled with *o* and sometimes *oo*)	Ʌ UH̲	ə >UHᴿ<	kə̃, flə̃d K>*UHᴿ*<, FL>UHᴿ<D	
about banana	ə uh	[ə] or [a] [uh] or [Ah]	ə'ba̰ṵt̰ or a'ba̰ṵt̰ uh.**B>OW<T** or Ah.**B>OW<T**	
☞ consider compare	[ə] in con and com prefixes	the first syllable is stressed and [n] or [m] is often dropped	'kõn.sị.də̰, 'kõm.pɛ or 'kõ.sị.də̰, 'kõ.pɛ	
	[uh] in con and com prefixes	the first syllable is stressed and [N] or [M] is often dropped	K*o*N.SḚE.DUH, K*o*M.PEH or K*o*.SḚE.DUH, K*o*.PEH	

Back Vowel Sound Shifts

	Back Vowel Shifts			
	*I thought my father would not stop being a bully but the truth is, I was wrong.*			

IPA: aĭ t̪ɔt̪ maĭ 'fa.d̪ə wʊd̪ nõ st̪op˺ bĩŋ ə 'bʊ.le bə d̪ə t̪ɹut̪˺ ɪz aĭ wɔz ɹɒ̃ŋ

SYMBOLS: Ah-Ĭ ToT MAh-Ĭ **FAh**.DUH WOͧOD No SToP BEENG uh **BOͧO**.Le B>UH^R< Duh TR>OO<T EͧEZ^S Ah-Ĭ WAWZ^S R*o*NG

Key Words	Detailed American English Accent IPA ----------- Symbol	Shift to Liberian Accent of English IPA ----------- Symbol	Key Words Shifts IPA ----------- Symbol	Your Key Words
f<u>oo</u>d gr<u>ew</u>, tr<u>ue</u>, tw<u>o</u>	u ----------- OO	ụ ----------- >OO<	fụd̪, gɹụ, t̪ɹụ ----------- F>OO<D, G>ROO<, T>ROO<	
⊶ f<u>oo</u>t p<u>u</u>t	ʊ ----------- U	ʊ̣ ----------- OͧO	fʊ̣t̪ ----------- FOͧOT	
⊶ th<u>ough</u>t t<u>a</u>ll, c<u>au</u>lk, <u>aw</u>ful	ɔ ----------- AW	ọ ----------- o	t̪ọt̪, t̪ọɤ, kọk ----------- ToT, To<o>, KoK	
⊶ cl<u>o</u>th *[ɒ]/[O] d<u>o</u>g, c<u>ou</u>gh, w<u>a</u>sh, h<u>o</u>rrid	ɔ ----------- AW	ọ ----------- o	klọt̪, d̪ọg, kọf ----------- KLoT, DoG, KoF	
f<u>a</u>ther	ɑ ----------- AH	a ----------- Ah	'fa.d̪ə ----------- **FAh**.DUH	
⊶ l<u>o</u>t *[ɒ]/[O] squ<u>a</u>d, w<u>a</u>nder	ɑ ----------- AH	[ɔ] or [o] ----------- [AW] or [o]	lọt̪, skwọd̪, 'wɔ̃n.d̪ə or lot̪, skwod̪, wõn.d̪ə ----------- LAWT, SKWAWD, **WAW**N.DUH or LoT, SKWOD, **WO**N.DUH	

Diphthong Sound Shifts

	Diphthong Shifts			

I'd like to fly away someday and go south to the mountains with the boys.

IPA: aɪ̯d laɪk tu̯ flaɪ̯ a'weː 'sɛm.de ã go sau̯t tu̯ də 'mãʊ̯n.tɛ̃z wɪ̯ də boɪ̯z

SYMBOLS: Ah-ĬD LAh-IK TŌŌ FLAh-Ĭ Ah.**Wē S>***UH^R*<**M**.De *Ah* Go S>OW<T TŌŌ Duh **M>***OW*<N.TeZ^S WĒĒ Duh Bo-ĒĒZ^S

Key Words	Detailed American English Accent IPA Symbol	Shift to Liberian Accent of English IPA Symbol	Key Words Shifts IPA Symbol	Your Key Words
☞ f**a**ce p**ai**n, d**a**y, w**eigh**t, st**ea**k	eɪ AY	[eː] or [ɪ] [e] or [I]	feːs, pẽːn, deː or fɪs, pĭn, dɪ FeS, PeN, De or FIS, P/N, DI	
pr**i**ce **eye**s, d**i**aper, fl**y**, g**uy**, h**eigh**t	aɪ̆ EYE	aɪ̆ Ah-Ĭ	pɹaɪs, aɪ̆z, 'daɪ̆.pʰə̯ PRAh-ĬS, Ah-ĬZ^S **DAh-I**.Pᴮ UH	
ch**oi**ce b**oy**s	ɔɪ̆ OY	oi̞ o-ĒĒ	ʃoi̞s, boi̞z SHo-ĒĒS, Bo-EEZ^S	
☞ g**oa**t s**ew**, g**o**, t**oe**	oʊ̆ OH	o o	got, so, go GoT, So, Go	
m**ou**th t**ow**n	aʊ̆ OW	a̞ʊ̆ >OW<	ma̞ʊ̆f, ta̞ʊ̆n M>OW<F, T>OW<N	

Diphthongs and Triphthongs of R Shifts

> **Note!**
> **On r-coloration**
> A Liberian accent has no r-coloration in diphthongs and triphthongs of R.

Diphthongs and Triphthongs of R Shifts				
Our friends st_ar_ted the f_ire_ n_ear_ _your_ n_or_th _or_chard an h_our_ bef_ore_ we got th_ere_.				
IPA: ˈa.wə̰ fɹɛ̰ɡ̊z̰ ˈstɑ:.tḛd ḍə ˈfaɪ̯.jə̰ nĩ:ʌ jɔˈ nɔ:t̰ ˈɔ:.ʃə̰d ãn ˈa.wə̰ bḭ.ˈfɔ: wi go ḍɛ				
SYMBOLS: Ah.WUH FR*EHZ*ˢ ST**ĀH**.TeD Duh **FEYE**.YUH *N**EĒ**.*UH YĀW N**ĀW**T **ĀW**.SH>UHᴿ<D *Ah*N Ah.WUH B**EĔ**.F**ĀW** WEE Go DEH				
Key Words	*Detailed American English Accent* IPA ---- *Symbol*	*Shift to Liberian Accent of English* IPA ---- *Symbol*	*Key Words Shifts* IPA ---- *Symbol*	*Your Key Words*
☞ n_ear_ b_eer_	ɪ˞ ---- EAR	i:ʌ ---- EĒ-UH	nĩ:ʌ ---- N*EĒ*-UH	
☞ h_air_ st_are_, p_ear_, squ_are_, th_ere_	ɛ˞ ---- AIR	[ɛɪʊ] or [ɛ] or [ɪʌ] ---- [EH-U] or [EH] or [I-UH]	hɛɪʊ, s̰t̰ɛɪʊ, pɛɪʊ, skwɛɪʊ, or hɛ, s̰t̰ɛ, pɛ, skwɛ, or hɪʌ, s̰t̰ɪʌ, pɪʌ, skwɪʌ ---- STEH-U, PEH-U, SKWEH-U or STEH, PEH, SKWEH, or STI-UH, PI-UH, SKWI-UH	

Key Words	Detailed American English Accent IPA ---- Symbol	Shift to Liberian Accent of English IPA ---- Symbol	Key Words Shifts IPA ---- Symbol	Your Key Words
☛ s<u>u</u>re p<u>oor</u>, y<u>our</u>	ʊɝ ---- UR	ɔː ---- A͞W	ʃɔː, pɔː, jɔː ---- SHA͞W, PA͞W, YA͞W	
n<u>or</u>th Ge<u>or</u>ge, p<u>our</u>, w<u>ar</u>p, <u>oar</u>	ɔɝ ---- AWR	ɔː ---- A͞W	nɔːt̪, ʒɔːʒ, pɔː, wɔːpˀ, ɔː ---- NA͞WT, ZHA͞WZH, PA͞W, WA͞WP, A͞W	
st<u>ar</u>t h<u>ear</u>t	ɑɝ ---- AHR	ɑː ---- A͞H	stɑːt̪, hɑːt̪ ---- STA͞HT, HA͞HT	
f<u>ire</u>	aɪɚ ---- EYER	aɪ.jə̣ ---- EYE.YUH	ˈfaɪ.jə̣ ---- **FEYE**.YUH	
h<u>our</u>	aʊɚ ---- OWR	a.wə̣ ---- Ah.WUH	ˈa.wə̣ ---- **Ah**.WUH	

362

Key Sentences for Practice

Note!
- By practicing the sentences below, you can work through the sound shifts for a Liberian accent in the context of a simple thought. I suggest you think, imagine and speak actively from a point of view. As you begin to work with the operative words in the thoughts, the rhythm and melody of the accent will begin to emerge appropriately.
- Note that less significant words are often unstressed, and articulation of vowels and diphthongs in these words may move toward the neutral *schwa* [ə]/[uh].

Note!
Consonants: Consonants are key to this accent, so the consonant sentences are customized.

The stuff there on table came from the first love.

IPA: ɖə stə ɖɪʌ ɔ̃ ˈteːbɤ kẽː fɹɛ̃ ɖə fɛs l̪ə̥ɣ

SYMBOLS: Duh ST>UH^R< DI-UH *AW̃* **TE**.B<o> Kē FR>UH^R< Duh FeS L>UH<V^F

Compare that judge to other and he bad.

IPA: ˈkõ.pɛ ɖa ʒɐʒ tə ˈə.ɖə̥ ã hɪ ba

SYMBOLS: **K***o*.PEH DAh ZHUHZH Tuh >**UH^R**<.DUH *Ah* HĒ̃E BAh

I'll meet you at the ferry in an hour with the ten children.

IPA: aɪ̆ˠ mĩt̪‿ʃʊ̞ ɛ d̪ə 'fɛ̠.ɹe ĩn ã 'a.wə̞ wɪt̪ d̪ə tɛ̃ ʃɪˠ.d̪ɪẽn

SYMBOLS: Ah-Ĭ -<o> MEET‿CHŎO EH Duh **FEH**.Re *ĔĔN Ah* **Ah**.WUH
WĔĔT Duh T*EH* SHĔĔ-<o>.DR*EH*N

Front Vowels: Vowels made by arching or cupping the front of the tongue toward
the front of the hard palate.

● **The thief will tell me after we trap him.**

IPA: d̪ə t̪if wɪˠ t̪ɛ̠ˠ mĩ 'af.t̪ə wị t̪ɹap˥ hĩm

SYMBOLS: Duh TĔEF WĔĔ<o> TEH<o> M*ĔĔ* **AhF**.TUH WĔĔ TRAhP
H*ĔĔ*M

Middle Vowels: Vowels made by arching or cupping the middle of the tongue
toward the middle of the hard palate.

● **In the summer, workers burned the underbrush.**

IPA: ĩn d̪ə 'sɘ.mə̞ d̪ə 'wɘ.kə̞z bɘ̃nd̪ d̪ị 'ɘ̃n.d̪ə̞ˌbɹəʃ

SYMBOLS: *I*N Duh **S>UH**ᴿ<.M*UH* Duh W>UH*ᴿ<*.KUHZˢ B>*UH*ᴿ<ND DĔĔ
>*UH*ᴿ<N.DUH.BR>UH*ᴿ<SH

Back Vowels: Vowels made by arching or cupping the back of the tongue toward
the back of the hard palate.

● **I thought my father would not stop being a bully but the truth is, I was
wrong.**

IPA: aɪ̆ t̪ot̪ maɪ̆ 'fa.d̪ə wʊ̞d̪ nõ st̪op˥ bĩŋ ə 'bʊ̞.le bə d̪ə t̪ɹ̣ut̪˥ ɪz aɪ̆ wɔz
ɹɘ̃ŋ

SYMBOLS: Ah-Ĭ ToT M*Ah-Ĭ* **FAh**.DUH WŎOD N*o* ST*o*P B*EE*NG uh
BŎO.Le B>*UH*ᴿ< Duh TR>OO<T ĔĔZˢ Ah-Ĭ WAWZˢ R*o*NG

Diphthongs: When two vowels are combined in one syllable.

● **I'd like to fly away someday and go south to the mountains with the boys.**

IPA: aɪ̆d laɪ̆k t̪ʊ̞ flaɪ̆ aʹweː 'sɘ̃m.d̪e ã go sɐ̞ʊ̆t̪ t̪ʊ̞ d̪ə 'mɐ̞ʊ̆n.t̪ɛ̞z wị d̪ə
boɪ̞z

SYMBOLS: Ah-ĬD LAh-ĬK TŎO FLAh-Ĭ Ah.W*ē* S>*UH*ᴿ<M.De *Ah* Go
S>OW̆<T TŎO Duh **M>*OW̆*<N**.TeZˢ WĔĔ Duh Bo-ĔĔZˢ

Diphthongs of R: A diphthong in which the second vowel is rhotic (e.g., has r-coloration in the final sound).

Example: near → nɪɚ/NEAR

Triphthongs of R: A combination of three vowel sounds, in which the third vowel is rhotic.

Example: fire → faɪɚ/FEYER

- ***Our** friends st**a**rted the **fi**re ne**ar** y**our** n**or**th **or**chard an h**our** bef**ore** we got th**ere**.*

  IPA: ˈa.wə fɹɛ̰z̰ ˈstɑː.teḓ də ˈfaɪ̰.jə̰ nĩːʌ jɔ˞ nɔ̃ːt̚ ˈɔː.ʃəḓ ãn ˈa.wə bɪ̰.ˈfɔː wi go ḓɛ

  SYMBOLS: **Ah**.WUH FR*EHZ*ˢ **STĀH**.TeD Duh **FEYE**.YUH *N**ĒĒ***.UH YĀW N*ĀW*T **ĀW**.SH>UHᴿ<D *Ah*N **Ah**.WUH B**Ē̃**E.**FĀW** WEE Go DEH

Additional Sentences:

The Liberian woman has a family she can care for and

trust all around her country.

IPA: ḓə la.ˈbɪː.ɹɪ̰ə̰n ˈwo.mẽn has ə ˈfa.mɔ̰.leː ʃĩ kã kjɪʌ fo ẽn t̰ɹ̰əs ǫl ə.ɹ̰ə̰ðn hɐɪ ˈkẽn.t̰ʂ̰ɹe

  SYMBOLS: Duh LAh.>**B**<**Ē**E.R**Ē̃**E.*uh*N **Wo**.MeN HAhS uh **FAh**.M*uh*.L**ē̄** SH**Ē̃**E K*Ah* **KYI**.UH Fo *EH*N >TRUHᴿ<S AWL uh.>**R**<*OW*N H>UHᴿ< **K**>*UH*ᴿ<N.>TSR<e

Making Your Own Map of the Accent

Listen to the Liberian accent samples provided and investigate the resources suggested in the *Introduction and Resources* section. Compose (or steal) *Key Phrases* from your listening/viewing that challenge and/or ground you in the accent. Then get more specific and check your sounds against the sounds in the Workbook.

Your take on the sound shifts may be slightly different. That is okay. The breakdown is a tool, not a rule. Recheck what you hear and, if you still stand behind your discoveries, go with them. This will help you to develop **your own** idiolect of the accent.

> *Note!*
>
> **What is an Idiolect?**
>
> Each of us speaks differently even if we have the same general accent. The individualized way that each of us speaks is referred to as an idiolect. For the actor, idiolect is part of what creates character. It is the "how" of the accent, and influences the way we craft our thoughts through language.

KEY PHRASES WITH KEY SOUND SHIFTS

Speak your *Key Phrases*, shifting back and forth between your own home *idiolect of English* and the *Liberian accent* you are building. **Observe** the shifts <u>ONE by ONE</u> in your Articulators, Focus of Articulation, use of Melody/Pitch/Lilt, Rhythm/Stress/Pace, and Source & Path of Resonance as you shift back and forth between the two accents. Make note of the shifts in the table provided. Putting your understanding of the shifts into your <u>own words</u> will encourage you to develop a more clear and personal idiolect.

LIBERIAN ACCENT *KEY POINTS OF FOCUS: VOCAL POSTURE AND CHARACTERISTICS*

JAW
LIPS
TONGUE
SOFT PALATE
PHARYNX

FOCUS OF ARTICULATION (TOWARDS TEETH, FRONT/MIDDLE/
BACK OF HARD PALATE, SOFT PALATE, ETC.)

MELODY/PITCH/LILT

RHYTHM/STRESS/PACE

SOURCE & PATH OF RESONANCE – Where does the resonance begin and
what is the apparent path it travels through your body (chest, hard palate,
sinuses, temples, crown, base of skull, etc.)? Refer to the Source & Path of
Resonance and Resonators in the *Liberian Accent of English: Down & Dirty
Warm-Up and Quick Look* on page 341.

OTHER CHARACTERISTICS (What are your observations?)

PERSONAL IMAGES (For many actors personal images can be the most
powerful and effective triggers for their transformation into an accent)

368

Glossary

This glossary of terms is a combination of (1) existing linguistic definitions and (2) words and phrases that have been crafted to refer to elements in the accent breakdowns of this workbook.

Accents
1) This workbook uses the word *accent* to refer to how the traits of speakers of one language – including melody, pitch, lilt, rhythm, stress, pace, resonance, phonemic variation and vocal posture – get carried over to a second language to create a distinct and somewhat predictable way of speaking.
2) The words *accent* and *dialect* are sometimes interchangeable when referring to how people from a particular place speak. The sample sentences and phrases for each accent in this book are constructed with dialect in mind, but our focus is on the accent, leaving the dialect to the playwright or screenwriter.
3) Accent also refers to how a particular group of people speak their own language and/or how they speak another language. So, a person from Mississippi will have a particular American accent of English and when s/he speaks a language that is not their native language, like French, they will be speaking French with a Mississippi American accent.

Aryepliglottic Sphincter
The flaps on the sides of the epiglottis that can make growling-type sounds; they are activated when creating twang in the voice.

Clicks
These are sounds made by raising the front, middle or back of the tongue against the palate then, with either the lips or the tongue, creating an airtight cavity while sucking and quickly popping the lips or the tongue away from the place of contact. One click common to English is used when you are condescendingly scolding someone, "tsk tsk tsk".

Creole
A creole is a *pidgin* (definition on page 371) that has been used every day over a long period of time and has begun to develop its own grammar and complex vocabulary. Historically creoles emerged largely as a result of slave trade.

Dentalized

Refers to a sound that is shifted in articulation so that the tip or blade of the tongue is placed against the back of the top front teeth. This often occurs on [t]/[T], [d]/[D], [θ]/[th], [ð]/[TH] in African languages.

Detailed American English (D.A.E.)

Refers to an accent model that *Dudley Knight*[1] synthesized to teach a form of American English that would employ the detail of pure American phonemes without regional variation. This is a model, and is used as one, since no one speaks this way all of the time. Elements of it are used or discarded depending on the character an actor is playing. The point is that it is a linguistic work-out for American English and a clear frame of reference. The Workbook refers to this model as the departure point for each accent.

Diacritics

Symbols that signify that a particular phoneme has changed from its pure form to something else. For instance if you were in Liberia, and you had a friend named "Skip" the final [p] would not have a release of air after it as it would in D.A.E. The following diacritic would indicate this shift: [p˺].

Dialect

The Workbook refers to *dialect* as the grammar, vocabulary and idiomatic use of words within an accent.

Diphthongs

When two vowels are combined in one syllable. Example: face → feɪs/FAYS.

Diphthongs of R

When two vowels are combined in one syllable in which the second vowel contains rhoticity. Example: near → nɪɚ/NEAR.

Hypo-nasal

To speak without nasal resonance; somewhat like speaking with a cold. A way to check if you are speaking with a hypo-nasal quality is to hold the nose with your fingers and inhibit any resonance from coming into the nose unless you are making a nasal consonant: [n]/[N], [m]/[M] or [ŋ]/[NG].

Idiolect

Refers to a person's individual accent. Each of us speaks differently even when we have the same general accent. For the actor, idiolect is part of what creates character. This includes the way the individual works with the elements of accent, as well as how s/he crafts those elements with the thoughts in the text.

International Phonetics Alphabet (IPA)

A sound-symbol alphabet that represents what are considered to be the predominant sounds in the languages of the world. Its value is that it is more specific in describing pronunciation than spelling. It uses a table that shows both the *place* the sound is articulated in the mouth or throat, as well as the *way* it is articulated. So an [m] is articulated on the lips (bi-labial), and it is called a nasal, which means the sound goes up through the nose, so it is categorized as a bi-labial nasal. As sounds move further away from our place of reference as speakers of English, this alphabet becomes extremely useful. Please refer to the IPA chart on page 18, in Chapter 1.

Larynx

The larynx is located in the neck and houses mechanisms for producing voice (including the vocal folds). It also helps in the actions of swallowing and breathing.

Lexical Word Sets

These are word sets that share the same sound. In the Accent Breakdowns, they are referred to as *Key Words*. For example, *love* and *cup*, although spelled differently, share the same vowel sound in D.A.E. [ʌ̈]/[UH] and therefore are a *lexical set* in this respect. They might not share the same sound in another accent of English, however, therefore would not be a *lexical set*. For example, in a Liberian accent of English, the vowel in *love* is pronounced [ɔ]/[AW], while the vowel in *cup* is pronounced [ʌ]/[>UH<]. Each first word under *Key Words* in the *Sound Shifts* section is borrowed from J.C. Wells' Lexical sets.

Lilt

Refers to a gradual up/down, down/up, up/down/up, etc. glide in pitch that can happen either within a word or within a phrase. If I looked at your new shoes and I liked them a lot I might say: *niiiiice* and lilt down/up/down on the *iiiii*.

Major Interval

Refers to a pitch distance that can be characterized as *sunny*. This refers to a perceived *sunny* interval of resolution in melody, as in the song *Happy Birthday*. (A minor interval does not have the same sense of *sunny* resolution as a major interval. It can often feel a little sad, as in The Beatles' song, *Yesterday*, as described below.)

Melody

Refers to a perceived combination in pattern of pitch and rhythm change in speech.

Minor Interval

Refers to a pitch distance that is unexpectedly smaller than that of a major interval and can be characterized as *sad* or *introspective* to the Western ear. This also refers to a perceived *sad* interval of resolution in melody, as in The Beatles' song, *Yesterday*.

Monophthong

Is a vowel that maintains a single position in articulation.

Operative Words

The words in a text that carry the message of the thought. For example, if one were to say: "In the past, he seemed to me to be rather insincere and suspect." The words that carry the message of the thought might be: *PAST HE INSINCERE SUSPECT*.

Pace

Refers to how fast or slowly someone is speaking.

Phoneme

This is the smallest unit of sound in a language that describes a single gesture of speech. Example: [l]/[L] in app<u>l</u>e or the [u]/[OO] in n<u>u</u>meral.

Pidgin

A pidgin is a language of necessity that is created when people who speak different languages are forced to communicate over an extended period of time. It is a "get to the point of what you need to say" way of communicating. Historically it has been a makeshift language for traders. It does not have a distinct grammar or a developed vocabulary.

Pitch

Refers to the highness or lowness of the voice. Pitch is determined by the length of the vocal folds and also by how quickly the folds open and close to make sound waves.

Plosive

A consonant that stops the flow of air and then releases it in an explosive manner.

Pulmonic Consonants

Consonants that are made with the breath being released out of the mouth or nose, from the lungs. The consonants of English are pulmonic. There are consonants in languages other than English that are non-pulmonic, which are made by drawing air into the lungs. Non-pulmonic consonants include 1) implosives: *a stop produced by drawing the air into the pharynx by closing the vocal cords and pulling the larynx downward*[2]; 2) clicks: (please see definition on page 121); and 3) ejectives: *a voiceless plosive with a simultaneous glottal stop*[3]. Both pulmonic and non-pulmonic consonants (implosives, clicks and ejectives) are found in African languages.

r-coloration / Rhoticity

r-coloration or rhoticity happens when a weak form of the consonant [ɹ]/[R] bleeds into the tail-end of a vowel. Example: Rhotic → bɝd/BUHRD, Non-rhotic → bɜd/BUHD.

Received Pronunciation

Refers to a non-regional English accent that was cultivated in relation to high status and education. In the early 20th century, Daniel Jones, the British phonetician, systematically defined R.P.'s characteristics. He favored a Southern English pronunciation as his frame of reference.

Resonators

Refers to the places in the body that one perceives vibration of sound.

Rhythm

Refers to an element in speech that is determined by pitch, pace, volume and pause. David Crystal goes further in the definition and points out that individual language will defer to either stress-timed rhythm (i.e. English) or syllable-timed rhythm (i.e. French).[4]

Schwa

A short, weak vowel made in the middle of the mouth [ə]/[uh]. Example: th<u>e</u>, <u>a</u>bout.

Soft Palate

The soft area on the back roof of the mouth. It is also referred to as the *velum*. It rises during a yawn.

Sound Shifts

Refers to the sound changes that occur for vowels, diphthongs or consonants in any given accent. In this workbook, the sound shifts are determined with D.A.E. as a departure point.

Source and Path of Resonance

Refers to the length and shape of the vocal tract and the shape that the tongue and mouth make to create a particular resonant quality. This quality is distinct for each accent. Normally, you can sense where this resonance begins, and the *path* it travels through different places of resonance (chest, hard palate, sinuses, etc.). This is a key element in speaking any accent.

Stressed

Refers to words or syllables that are emphasized.

Strong Form

Refers to the strong version of a vowel. In American English, strong forms of vowels normally occur in the stressed syllables of operative words.

Syncopated

Refers to an unexpected shift in rhythm where the expected weak accent in a musical passage is strong.

Tapped R

A single tap of the blade of the tongue against the alveolar ridge.
Example: the Spanish words pero and amarillo

Tonal Language

A tonal language is one that knits tone (pitch) to its smallest units of speech. This tonality is one of the linguistic elements that helps determine the meaning of the word in tonal languages.

Trilled R

Multiple taps of the blade of the tongue against the alveolar ridge.
Example: the Spanish words Roberto and perro

Twang (Oral)

Oral Twang is present in most languages. Twang can be created by narrowing the *aryepiglottic sphincter* which is located on the sides of the entrance to the *larynx*. The *vocal folds* live within the larynx and are affected by this narrowing. (A pure twang has the sound and feel of bagpipes playing). Another way to experience oral twang is to sing like an opera singer without vibrato. Nasal twang is the twang characteristic of country western singers.

Velum

See *Soft Palate*.

Vocal Folds

Are two mucous membranes that stretch horizontally across the larynx. When air is expelled from the lungs, the vocal folds can open or close as the air passes through, and vibrate. This results in sound and, if modulated, phonation. The vocal folds are also called vocal cords.

Vocal Posture

Refers to how the tongue, lips, jaw, soft palate, and pharynx participate in the articulation of speech. This process for the actor is unique, as s/he applies it to character. Along with the elements in *Accent Characteristics* in the accent breakdowns, *Vocal Posture* is key in helping the actor to find idiolect. Most importantly, it enables the actor to integrate the accent through physical transformation rather than by a mathematical matching up of each sound change. The *Mapping Your Accent* section of the Workbook guides the actor building his/her individual *Vocal Posture* for each accent.

Weak Form

Refers to the weak version of a vowel. In American English, weak forms of vowels normally occur in unstressed syllables and/or in words that are not operative words. The vowels in weak forms tend to move towards the central schwa [ə]/[uh].

Notes

1 The co-founder of Knight Thompson Speechwork. His book, *Speaking with Skill*, and articles and chapters in *The Vocal Vision* and *Standard Speech*, and *Voice and Speech Training in the New Millennium* encourage speech training to move from what he considers has been a largely prescriptive process to a more descriptive process.
2 *Glossary of Linguistic Terminology*, p. 368.
3 *Glossary of Linguistic Terminology*, p. 79.
4 *The Cambridge Encyclopedia of the English Language*, p. 4.

Bibliography

"Akan (Twi)." AMESALL: African, Middle Eastern, and South Asian Languages and Literatures. Rutgers School of Arts and Sciences. 19 February 2014. Web. <http://www.amesall.rutgers.edu/languages/128-akan-twi>.

"Afrikaans." *About World Languages*. 2014, The Technology Development Group. Irene Thompson. 3 February 2014. <http://aboutworldlanguages.com/afrikaans>.

Background Note: Liberia. U.S. Department of State Diplomacy in Action. 30 August 2011. Web. 1 July 2011. <http://www.state.gov/r/pa/ei/bgn/6618.htm>.

Background Note: Zimbabwe. U.S. Department of State Diplomacy in Action. 14 October 2011. Web. 27 November 2011. <http://www.state.gov/p/af/ci/zi/>.

Blumenfeld, Robert. *Accents: A Manual for Actors*. New York: Limelight Editions, 2002. Print.

Campbell, George L., and Gareth King. *Concise Compendium of the World's Languages*. London: Routledge, 2010. Print.

"Consonants (Pulmonic)," "Vowels," and "Diacritics." *IPA Chart*. 2005, International Phonetic Association. Web. 25 July 2012. <http://www.internationalphoneticassociation.org/content/ipa-chart>.

Crystal, David. *The Cambridge Encyclopedia of The English Language*. New York: Cambridge University Press, 1995. Print.

"Dholuo." *About World Languages*. 2014, The Technology Development Group. Irene Thompson. 20 June 2014. <http://aboutworldlanguages.com/luo>.

"Ganda (LùGáànda)." OMNIGLOT: The Online Encyclopedia of Writing Systems and Languages. 26 February 2014. Web. 1 March 2014. <http://www.omniglot.com/writing/ganda.php>.

Gaynor, Frank, and Mario Pei. *Dictionary of Linguistics*. New York: Philosophical Library, 1954. Print.

"Ibo." *Accredited Language Services*. 2014, Accredited Language Services. np. Web. 9 June 2014. <http://www.alsintl.com/resources/languages/Ibo/>.

Jones, Daniel. *English Pronouncing Dictionary*. New York: Cambridge University Press, 1997. Print.

Katzner, Kenneth. *The Languages of the World*. New York: Routledge, 2002. Print.

Kimenyi, Alexandre. *A Tonal Grammar of Kinyarwanda*. Lewiston: The Edwin Mellen Press, 2002. Print.

"Kinyarwanda." *About World Languages*. 2014, The Technology Development Group. Irene Thompson. 1 March 2013. Web. 3 August 2014. <http://aboutworldlanguages.com/kinyarwanda>.

Knight, Dudley. *Speaking With Skill*. New York: Bloomsbury Methuen Drama, 2012: 237. Print.

Knight, Dudley. "Standard Speech: The Ongoing Debate", in M. Hampton and B. Acker, *The Vocal Vision*. Applause Theatre Books, 1997: 182, #6. Print.

Kopf, Ginny. *The Dialect Handbook: Learning, Researching and Performing a Dialect Role*. Orlando, Fl.: Voiceprint Pub., 2003. Print.

Koutonin, Mawuna Remarque. 63 African Symbols For Creative Design. *Silicon Africa*. np. 4 June 2013. Web. 4 August 2008. <http://www.siliconafrica.com/african-symbols-for-creative-design/>. Symbol #44.

Lane-Plescia, Gillian. *South African for Actors*. [Boston]: [Baker's Plays], 1993. Print.

"Language and Religion." *Ghana Embassy*. 2014, Embassy of Ghana and Globescope Inc. 14 May 2014. <http://www.ghanaembassy.org/index.php?page=language-and-religion>.

"Language of the Wolof of Senegal." *Wolof of Senegal*. np. nd. Web. 9 July 2014. <http://wolofresources.org/>.

"Liberia." *Wikipedia, the free encyclopedia*. 22 July 2011. Web. October 2009. <http://en.wikipedia.org/wiki/Liberia>.

"Lingala." *About World Languages*. 2014, The Technology Development Group. Irene Thompson. 20 June 2014. <http://aboutworldlanguages.com/lingala>.

"Lingala language." *Encyclopedia Britannica Online*. 2014, Encyclopedia Britannica Inc. Salikoko Sangol Mufwene, 26 September 2013. Web. 9 July 2014. <http://www.britannica.com/EBchecked/topic/342347/Lingala-language>.

Linklater, Kristin. *Freeing Shakespeare's Voice: The Actor's Guide to Talking the Text*. New York: Theatre Communications Group, Inc. 1992: 25.

"Luo." *Countries and Their Cultures*. 2014, Advameg Inc. Web. July 2014. <http://www.everyculture.com/wc/Japan-to-Mali/Luo.html>.

McDonald Klimek, Mary. *Estill Voice Training System Level Two: Figure Combinations for Six Voice Qualities*. Think Voice Series. With Kerrie Obert and Kimberly Steinhauer. Pittsburgh: Estill Voice Training Systems International, LLC. Print.

McWhorter, John. *The Story of Human Language: The Great Courses*; 3 Volumes. Chantilly, VA: The Teaching Company, 2004. Audio and Print.

Olivier, Jako. *South African Languages*. <http://www.salanguages.com/>.

Pei, Mario. *Glossary of Linguistic Terminology*. New York: Columbia University Press, 1966. Print.

Russell, Tony, Allen Brizee, and Elizabeth Angeli. "MLA Formatting and Style Guide." *The Purdue OWL*. Purdue U Writing Lab, 4 April 2010. Web. 22 June 2014. <https://owl.english.purdue.edu/owl/resource/747/01/>.

"Rwanda language." *Encyclopedia Britannica Online*. 2014, Encyclopedia Britannica Inc., 2014. Web. 14 December 2014. <http://www.britannica.com/EBchecked/topic/514454/Rwanda-language>.

Scheeder, Louis, and Shane Ann Younts. *All the Words on Stage*. Hanover, New Hampshire: Smith and Kraus, Inc., 2002. Print.

"Shona." *About World Languages*. 2014, The Technology Development Group. Irene Thompson. 16 May 2013. Web. 2 August 2014. <http://aboutworldlanguages.com/shona>.

"Shona (chiShona)." OMNIGLOT: The Online Encyclopedia of Writing Systems and Languages. 26 February. 2014. Web. 3 August 2014. <http://www.omniglot.com/writing/shona.php>.

Skinner, Edith. *Speak with Distinction*. New York: Applause Theatre Book Publishers, 1990. Print.

Soave, Matt. *Luganda*. Trans. S. H. Butcher. *The Internet Classics Archive*. np. 19 March 2009. Web. 1 Aug. 2014. <http://mattsoave.com/projects/luganda/content/Luganda.pdf>.

"THE LUO: Know Your Tribe – Know Your Roots." *African Press International*. 2014, African Press International, Wordpress.com. 14 May 2014. <http://africanpress.me/2008/09/25/know-your-tribe-know-your-roots-the-luo/>.

Wells, J.C. *Accents of English. Vol. 1: An Introduction*. New York: Cambridge University Press, 1982. Print.

Wells, J.C. *Accents of English. Vol. 3: Beyond the British Isles*. New York: Cambridge University Press, 1982. Print.

"Wolof." *About World Languages*. 2014, The Technology Development Group. Irene Thompson. 9 May 2013. <http://aboutworldlanguages.com/wolof>.

"Zulu." *Accredited Language Services*. 2014, Accredited Language Services. nd. Web. June 2014. <http://www.alsintl.com/resources/languages/Zulu/>.

"Zulu." *South African History Online*. South African History Online. nd. Web. June 2014. <http://www.sahistory.org.za/people-south-africa/zulu>.

"Zulu language." *Encyclopedia Britannica Online*. 2014, Encyclopedia Britannica Inc., 2014. Web. 14 December 2014. <http://www.britannica.com/EBchecked/topic/658378/Zulu-language>.

Index

Note: Page numbers in **bold** refer to the definition of the term in the Glossary.

Taylor & Francis eBooks

Helping you to choose the right eBooks for your Library

Add Routledge titles to your library's digital collection today. Taylor and Francis ebooks contains over 50,000 titles in the Humanities, Social Sciences, Behavioural Sciences, Built Environment and Law.

Choose from a range of subject packages or create your own!

Benefits for you

» Free MARC records
» COUNTER-compliant usage statistics
» Flexible purchase and pricing options
» All titles DRM-free.

Benefits for your user

» Off-site, anytime access via Athens or referring URL
» Print or copy pages or chapters
» Full content search
» Bookmark, highlight and annotate text
» Access to thousands of pages of quality research at the click of a button.

REQUEST YOUR **FREE** INSTITUTIONAL TRIAL TODAY

Free Trials Available
We offer free trials to qualifying academic, corporate and government customers.

eCollections – Choose from over 30 subject eCollections, including:

Archaeology	Language Learning
Architecture	Law
Asian Studies	Literature
Business & Management	Media & Communication
Classical Studies	Middle East Studies
Construction	Music
Creative & Media Arts	Philosophy
Criminology & Criminal Justice	Planning
Economics	Politics
Education	Psychology & Mental Health
Energy	Religion
Engineering	Security
English Language & Linguistics	Social Work
Environment & Sustainability	Sociology
Geography	Sport
Health Studies	Theatre & Performance
History	Tourism, Hospitality & Events

For more information, pricing enquiries or to order a free trial, please contact your local sales team: www.tandfebooks.com/page/sales

 Routledge
Taylor & Francis Group

The home of Routledge books

www.tandfebooks.com